Love Bade me Eat

ONE WOMAN'S ENCOUNTER WITH LOVE ON A JOURNEY THROUGH ANOREXIA.

ALYS CAVANAGH

September, 2025

Ark House Press
arkhousepress.com

Some names and identifying details have been changed to protect the privacy of individuals.

Cataloguing in Publication Data:
Title: Love Bade me Eat
ISBN: 978-1-7645620-1-0 (pbk)
Subjects: REL012170 RELIGION / Christian Living / Personal Memoirs; PSY011000 PSYCHOLOGY / Psychopathology / Eating Disorders; REL012040 RELIGION / Christian Living / Inspirational.

Design by initiateagency.com

LOVE bade me welcome; yet my soul drew back,
Guilty of dust and sin.
But quick-eyed Love, observing me grow slack
From my first entrance in,
Drew nearer to me, sweetly questioning
If I lack'd anything.

'A guest,' I answer'd, 'worthy to be here:'
Love said, 'You shall be he.'
'I, the unkind, ungrateful? Ah, my dear,
I cannot look on Thee.'
Love took my hand and smiling did reply,
'Who made the eyes but I?'

'Truth, Lord; but I have marr'd them: let my shame
Go where it doth deserve.'
'And know you not,' says Love, 'Who bore the blame?'
'My dear, then I will serve.'
'You must sit down,' says Love, 'and taste my meat.'
So I did sit and eat.

George Herbert

Please note, readers who themselves experience mental health illness may find some themes in this book triggering to read. Where this is the case, the chapter heading has been footnoted to give prior warning.

With the exception of the author, names have been changed throughout this account to preserve the privacy of individuals.

Contents

Acknowledgements

To the many friends, mentors and spiritual leaders who have generously shared their time, wisdom and support in the writing of this book, thank you so much. Your input, however small you might feel it to have been, has been a tremendous gift.

To Nicole Partridge and Ruth Athanasio.... I know you are both aware how close I was to giving up on completing this book. Were it not for your gentle but insistent encouragement to keep going and, Ruth, your diligent, thoughtful editorial input, I probably would have. So ... thanks a million.

To the Ark House Publishing family, your vision and courage to help authors like me have a crack at sharing their stories of hope and inspiration with others has made this book possible. Thank you for the encouragement, creativity and commitment you have provided in turning one person's dream into a reality.

And to Mike. Words can't express. Thank you for waiting, praying, loving relentlessly, hoping against all hope, and, ultimately, taking me back. I won't embarrass you by saying any more. Except – how could I not? - I love you.

Preface

I've been told I apologise too much.

Sorry.

Nevertheless, a preface seems like a perfect opportunity to offload a few disclaimers to what you are about to read. So here goes.

When I first thought about writing my story, I was propelled by the realisation that there really aren't that many books out there for people who have eating disorders, particularly severe and enduring ones, and especially in the faith space. I felt like there was a gap that I wished had been filled when I was at my sickest.

So, my biggest motivation for writing this book was to help fill that gap in some small way. Which paves the way for my first disclaimer: who the book is written for.

I really hope this story encourages any and everyone. I believe it can.

Notwithstanding, the person I have held most in my heart as I write is the reader who struggles with an eating disorder themselves – diagnosed or not. Particularly one for whom recovery has seemed perpetually out of reach.

For that reason, I have unashamedly unearthed all the layers of that illness, accompanied with multiple reflections on the journey of malaise, treatment, relapse, recovery, that such a reader may be familiar with.

For those of you without eating disorders who have come along for that ride, you are so welcome. You will discover that none of us are really that different from each other. We all struggle with the same wounds – they just manifest in different forms.

All the same, bear with us as I and my fellow sufferers unpeel the eating disorder onion in all its ugly complexity. The One I write of has balm for each of its layers, and it wouldn't do to miss some of them out. If the journey feels a bit laborious, skim away, or put down altogether and watch some Netflix. Apologies all the same.

Second disclaimer: Sentimentality. You hold in your hands my most precious and intimate relationship. Try as I might, I cannot describe it in terms anything other than those you will find; terms that may seem unbearably sentimental. If this is the case, again, please, take a breather and grab a good academic theology book instead. I certainly don't profess to have written one here. All I can do is share my experience. And I probably haven't done that with the greatest literary skill. Apologies again.

Third disclaimer: On all matters spiritual. To those of you who have had a belly-full of religion, or who don't identify with holding a particular faith of any kind, I have done my best to remove religious jargon from this account. I may have missed the bar at times on that – I apologise if so.

To my Protestant brothers and sisters, you may find here some Catholic concepts that make you twitch. And to my Catholic family, you may stumble across some nonconformist language that doesn't sit entirely comfortably with you. My faith walk has had me grazing in a plethora of denominational pastures. I am unable to hide that. Bear with me if you can and, if in doubt, take what helps and leave the rest. Apologies for any offense taken.

Fourth disclaimer: References. We seem to live in the 'Tower of Babel' these days – voices screaming truths from left right and centre. It confused me. A lot.

So, I wanted to make sure that the things I have heard in my journey haven't just been conjured up in my own addled brain. I wanted to know they could be found from a Source that is more solid, more reliable. Hence the plethora of biblical references. Most of them are from the New International Version (NIV) of the Bible unless otherwise stated. These may be a distraction as you read or, if you have a brain that is a glutton for detail like mine, you might enjoy browsing that book for the passages I have alluded to. Either way, I may have gone over the top. So, apologies again.

Finally, readers may notice that I describe a period where I needed to step back from medical treatment for my condition. It was a particularly risky decision. I want to urge those of you who are currently in treatment to listen carefully to the One I write about on that one. And to those around you who love and care for you.

The help you may be receiving right now might not be perfect. But, like me for 30 years, it might be the only thing keeping you alive. Please don't read part of this story and use it as a reason to rashly give up on what you have.

If you keep reading, you'll see that I reengaged with treatment. I still see a psychologist; I still take my meds. And I am hugely grateful for them both, together with the army of professionals that fought to keep me alive for the decades during which I languished. So, if I am at all misleading in that regard, I apologise again.

Please know that sometimes any treatment, however painful it might be, is better than none.

Okay, I think that's as much apologising as we need for now. I hope you find this story helpful. And if you don't, be gentle. It's my life on a plate.

Literally.

Love story

Beginning

I flick the lighter. It sparks once. I flick again. It flares.

I lean it into the candle wick, trying to avoid a burn. It catches. I put the lighter down and lean back in my chair, transfixed for a moment by its flame.

It's not a holy moment or anything. I'm not a very holy person. I just like a candle by me some days. Reminds me He is here. Gives me a still point to focus on when my brain is pulled in five or twenty different directions.

'I don't know where to begin.' I whisper. I slump in my seat, daunted.

'I don't know what to tell or how to tell it.'

Silence. Loving silence.

What's going on?

'I don't have a story to tell… or at least not a clean one. I don't have a perfect recovery. I don't have a '5-steps-to-freedom' formula. The medical fraternity will call this baloney. So will half the Christian community. My faith is all over the place. My life has been all over the place.'

I know.

Another pause. Patient.

'And what about my family? My parents? They are incredible people—so talented, giving and creative. They've helped so many through their work, and they have been through so much themselves… both with their childhood traumas. They never meant for me to get sick. All they wanted was the best for me. If I had just processed things differently… if I had just been more resilient, less sensitive… none of this would have happened.'

I pause.

'I don't want to bring them down… I don't want to hurt them.'

Breath.

'I love them… I want them to know I love them.'

I know.

Silence.

It is possible to be wounded when the wounds were never intended. When people were doing their absolute best.

Pause.

And it is possible to love those people deeply. With wounded love.

I open to His words for a moment.

Then fear overwhelms me.

'I don't even know why I am writing this! Damn it - it makes me feel like shit thinking about it! I'd forgotten about this stuff and now it feels like yesterday all over again. And how do I know it's really You I am hearing, have been hearing all along? People will think I'm mad – and that I always have been.'

He waits. Breathes. Then whispers.

Alys.

A thousand loving words contained in a name.

'Okay .... I know it's You, I know it has been You. But how the heck do you write that on paper? Without it sounding like some trite, contrived, pious set of platitudes? Or some evangelical tract – the stuff I have always hated?! I don't even know where to begin.'

Pause.

In my mind's eye, I see Him take my hand.

I look up. Our eyes lock.

Why don't you tell them a love story? Our love story.

Why don't you start there?

Something in me loosens, relaxes. My shoulders drop a little.

'Yes... I guess ...I could tell them that.'

I pause some more.

'But it's awful intimate and private and all! What if someone shoots it down? I don't know if I could deal with embarrassing myself in public all over again.'

Maybe they will. Do you have something to lose?

I reflect on all that I have laid bare before others over the past few years. I remember the freedom that came in those early days with Him. When I found that to lose myself in Him - to throw caution to the wind, to not care anymore about the self I had been guarding, creating, fighting to hold onto - was the ultimate release.

'I guess not.'

Well then. Why don't we begin?

'Okay. A love story.'

I pause.

'Please… help me do this… I'm… scared.'

I know.

He embraces me. I melt.

The candle is burning brightly now.

I am ready.

Emmaus

He was there all along – I just didn't know it. Or maybe I knew it… but stopped believing it.

I don't think I am different to any other human being. I was born with that sense of magic I think every child has. That sense of knowing where I came from and where I would ultimately return to. No-one told me. I just knew.

In my flying dreams I would soar up, up, up into the sky, beyond the stars, right to the borders of the universe. To a point where I knew I was to stop. It was not time to come home yet.

He was there, but He wanted me to find Him here – on this soil, this ground. Loving, but firm, I would hear Him say,

Not time yet Alys. Go. Live the life I have given you.

I carried the magic into my later childhood. I found it in the Narnia books[1]. They were, for me, a world of escape where He was always to be found.

He would come to me as the Lion, Aslan[2], during my sleepless nights at boarding school. I would jump on His back, and we would gallop and fly far, far away from that place. I read those books voraciously – through lessons, assemblies, in my dormitory, during the performance classes,

---

1 The Chronicles of Narnia. C.S. Lewis. (1950-1956)

2 The creator and overarching force for good throughout the entirety of those Chronicles.

in the warm-up rooms while I waited for my concert stage call. I read them in my bedroom at home to blot out the arguments and crashing and bashing. I read them in the cool, hidden groves that were splattered throughout the Welsh woodland that surrounded us.

He was my refuge. My lifeline.

But there came a time when the lights went out. I couldn't see Him anymore.

I tried so hard. I listened to other people's versions of Him and tried to fit Him into their mould. But I ended up with counterfeit upon counterfeit; gods that demanded much and gave little, that were disappointed, not delighted. That drove rather than released. Gods that were waiting, impatiently, for me to do well, fix myself and get well.

I couldn't please those gods.

And so, I thought He, like them, must have given up on me. I figured I had to go it alone, work everything out alone. My illness, this life, who I was. Everything.

But He stayed with me all along. Music school. Fights at home. Sexual trauma. Breakdowns. Anorexia. Borderline personality disorder. OCD. Self-harm. Overdose. Admission on admission. Separation. Crippled parenting.

He never left. He was always there.

There was a time when I was tempted to shake my fist at Him about that.

'If You were there why didn't You do something? Why didn't You stop that happening? Why did You let me get so sick? Why did You let me screw up so bad?'

But I can't shake my fist at Him anymore.

He wooed me and I fell in love. Completely, head over heels, in love.

And I can't get mad and demand explanations and justifications from the One who gave me everything.

I've learnt to trust in His silence these days. It is warm, not cold. It speaks more wisdom than the most carefully crafted of words.

He was there all along.

Love was there all along.

I just never knew it.

ONSET

The Black

Just as He was there all along, so too was a brewing darkness. Storm clouds that were hungry to twist, spoil and conceal the awareness of Him that I had when I was so young.

Sometimes it would attack me in my sleep through nightmares that shattered the wonder of my flying adventures. In them, a dark force would draw me in and seek to consume me. Every fibre of my being knew it was not safe, but I felt utterly powerless against it.

Yet always, at the point at which I felt completely defeated by this being, Someone would enable me to call out for help. I am not even sure of the name I used for Him then, but I would speak it in desperation. Sometimes only a whisper.

In an instant the darkness would vanish. I would awake, bolt upright, sweating and panting. But safe.

'The Black[3]' I encountered in my early night terrors, and on many occasions after, was not some 'part of myself'. Nor was it the early signs of mental health illness. It was something entirely separate to me. A being that was insatiably jealous of the One from whom I came. hell-bent on taking me – and every other human being - away from Him.

The instigator of Eden's trauma[4].

---

[3] Some may know this entity by the name of Satan, the enemy, or evil.

[4] The Bible, Genesis 3.

The author of the lie that we are all to be forever separated, wrenched, cast out from our eternal home. That we were never truly loved. We were never really wanted. And that we have no hope of return.

As I grew up, the Black became more nuanced, subtle in its methods.

It replaced terrifying dreams with the everyday messy circumstances of a human life. Difficult experiences became the seedbed of a web of lies. Lies for which anorexia, self-harm and a plethora of other compulsive behaviours were simply a desperate, but lethal, antidote.

Hold everyone together

They are fighting again. I don't understand it – I am only three. Mum is crying. Her voice goes high and squealy when she cries. She is begging him about something – I am not sure what.

Dad is angry. I think he is crying too. He is stamping up the stairs. Sometimes he gets mad and throws things, bangs things. Once he threw the TV out the window. It is scary.

Mum grabs me and cries into the sweater I am wearing. I see Dad walking away angrily. I don't want him to walk away and leave me here. I love him. I love Mum. I don't know what to do. I feel bad that Dad is sad and I am not helping him. I feel bad that Mum is sad and I don't want her to cry into me. I don't want to be held like this. I feel trapped.

But I figure this is what I've got to do.

I must soak up Mum's tears. And then when I am big enough, I will run after Dad and check he is alright. I will keep doing that. I will try and take care of them both. Hold them together. Keep the family together. That is what I will try and do.

Over the years that follow I find many ways to do this.

I figure a messy house can be the trigger for an argument or an outburst of frustration from Mum or Dad. I hear Dad call us 'staff'. He is only joking but I am autistic, very literal in the way I think. I don't know it yet – nobody knows it[5]. But that is how my brain is wired. So, I take his words seriously - just in case. He reminds us that we are guests in his house. It is a good thing. It's so we help and pull our weight. I take that literally too, just to be sure. I want to be as helpful as I possibly can.

I figure that if I get ahead of the game and clean the house before the outburst, that will keep everyone happy. I will have earnt my place. If I do the dishes and cook the dinner before being asked, we will have a peaceful home, and I will get my approval fix. I get my sister into trouble doing this because Mum and Dad compare us often, and she doesn't like doing the housework. She is more of a rebel than me. She always looks bad when I do it and that is my fault.

But I can't help myself.

Cleaning, tidying and doing things before I am asked are my obsessive compulsions. Sometimes I do them in tears, telling myself how much I hate myself. I don't understand why those words tumble out of my mouth.

I don't understand my behaviour at all. I just figure I should be more helpful.

As I grow older, I try being a good listener to everyone. I triangulate without realising. I listen to Mum and the stories of her painful childhood, consoling her to the best of my ability. I listen to Dad as he vents his frustrations with Mum and his concern that they are going to have to divorce. I listen to Mum and Dad as they share their concerns about my

---

5 I did not get my formal diagnosis until I was 40, soon after my then seven-year-old son was diagnosed.

sister who is drinking and smoking and acting out at school, clocking the necessary information I need to know to make sure I don't upset them by making the same mistakes.

I get called 'Al the Pal' because I am such a great listener, and I figure if Mum and Dad can talk about all their problems with me, then they will fight less and maybe they won't split up.

Listening and triangulating becomes another way I get the attention and the approval I want. I figure I have nothing important to show for myself when Mum and Dad and my sister all have so many big problems. So, this is a good alternative.

Life gets very tiring, trying to hold my family together. Nobody in my family asked me to do that, but I feel I have no alternative.

One day I will crack and no longer be able to be Al the Pal. But for now, I must keep trying.

Do it again

It is my piano lesson, and I am trying to play the Chopin Nocturne perfectly. I am ten, at one of the top music schools in the UK. It is a boarding school, so I am away from my home in Wales.

Me and my sister, we both got scholarships here. We were talent scouted after Mum got us playing music when we were little. She wanted us to be musical and to have the chances she never had as a child. No one believed in Mum, so I am very fortunate and lucky that I am here at this music school, I tell myself. I should be grateful.

My teacher is upset today – more than usual. She is frowning and her voice is shaky, as though she is about to cry. I don't know why. Maybe it's me. Maybe I've done something wrong.

"Play it again," she says, impatiently.

I am nervous. I take a breath, place my fingers on the keys, and begin.

It is not right. I miss a note.

'Wrong!' she snaps. 'Play it again!'.

My hands start to shake, and I have butterflies in my tummy. I play it again but this time I miss two notes.

'How could you be so stupid? Play it again!' she orders, louder now. Her hands touch mine as she points angrily at the notes I missed.

The more she shouts, the worse it gets. I play, I miss, she yells. Over and over. My fingers keep stumbling – I can't control them – and the walls of the practice room seem to close in around me. There is no way out. No way to escape the endless cycle of wrong, wrong, wrong.

I am scared and I am homesick. I don't want to be here, but my sister is here, and I didn't want to be apart from her because she keeps me safe when Mum and Dad fight. So, I think I should be happy here, I should be grateful.

I should do better and play it perfect. Then my teacher will be happy with me.

But she is not happy now.

She just keeps screaming, 'Do it again, do it again!'

I can't remember how I got out of the situation.

Maybe the bell went. Maybe she gave up on me and finally let me go.

I must practise more. I have to be better.

Which one's Dad?

Dad works in the theatre. He is so artistic and clever. Everyone knows it. I am proud of him. Proud he is my dad. I get to go on stage sometimes and see his show designs. It is so cool. He is so cool.

Sometimes Dad can get angry. He went through a lot as a child. He saw his father drown in a boating accident on his 10th birthday. Then his mother passed away from alcoholism decades later. He says he is okay about it all now, but I am not sure. It breaks my heart thinking about it.

Maybe he gets angry because he and Mum push each other's buttons. Or because he works so hard to provide for us and he is under so much pressure all the time. Or maybe it is because he is an artist – he says artists often let it all hang out and it is kind of normal to get mad if you are creative.

I don't know.

He doesn't want to get angry. He hates himself when it happens, and I feel sad for him about it. I don't want him to feel bad.

But it happens all the same.

It starts in his office, below, while he is working. There is money trouble, and he is worrying about the bills. Then he finds it hard to design his theatre sets. He starts swearing and it gets louder and louder and then we hear him stomping up the stairs and we all know to get out of his way. Get out the house or hide in your room or something.

Mum always says that the best thing about Dad is that he can turn anything into a joke and that is how he comes down from being mad.

But I find it confusing. You never know when he is joking or when he is mad. Sometimes he acts mad, and I think he is joking, and I laugh, hoping, praying this time it is a joke, and he is going to calm down and smile and be fun again. But then I am wrong, and he gets even madder.

Then other times, he does make a joke, he turns it all into a crazy joke and everyone laughs with relief, and it should all be better now, shouldn't it? But I don't feel better – because I never know which one he is in any given moment. Is he mad Dad or clown Dad? I don't know and I don't want to upset him by getting it wrong.

It is all so random.

Like I said, I am autistic, and I am seeing everything literally, black and white. I don't understand when someone is angry and then they tell you they were just joking. I don't go well with the unpredictability all the time. And the fear.

I feel like I need one thing I can control in my world. Just one thing. And then I will be okay.

But I can't find that thing.

So privileged

I am eleven and it is the junior house meeting at music school. We have them every Sunday morning. We must go. And it is something to fill the time. On weekends, we kick around in empty rooms and empty halls, feeling empty, wishing we were home, but filling the void with practice.

Mr. Griffiths, the housemaster, is giving us the Sunday talk. I think it is meant to be, like, a church sermon or something.

He is ranting and raving. 'You're all so molly-coddled,' he says. 'You all worship your instruments,' he says. 'Sunday should be for worshipping the Lord but here you all are, practising away in your little cubby holes playing like that is the only thing in the world! Your music is an idol!'

He used to be an actor. He is very good at screaming and scaring us. One time he screamed at me as a joke on my birthday and I wet my pants, literally. I had to stay sitting to cover up the puddle until he had gone.

I find Mr. Griffiths' Sunday talk hard to understand.

I don't want to be here. I said I would go to the music school because I missed my sister, and I didn't like being alone at home with the arguments. I never wanted to be here on a Sunday practising away in my practice room. But if we don't practise, the teachers will yell at us at our next lesson. The concert won't be perfect. The assessment will fail.

We don't have any choice.

But Mr. Griffiths shouts at us and tells us we are lucky; we are molly coddled.

I don't understand his words, too, because things go on in the practice rooms that nobody talks about, nobody mentions.

The way the head of music grooms us, singles out the chosen ones. Me and my quartet had to stay at his house one holiday – I can't remember what happened, I blacked it out, but one of the older students was there too and they looked really sad. So did his wife.

We have to work hard to please our teachers. Then, when we hit ninth or tenth grade, or I guess whenever we look kind of grown up and attractive, those teachers start doing things with the students. We whisper about it and are afraid, but we don't know what to call it. I am only eleven, so I don't really understand it at all. It just feels scary. It's not until it hits the newspapers, years later when I am a grown up, that it all makes sense.

For now, I don't feel safe. And I feel guilty that bad things are happening to the older kids and not me.

But Mr. Griffiths keeps screaming at us that we are lucky, we should be grateful, we don't know how good we have got it. Being here in one of the top music schools in Britain.

Bathroom

I forgot my music case.

I realise it when we are an hour into the car journey back to music school. A wave of panic floods through me. My teacher will be so angry, so disappointed with me. I will not be able to practice or do anything without it.

I melt down completely. We drive all the way back to Wales to get it. I have upset my sister. I didn't mean to upset her. I didn't mean to forget it. I can't get rid of the sorry feeling. And the panic.

Now I am even more panicked because I hate going back to school, I don't want to go there at all. But if I get back there late that means that it is bedtime straight away. I hate bedtimes, lying in bed, not being able to sleep with that gnawing homesick feeling that I can't get rid of.

We get there after dinner. Everyone is settled in, all the kids in their pyjamas. Mum rushes to unpack me. I don't want her to unpack me because I don't want to stay. I want to go home.

There is a house meeting again telling us all the rules for the term. The housemistress knocks on the dorm door and tells me I must go to the house meeting now.

But I don't want to go. I am not ready. I haven't unpacked. I am a good girl, but I start screaming, screaming that I don't want to go. I cling to my parents, and the housemistress grabs my hand as I scream and scream. Eventually she pulls me off them and I see them turn their backs and walk away.

I see them leave. Gone.

I know they are sad; they are doing what they think is right, but I don't know where to go with this pain, this aloneness, this left-behind-ness. I go into the house meeting sobbing.

I can't remember any of the new term rules they talk about.

That night I can't sleep. I go to the girls' bathroom. I am scared because I will get into trouble if I am found out of bed. I want someone to comfort me. I am looking out the window wishing my dad's car would come back. But it never does. I could go knock on the house-mistress's door, but if I knock, they will probably be angry and yell at me like they do the other kids. So, I cry and cry. I cry so loudly. I sob, hoping someone will hear and comfort me.

But nobody hears. Nobody comes.

I don't know how long I am in that bathroom sobbing and howling. But I figure if no-one is going to come, I must do something with this feeling myself. I have to numb it. Shove it down.

It took me I-don't-know-how-many nights of crying with nobody coming before I made my decision.

I will stop crying.

I will stop feeling.

Nobody is coming to get me.

As the years pass, I vow not to go home anymore.

Then I won't have to feel this pain. I will practise my way through the holidays, the weekends. Whatever it takes to numb that feeling. To get rid of it.

To kill it.

Go it alone

I love Mum. She had a very painful childhood. She came from a wealthy, deeply unhappy family environment in which she and her sister were abused and neglected on multiple levels.

Mum never allows herself to get the professional help she needs to heal from what she has been through. At least not for long enough. She says she doesn't want to put her family through the burden of her doing therapy.

Maybe that is why she talks about it with me so much.

I want her to heal – I want it so bad, because Mum's past and her wounds make her teary, emotional, hot and cold, unpredictable and I get afraid of her. I listen as much as I can because maybe that will help. Maybe it will make her happy. And then she and Dad will fight less.

I am eight and she has found a faith for herself. A Christian faith. She becomes a lay reader[6]. Runs prayer groups. Preaches sermons. It is very important to her. She says prayer is all she needs to solve her past. Prayer is enough. God is enough. She'll become a priest someday. She'll help a lot of people.

I want to support her, but I feel confused. She prays fervently every morning for an hour and gets angry if we disturb her while we get our breakfast. She cries even more, especially during Lent and Easter, and I don't understand why. She spends stacks of time at the local convent. She

---

6 A lay person in the Anglican Church who has been licensed to assist in worship, preach and teach.

tells me that if she didn't have us, she would become a nun. I don't think she means it in a bad way. All the same, I figure she would rather have been a nun than have us and I feel guilty for being in the way between her and God.

Mum and Dad fight a lot about her new faith. Dad cannot journey with her on it – not till later in their lives. He tells me she is not the woman he married, that they are going to separate because of it. They never do separate, but I always feel like it is going to happen. I feel like it is pulling them apart and I must hold them together.

Mum talks to me heaps about God and I go with it. I think maybe if I do this, she won't talk about it with Dad, and they won't argue or separate like they say they might. And I want to support her. She has been through so much, I want to be there for her.

I become her 'spiritual friend'. I'm bright, so I cotton on to a lot of these 'God' concepts. I talk her talk, walk her walk. Mum says she has a special relationship with me, different to everyone else in the family. I feel a bit overwhelmed and scared by that. Scared that I will fail and let her down. Then she will be hurt and disappointed. Then she will be angry with me. I will have betrayed her.

I want so bad to have time with Dad too, but he is often busy, away working and it is hard to get time with him. I don't want Dad to think that I don't care about him. But listening to Mum about her God stuff, her painful childhood, it keeps her happy and I figure that is a good thing, because things can feel cold, very cold when she is not happy.

Sometimes Mum is upset at dinner times. She tells the rest of the family that I am the only one who listens to her. The only one who understands her. I feel guilty because I have gotten my dad and my sister into trouble. Sometimes it causes another argument between Mum and Dad, and I am trying to stop that, I am trying to help, but I am failing. I am only making things worse. It is my fault. It is all my fault. I am a bad daughter.

But I don't want to disappoint Mum, so I listen and keep talking all this God stuff even though I am not sure it is really me that is talking.

When I am at boarding school Mum studies to go to university to do a Theology degree, then to become a priest, then to do a PhD. I figure it must be important to her that we aren't at home because that gives her time to do her study and to follow her calling from God. I don't want to get in the way. No-one ever believed in her when she was a kid, and I don't want to stop her following her dreams.

Some days Mum is so excited about her faith. She says, in this super intense voice, 'Oh Al, I am just so in love with God!' and there are tears in her eyes. I start to figure that God must be much more important to her than us. That God must be very busy with her. That God is all hers and she is all God's and there is no space for my sister and I, so we mustn't get in the way.

I try to pull off the spiritual friend thing as long as I can.

But as the years go by, I find I can't do it. I start to shut down. I can't be who she wants me to be. I struggle with the funny voice she has when she preaches from the pulpit or when she leads family prayers, and I feel guilty that I don't like it. I feel anger when, at church, she is a holy person that everyone loves and admires, but back home she seems unpredictable, emotional, scary. I see her pushing Dad's buttons and then fights happening. I don't understand it. It doesn't make sense.

Mum gets cross and upset with me for my anger and my sadness even though I try so hard to cover them up. She says I have no reason to feel those things – I have everything she didn't have. So, I push it down even deeper – I don't want to turn her against me.

And I try and try to keep doing the God thing.

But eventually something snaps. I think it is when I hit ninth grade. I am tired of being teased at school for being religious. And I think God must be angry because I am starting to have scary, angry feelings towards my mum. He must be angry because I don't want to be her special friend or her listening ear anymore.

God must want me at boarding school so she can become a priest and all. But I cry a lot at boarding school. So, I figure he must be mad at me for that too. My tears are getting in the way of his plans with her.

Anyway, he is all Mum's not mine, right?

So eventually I handball him to her in my mind. I let them do their thing, write their books, preach their sermons, go their way.

I give up being Mum's spiritual friend. And I give up on God too.

Gifted

I am in ninth grade, at a second music school now. There are four top specialist music schools in Britain, and this is another of them. I was moved here after my sister got a debilitating arm injury from the practice regime at the first. Mum and Dad hoped this school, also a boarding school but closer to our home in Wales than the first, might soften my homesickness.

I'm told I'm gifted and exceptional – not just at music, but academically too - and fortunate to be so.

I take this to heart and rush from one subject lesson to the next, then on to the music rooms to cram in hours of daily practise on the piano on top of a regular school timetable. I figure if I'm talented and bright I must try and be the best at everything. My mind sees everything in black and white and extremes. Every standard thrown at me I ramp up threefold.

I have stomach cramps, headaches and insomnia all the time.

I feel like my autistic brain is an untamed beast. It absorbs things like a sponge – things that my friends can't remember. I read a book, shut my eyes and read it again as if I can see it right in front of me. I'm oversensitive to all kinds of sensory stimulus, especially smells, noise and lights. Environments like the clattering, boomy school dining room, or the glaring dazzle of a concert platform, are overwhelming, but I can't put a name to this overwhelm. We have fire drills in the middle of the night, and it takes me a week to recover from the startle effect and the sound. I don't know that I am autistic. I just think I am weird.

At the same time as this sensory overwhelm, I'm painfully bored in my school lessons. My mind chatters to me constantly and bombards me with concepts. It's insatiably hungry and needs a continual stream of new information and learning. The slow pace of schoolwork feels excruciating, like fingernails scraping on a chalk board. I irritate my friends and teachers with relentless questions, but I can't help myself. I wish I could switch my brain off. I wish it would shut up.

The music teachers tell me my playing is outstanding. 'You'll go far if you stay committed,' they promise. 'Just keep working and you will get there. You will win Young Musician of the Year, and you will be one of the youngest to do it.'

A TV company makes a documentary about me. It is a series about 'gifted' children. The company approaches the school looking for a precocious musical child for one of their episodes. I am the lucky one to be picked. The crew come and live with our family for two years, filming everything we do. Except the arguments, the explosions, the bangs and crashes and the tears that go on between every cut scene. They film church services we go to, prayer times Mum runs in our home. They film me being the good girl, being Al the Pal, being the spiritual kid that can talk deep stuff with her parents. They film us playing music at London's Southbank, busking on the streets, playing to the nuns.

They film me as if I am a child prodigy. It makes for a good reality TV show.

But it is not real. I am not a prodigy. In a few years' time I will have a nervous breakdown.

They never film that.

Just keep working

A year has passed, and I feel tired. I get straight A's for my exams but nobody is surprised or impressed. It's the same with the 'A*'s' I get in the piano performance assessments. Teachers and family know I am gifted, so of course I would ace both.

But they don't realise how hard I must work. The hours of study and practice required to pull off this perfection act.

The never-ending anxiety about the next exam and performance is exhausting. One slipped note is a failure I can't tolerate. One dropped grade and I'm nothing. I'm goaded by a slavedriver, a tyrant in my mind. It is never satisfied. Nothing I do is ever good enough. I must do better. Always better.

The Parable of the Talents[7] haunts me. Every Sunday evening at school we must go to Evensong in the Cathedral and worship this boomy terrifying god. The chaplain reminds us how fortunate we are to be so gifted. How we must not bury our talents like the man did in that parable - and was cast out by his furious master. I don't want to fail this god.

But I feel like I can't keep going. I can't pull off this 'gifted' thing for much longer.

One bedtime at lights out, the housemistress spots me hiding under my covers looking stressed. She reminds me I have no reason to be sad or upset.

---

7 A story found in the Bible, Matthew, 25:14-30.

'You're so talented, Alys,' she says. 'Just think about the rest of the world. Think about other kids out there. They don't have the opportunities you have. You should be grateful, not stressed, for being so fortunate.'

I feel guilty because I wish I was one of the other kids. I wish I wasn't talented. I wish I had a normal brain and went to a normal school. I wish I was just 'average', whatever that is. I wish I could watch TV and make model aeroplanes and play in the woods. Not work day and night like this.

At home Mum reminds too. Nobody ever believed in her. But look at me, gifted, musical, with a top education she never had.

I figure if there is a god I must owe him a lot. He must want me to be the best. I mustn't disappoint him by failing.

Everyone at home has lots of problems. In the holidays they talk and cry and argue about them around the dinner table. I don't have any problems. I just sit there real quiet and do the washing up because I believe I don't have anything they would want to hear. I figure I need to be the best, be brilliant, to get noticed.

Only it doesn't really work. If I had the kind of difficulties my mum and dad and sister had, I could get to say stuff around the dinner table too. But I don't because I am the good girl, the smart one, the lucky one.

So, I just keep working.

What do normal kids do

I look out the practice room window on a Sunday morning. All the day-kids have gone home.

I wonder what those kids do on a Sunday.

I can see a family through the window of a house opposite the practice block. They are having Sunday lunch. Watching TV. Playing with toys. I can't do that – there isn't much to do for boarders on the weekend. It is empty and lonely, so I practise and practise to fill the hole.

I see a kid walking down the street. They look carefree. They are the same age as me and I wonder,

What in the world do you do if you are 14 and not a musician with a gifted brain?

What do you do with all those hours I spend studying and practicing?

Crack

I'm 15. One of my dorm-mates has a quiet word with me, saying I've got chubby thighs. I think she is trying to help, because I get teased for being daggy and a bit of a nerd.

A week before, the popular boys play a prank on one of their mates and set them up for a slow dance with me at the school disco. They often call me a space-cadet, ugly and uncool. Pity the person who gets a dance with me. When the song plays, the boys stand lined up along the wall laughing at me and their friend as we sway awkwardly. It's humiliating.

I guess my friend must be right.

One early morning, as I rush to get the first breakfast in the line before practice time, I see myself in the mirror in the boarding house bathroom.

And I see a scale.

I wonder what would happen if I missed a few meals each day. I would get the best piano in the practice block – it's first come first served so I would have a head start to beat the others. I might even lose some weight. Then maybe the boys wouldn't laugh at me.

I try it for a week, and I weigh myself.

Magically, the number has gone down.

I suddenly realise I may have a solution for all this pressure. If I don't win that competition, if I slip up in that concert, if I miss a mark in that maths exam, it won't matter – because I can become the best at being thin. I can control what I eat like no-one else. No failure will be able to touch me.

I wonder for a moment if that god who booms out of the terrifying organ in the cathedral will accept this as my substitute if I am not good enough.

I figure I have no choice. I don't know how to cope with the stress. Controlling my weight becomes the new drug to nurse my anxiety and self-esteem.

The slippery slope has begun.

Enter Anorexia

I go hard and quick at this skipping-meals thing. I want instant results. I want more piano practice, and I want people to see that I am not the ugly chubby nerd. I can do something they can't.

So, I drop more meals in my day. Cut lunch and I get an extra hour of practice. Cut dinner and I can roll two hours into three. The pain of the hunger searing through my body is agony. But I must stick with it. I have no choice.

The only way to override my body's desperate cries for nourishment is to listen to a new voice in my mind. Like a computer virus, it overwrites all that my body is hardwired to do to live.

The voice trains me to tell myself feelings of hunger are good. Feelings of hunger make me worthy. Clean. Self-controlled. Committed. Hard-working.

It tells me hungry is safe. Full is dangerous – terrifying, even. If people don't notice I'm thin, I am not trying hard enough. I need to double down. I need to starve harder.

All kinds of foods become dangerous. Foods I had loved, home-cooking that I had yearned for during my homesickness – none of it can be trusted now, because of the tirade of punishment and reprimand it will elicit from this new master in my mind.

When I start to feel perpetually cold, the voice tells me that is not good enough, I should have less flesh on me.

When I reel with exhaustion walking back and forth from the practice block it tells me to walk more, go for morning runs – nobody has noticed anything yet, so I must still be fat.

The voice warps my perspectives of other people. Everyone is thinner than me. I need to see more of my bones, less of my flesh, look as petite as that girl or this girl.

Weeks pass and the boys have stopped teasing me now. If they look at me at all it is with looks of alarm and fear at the pale, gaunt appearance of my face, rather than ridicule. The voice tells me this is a good sign – a sign that what I am doing is working.

My closest friends start to express their concern. One night I return to my dormitory after hours of practice. My best friend is sitting on her bed looking at me and crying. She won't tell me why. She says it is nothing, she just had a bad cello lesson.

Years later I find out it is because she had expressed her concern for me to the housemistress, and the housemistress had told her to stop being such a sook. My friend was making mountains out of molehills, she said.

I stop going home for holidays, free weekends, half terms, any break, as much as I possibly can. I made that deal with myself years ago – because I couldn't bear the homesickness. Now it is because I am utterly terrified at the prospect of having to eat what my family would expect me to eat.

Months pass and my weight has dropped dangerously low. The feeling of mastery that I had at the start of this exercise has been replaced with fear.

I start writing in a journal and on its pages, I pen the words, 'I think I have anorexia, and I don't know what to do.'

The voice in my head screams at me, 'No you don't you stupid idiot – you're too fat for that! How pathetic you are to think such a stupid thought.'

I cross out the words I wrote in shame. Then, in the tiniest of font, I whisper,

'I just wish someone would notice. I want someone to notice but no-one is noticing.'

And it really seemed like no-one was.

Some teachers comment in a jokey way that I looked like a waif and was I eating enough? To which I nervously laugh back 'Oh yes, of course!'

I am muzzled by the voice. I don't know how to ask for help.

During our routine vaccinations, the school doctor comments that there isn't much flesh on me. I think to myself, desperately, 'This is the point he will step in and help me. This is the point he will make the voice go away, the physical pain, the starvation.'

But no, he doesn't say anything else.

So, I figure I am not worth noticing.

I ramp up my efforts – to practice, to win, to excel. And to lose weight.

The voice has become a monster. A tyrant I can't get rid of.

Bus

I'm 15. It is 7.30 am and I am sitting in my practice room in front of the shiny, polished Kawai[8].

Every day I have eight hours in this room to knock off. I get to the end of the day, exhausted but relieved that I have earned a temporary reprieve till the next morning. I've paid my dues to the monster in my head that demands I practise and starve and practise and starve.

But right now, it's not the end of the day, it's the beginning. We are at the bottom of the mountain with eight hours to go all over again, packed between a full school day of lessons, then studies till 2 am.

I've been living Groundhog Day for months now and I'm done-in, defeated and hopeless before I begin.

I start with the usual routine: Beringer exercises, then scales, arpeggios, all inversions, double triads, double sixths, dominant sevenths, diminished sevenths. It's all so boring and mind numbing, but I have to do it. I must get these fingers in shape and make them do what they should do. Only then will I be ready for the next assessment, concert, masterclass, and competition.

Then my piano teacher will believe in me. She'll give me more time, attention, and approval.

I live for my piano lessons. I live for my piano teacher.

---

[8] A top Japanese brand of concert piano.

If Miss Wilks is pleased my heart and my self-esteem soar - for a few hours. Until I'm back in this room, in front of the Kawai, doing the next round of drudgery so I can perform greater feats at my next lesson.

But if I disappoint her, my world is dark. I feel like I have nothing to live for. Her opinion of me fills the hole I guess might have been filled if I was at home. I'm not home, so she's all I've got.

Miss Wilks says my playing is unique, outstanding. I will go far. There is a bright future of success ahead of me. I hunger, reach and grasp for it in these hours of practice and more practice.

When I play on the concert platform my hands take people places nobody else can. I get standing ovations. I win competitions. People cry. They are touched. They gasp at what I can do. Their eyes widen.

Miss Wilks gets me masterclasses with the top pianists in the world. In the holidays I stay at her house for extra lessons with her and her husband, a prestigious teacher, too. I feel special when I'm with her, winning her praise. I need the fix of her affirmation like a drug. I can't get enough of it.

But it comes at a heavy price.

Because beneath all this talent and brilliance I carry a secret that torments me.

My gifted brain has a glitch. And I never know when that glitch is going to show up. I never know when my fingers are going to trip over each other. I never know when I might have a memory lapse in front of the full auditorium. Or play clumsily, or too loudly, or too fast or too slow.

And whenever it does show up, I feel like I'm stripped naked, seen for the fake that I believe myself to be. My fix of approval, of winning, of momentary success, is replaced with an abyss of worthlessness, shame, and failure.

So, I practise and practise and practise. I must practise more than anyone else, because of my glitch. And when I practise, I create a bully in my mind that amplifies every criticism I might ever receive.

Its job is to beat out the glitch.

Its methodology is brutal.

I miss a note…'You stupid idiot'. I ace a performance …'That was terrible, you sounded awful.' I have a memory lapse 'Shame on you – how could you be so dumb?' On and on.

My 8 hours in the practice room become 8 hours of relentless self-abuse.

I know there will come a point when I can't keep going like this.

Young Musician of the Year is coming, and I am forecast to win the piano section. A concert tour in Europe is scheduled with me as the star soloist. The TV program they spent 2 years making about me has just been broadcast. It's called 'In a Class of their Own'. It seems the world awaits my imminent success.

But right now, on the piano stool in front of the Kawai, being beaten to shreds by the bully in my mind, I can't go on much longer.

I look out the window at the road that snakes past the practice block towards my boarding house. Every few minutes buses go along that road.

I wish that I had the courage to run out onto it and be hit by a bus. I wish that I would die.

Because I can't see a way out of this drudgery. If I fail, I lose my scholarship and I will be sent home. And I believe my parents don't want me home. Something deep inside believes that that is why they sent me here in the first place. It's a lie, but I believe it. And the shame would be unbearable.

So, I wish more and more that something would take me out, put an end to this.

I keep imagining that bus.

A bang and then it all goes away.

Crash and burn

It's not the national competition I'm working tirelessly for that brings my me to my knees. It's the inconspicuous local one. The dry run for the bigger show. The one that shouldn't matter at all.

I'm playing Beethoven's 3rd for the concerto class. I have been told I should win this, hands down, in preparation for the competition that is to follow. Miss Wilks accompanies me with the orchestral part, and I do everything I possibly can to please her.

By now, the thought of failing – of not winning – is the thought of losing my world, my soul, my entire reason for being.

But that day I do not win. I come third.

Third, not First.

And my world collapses.

Maybe it's because I'm so underweight by now. I get dizzy playing. My mind goes foggy. I can't hear the sounds from the keys anymore – all I can hear is their mechanical clunk. No tone, no note. The glitch in my brain hijacks me. It keeps talking, bossing, directing my hands while I try to make the music fly and soar – and I can't.

I am like a plane low on fuel that cannot take off. I bounce and splutter along the runway with the notes, but I never get lift, never go anywhere. The magic that usually wows the judges isn't there.

I sob all the way home in the school bus. I can't stop sobbing. All the way back to my dorm. All the way through the pathetic dinner I allow myself.

There is nothing to me now. Absolutely nothing. Without music, without winning I am nothing. I've reached the end of the road. The keys don't make music for me anymore. They simply tie my monkey hands and heart up in knots. They tantalise me with magic and yield wooden clunks. The keys bind me, imprison me.

'Maybe you're just not cut out for this,' says Miss Wilks, sweetly, in the pub that night when she insists we go out for a drink. A calorie-less tomato juice, rather than my usual dopamine-inducing lesson slot.

The words shatter my soul. I've sold everything – my home, my friends, my family, my entire childhood to this false god of music that I thought everyone wanted me to obey. And now I discover it was all for nothing. I 'm a crumpled heap, too sick to remain at school, with nothing to show for the years of labour.

A month later I am gone.

Competition entries, concert tours, masterclasses, summer school scholarships all cancelled. Gone from school. Gone from any friends I had. Gone from the practice room where I had been shooting up all these years. To a home that had been replaced by an adolescent mental health unit.

I don't play again for thirty years.

And something in my heart dies.

FIRST INTERLUDE - STOP

'I need to stop! I can't do this.'

I push the laptop away angrily. It is 4 pm. I have Sam settled, back from school. I should be focusing on him in any case.

I feel Him listen. Intently.

What's going on, Al?

'I can't talk about this stuff anymore. I'm done.'

My stomach is clenching. The nausea is coming on again. Which means dinner is going to be hard.

'Great,' I mutter to myself.

I try some deep breathing to get it to settle. In, count to 4. Hold, count to 7. Out, count to 8. Repeat three times.

It semi-works.

'I mean why am I writing it anyway? Nobody meant any of that to happen! My folks loved me – love me. I love them! They were just doing their best – trying to give me everything they didn't have. Trying to feel their way through raising a 'gifted' kid. None of this was their fault!'

I know.

'And they're amazing people – I always used to brag to the other kids that I had the coolest family in town. And they were. They were so smart, so funny…'

Nausea and guilt intermingle.

'I never had a reason to get sick! I should have known better!'

I see Him sitting next to me in the corner of my eye. He looks thoughtfully at me.

'And the school and the teachers – they didn't know any better – they were just part of a crazy system they have in the UK that … I don't know, don't know why it exists, but they were just trying to do their best too! They were just human – broken – like me. Even the ones that got caught...'

My voice trails off.

You're right.

'So why does anybody care? Who needs to hear this stuff? Everyone has their own shit – who cares about mine? How's it going to help anybody?'

I care.

And… you might be surprised what I can do with …stuff.

I sigh.

'I just feel like I can't do this.'

He doesn't say anything. He holds me.

I slump back in my chair. I breathe again.

A bird warbles outside and the aircon creaks. It's a hot summers day in Melbourne. Sam has his headphones on and jumps off the couch.

'Love you, bye.' he says. He always does that when he goes to the toilet in the middle of a gaming session. It's kind of sweet.

I hear Him whisper,

My strength is made perfect in weakness[9].

We sit together a bit longer.

'Okay. I'll keep going.'

---

[9] 2 Corinthians 12:9-10.

Surviving

Help curtailed

'I have to get back and finish my A-levels. I have to get back and finish my A-levels. My A-levels. Have to finish them.'

I am rocking back and forth on the floor of the psychiatrist's office. He heads up the adolescent mental health unit I have been sent to. He is kind to me. Everyone is here. Too kind. I don't deserve it.

'Alys, you are incredibly sick right now. You need rest, not A-levels.'

I want to believe him, but I can't. Since the school got panicked and sent me home, the shame of failure has been overwhelming.

The dentist asks me how I could possibly do this to Mum. The local priest questions when I am going to get my act together and go back to school. Family friends share what a pity it is I'm not playing the piano anymore. What a waste. Mum exclaims in desperation, 'This is the only 'illness' you can actually get yourself well from! So why can't you just eat?!'

I have delayed her university admission. I feel her disappointment and pain acutely. When she finally does go, I'm relieved – at least I don't have to blame myself for that anymore.

But the staff at the adolescent unit don't blame. They are kind. We do fun stuff – stuff I haven't been able to do for a long while. We play. We go down the creek and float leaves. We make stained glass. We go to the beach. We go kayaking. They give me permission to eat. They give me back up against the voice. They help me put words to my feelings and my sense of failure.

And I don't deserve it. I must show my family and their friends that I will be good again, I will get my life together. The guilt for receiving this kindness, this help, is too much. So I stay only for a few months.

Not long enough to heal.

Getting it together

I try and get it together. I throw myself into study at a local sixth form college. I'm well enough to learn, but too sick to do much else. I study in my usual obsessive way and land myself a place at a top university in London doing a subject I have no real passion for. I don't care. It makes me look like I'm shaping up and getting my act together. It muffles the shame.

Two years on and I'm at that university, studying like I should.

But my autistic brain hates the whole, unstructured, thing. Nothing is clear, directed, black and white, like I need it to be. There seems no end to the amount of study you can and should do. I hate the relentless hours in libraries reading every book on the book list because that's what my brain does – it ticks off all the boxes no matter how hard that is. I figure I still have the glitch that nobody knows about. My brain can still short fuse, so I better rely on knowing the lot.

My world has gone grey. The spark and brilliance I had as a kid, that won me scholarships, friends and admiration has gone. I numb the sense of failure and the shame for having unresolved anorexia by drinking and smoking secretly, alone, away from the pubs and clubs where most students hang out to have fun. I can't handle the noise and the socialising, or the possibility of having to eat with others. I hide. I restrict my food more. I exercise.

I have boyfriends, not because I want to, but because I figure that is what you're meant to do to show you're pulling off life. They want sex, and after saying no over and over I give it to them, figuring I am not worth waiting for in any case.

I hate every act of forced intimacy. And I hate myself for it.

Stab[10]

I am 21. It is late at night in my student digs.

It's exam season and I have been studying hard for finals – too hard. I'm exhausted, still trying to make up for myself and this illness.

He comes in around 3am. He's been clubbing with his mates and my student residence is closer to the city than his.

I think I love him. Everyone loves him. He's been my boyfriend for 2 years. A medic. Smart, funny, good looking. I have no idea why he is with me.

I don't know he is coming that night, but the door bangs open, and he staggers in. I can't remember whether he says anything or not. I can smell the beer. The smoke. I should have gone with him, but I hate the clubs. They are too loud and claustrophobic. I don't know how to be sociable. I don't know what you are meant to do or say in those environments. I feel awkward. I am such a boring girlfriend.

I hear him pull off his clothes. Climb into the bed. It's a single bed – not comfortable for two, but I let him.

I can't really remember the rest. I think I said no. Maybe I didn't. Nobody ever listened when I did in the past, so maybe I gave up trying. I know he said it wasn't worth being with me if I wasn't going to give him sex. So, it might not have been safe to say no that night.

[10] Please note there is a trigger warning with this chapter. If you have experienced sexual trauma and feel vulnerable in this area, skip and go on to the next.

There was that time a few weeks back when he got angry about it, punched the bed because the sex wasn't good enough and I ended up cowering in a foetal position….

I don't want that to happen again.

I'm scared. I might have said I was tired. I'm not sure. I'm so stupid. I should have said no.

I can't breathe. Everything is black. I want it to be over. It hurts. I can't stand the smell, the pain. It must be me, something wrong with me, to hate it so much. I should try harder. I should be better. It goes on and on. I am hurting so much I feel like daggers are going into me with each thrust.

Finally, he is done.

He rolls over and goes straight to sleep. He snores.

My alarm goes off a few hours later. It's early because I must study. I have to get a First, I have to do better. I climb over him and go to the showers. I'm walking funny because I am in pain.

I wash myself in the shower. Over and over and over. But the dirt, the shame, the physical pain, it doesn't go away. It's still there, stuck to my body.

God, I am such an idiot. So many times, this happens. So many times.

One day I will discover I can sear the shame away by burning.

For now, I will keep trying to starve it.

*

A NOTE TO THE READER: ON SEXUAL TRAUMA

Only in my late thirties did I finally begin to acknowledge that so many of my early experiences of intimacy with men, like the one described in the previous chapter, were traumatic.

Up until this point, I felt I lacked the right to use the seemingly dramatic label of 'sexual trauma' in describing any of them. I was convinced I was making mountains out of molehills.

After all, I wasn't sexually abused at home. I don't think I was sexually abused at school like so many other kids were – though with blacked out memories I guess I will never know. And in all the multiple relationships I had with guys during my late teens and early 20s, not once could I label any of them as criminally abusive. They were just overgrown boys responding clumsily to their own wounds and unmet needs. They were no different to me.

So where was the trauma?

Two characteristics of mine might help answer this question.

The first, a desperate need to please people that was coupled with a lack of self-worth.

It's a lethal combination when it comes to intimacy. You feel so unworthy of the affection and attention you crave that you will do literally anything to keep that person happy – whether you want to or not.

The second? Being a young adult who was not-yet-diagnosed autistic. (My diagnosis did not come until my late thirties, when my seven-year-old son, Sam, received his.)

I had no idea about the experiences of sensory overwhelm, aversion to touch and the host of other body sensations that so many neurodiverse people can struggle with. I just thought there was something deeply wrong with me for hating any kind of sexual contact. I was frigid – that's what the boys had said when they teased me years back in boarding school. Or maybe it was my darned eating disorder.

Neither, in my mind, were good enough reasons to insist on the 'no' that screamed in my mind every time I had sex. Especially when my first feeble attempts to say it got overruled in any case.

It wasn't until I was 37, when flashbacks of my early adult relationships had become so intrusive and debilitating, that I had no choice but to start talking about them with the mental health professionals working with me. And when I did, the experiences that tumbled out of my mouth, like the one given in the previous chapter, *were* traumatic.

Innumerable memories of feeling suffocated. Of contact with moistness that I could not stand, smells that repelled me, pressure that felt overbearing. The grazing scratch of stubble. The feeling of being completely out of control, pinned to the bed, with no way out.

And, of course, the pain. Anyone can tell you that if you have sex when every fibre of your body doesn't want to, it hurts. A lot.

Nevertheless, the 'trauma' label *still* felt incredibly difficult to own.

Because wasn't it all my fault? I should have said no but, after two or three attempts to assert my wishes, I gave up trying. So that's on me, right? In some cases, I became so scared of not pleasing the guy, of them getting angry, or fed up with me, that I offered it before they even asked. Surely, I don't get to tout the sympathy card for sexual trauma when it was all because of me – *my* people pleasing, *my* low self-worth, *my* yet-to-be-known autistic sensory profile?

I was sure that, if I named it as such, someone would catch me and say:

'Sexual trauma?! Don't be stupid, you've got it all wrong! You're not the real deal! Listen to what *I* went through if you *really* want to know what sexual trauma is.'

But I have come to realise that trauma is a kind of shattering. Like your brain is a vase, and something happens, and it shatters all the way through. Vases can get cracked in lots of ways. They don't only shatter when a thief breaks into the house and trashes the place. They can shatter when an unassuming friend – or boyfriend – knocks them to the ground accidentally. Thief or friend, the vase is still shattered.

Naming my experiences as sexual trauma was integral to understanding why I felt so persistently dirty. And why I could not seem to kick the habit of trying to cleanse myself of that dirt through the searing pain of hunger induced by anorexia and, in later years when even that was not enough, self-harm.

Perhaps you, the reader, feel shattered in this whole regard too. And maybe, like me, you have chided yourself for feeling that way, because you're convinced what you experienced was not the 'real deal' – whatever that might be. Possibly you hear thoughts in your mind such as:

'Don't be stupid – that wasn't really trauma because no-one meant it and you should have said no and you didn't know it would be that bad,'

Or others that are even more painful than these.

I am so sorry if this is the case.

But if it is, I hope that in reading these words, you might be gently touched by one truth.

You are not alone.

*

Faith but no reprieve

I am 22, living in London, giving myself over and over to guys when I don't want to. I feel like a ragdoll. Everybody's comfort toy.

I want something to ease the pain – the worthlessness, loneliness and shame.

My sister recommends a Christianity course. She's been watching me struggle all these years. I think she wants to help me. Despite all she's been through – she lost the functional use of her arms for several years because of music school - she seems to have pulled up a whole lot better from our childhood than I have. She has an Oxbridge degree. She's a successful journalist, excelling in her career. I call her 'superwoman' when I talk about her to people I know. I should listen to her advice.

And it's unusual for her – she never got into the religion thing when Mum had her conversion. So maybe she's found something worth finding. Maybe I should try it.

So, I go. I do the whole thing - except the meal part[11], for obvious reasons. It comes to the decision point – where the speaker explains what happened on the cross and how that means we're forgiven.

My mind fixates on that – not so much the love part, just that I might be forgiven. This angry god I pictured in the booming cathedral at school - who was so disappointed with me for the anorexia, for not making it

[11] Many introductory courses for Christianity involve a shared meal prior to the talk in order to foster connection and friendship.

as a concert pianist, so disgusted with me from all the times I have given myself to these guys - might have forgiven me…

I had assumed I would go to hell when I stopped pulling off the spiritual thing with Mum. I figured maybe that wasn't so bad, because this god must know best, so if that's for the best then so be it. I didn't care enough about myself for it to bother me.

But for some reason it really bothered me that he might be mad.

When I hear the forgiveness message it seems too good to be true – that God might not be as angry as I thought. I don't quite believe it, but I figure I could just act as if – as if I believed I am forgiven.

So, I say the 'sinners' prayer' and follow a new way of living.

Many great things happen.

I love this God so much and I am so thankful to Him for forgiving me. For not being mad with me when he should. For putting up with me. I want to do Him proud. I share a version of the gospel with those I meet. I give words from the Bible to encourage others – the ones that don't scare me, at least. I work as a youth worker with troubled teens in Brixton, a suburb in London known for its drug gangs, crime and other socio-economic difficulties. I teach in rough schools in the East End. I work with kids that can't handle school, because I couldn't handle it either. I volunteer in soup kitchens and on a phoneline for the suicidal.

I want to help others, because God has helped me by dying for me and forgiving me for all my sins. Me with all my dirt and mess and failure.

I want very much to get well for God. I figure that if I'm really saved, I won't have this anorexia thing. I hear people say that anorexia is a sin. So, I desperately try to beat it myself. I gain some ground, manage to eat a bit more, gain some weight and look quite healthy.

But beneath all the progress and testimonies that I share, I know the illness is still with me. Like the glitch in my brain, it makes me a fraud.

I'm still terrified of food. Of spontaneity, flexibility and eating with others. I'm still afraid of eating meals that are different to the 'safe' ones I stick to; I eat meals that nourish me enough to keep me alive but are rigid enough to give me an illusion of control.

I'm deeply ashamed of this. I feel I have failed God. I repent of my anorexia again at the advice of a Christian counsellor. But nothing changes. There must be something wrong with me. Maybe God has not forgiven me after all.

I get prayer ministry. Lots of prayer ministry. People pray for breakthrough. I confess my sins – everything I can think of. I confess the sexual trauma I experienced in my past relationships as though it was all my fault. I cast out demons. I renounce lies. I try so hard to beat this thing for God so He will accept me, be proud of me, not be disappointed in me.

But despite all the trying and all the prayer, nothing seems to work. And because I think my illness is a sin, I figure I should probably do whatever it takes to beat it.

So, in the decades to come, well into my married years, I start looking outside of Christianity.

I try Buddhism. It appears very compassionate, accepting, and nonjudgemental to me – which is a relief, because I have a skewed perspective of Christianity that carries a lot of guilt. I throw my all into Buddhist teaching, reading copious Dharma books and listening to renowned lamas and gurus. I learn to meditate and am pleased when mindfulness buys me some peace. I find out there are all sorts of things you can do to change the direction of your karma – pujas, mantras, offerings. Maybe changing my karma will get me well. I bow down to Buddha statues, telling myself what the Buddhists say in their writings – it's not worship, it's a sign of respect for the Buddha's teachings.

The psych professionals I see in my later twenties and thirties think this is a great step – real progress, to broaden my rigid Christianity and incorporate other religions. God would be proud of me. So, I keep at it, hoping that the end justifies the means and if this works, I will have got myself well for God. Then maybe I will be good enough for Him.

And God wants me to be well and happy, right, so whatever it takes ought to be okay?

But eventually Buddhism becomes too much for me. I can't do it well enough. I'm not great at keeping the five precepts[12]. They include not drinking and I still need alcohol to numb my hunger. A Dharma teacher tells me I shouldn't be on medication – which I am by now – and can I please sit a little further away from him when he speaks because I am giving off a bad vibe or something.

[12] 'Five Precepts': guidelines for ethical conduct in Buddhism and the premise for an individual's ultimate liberation from suffering and attainment of enlightenment. They are: not killing, not stealing, not engaging in sexual misconduct, not lying and not using intoxicants.

I realise that the goal of the whole philosophy doesn't make me happy. It makes me sad. I try and trust that enlightenment - seeing reality as it really is, that the 'self' that binds me is simply an illusion, that everything is 'empty', non-being – I try and trust that if I get my head around all of this, I will feel happy, and then maybe I will get well.

But there is something - or Someone - missing.

I give up on it and try other things. Esoteric beliefs. Writers that talk a lot about universal energy. Manifesting your desires. How we are one, everything is one, the universe is one, is God, is love, is us. How happiness is our destiny if you just think right. I try crystals. I read astrology charts. But none of it stops the restriction, the acting out.

And I still have this gaping hole in my heart for that missing Person.

By the time I hit my early forties, I realise that for all the talk in the world I don't want to be enlightened or awakened to my place in a primordial energetic soup of oneness. I don't want to be my own saviour.

I want someone to rescue me. I want someone to take me home.

I am lost.

Wedding

I am 28 and it is the night before my wedding.

I have no idea why he is marrying me. A voice tells me I should never have allowed him to. He is as close to perfect as a man can be. Good to the bones. Gentle. Giving. I am soiled, second-hand, complicated, messy. I don't deserve him. But I am completely in love with him.

*

I fell for Mike the day I met him, three years prior to our wedding night.

I knew better than to say anything at the time. I was terrified he might find out and I would make a fool of myself. We were at a church small group meeting soon after I had become a Christian. I hadn't yet drifted off into other religions and spiritualities. Mike sang and played the guitar that evening, simply, beautifully and with passion. It blew me away. He seemed so gently in love with God, but a different kind of God than the one I was hounded by. A God of grace, tenderness and compassion.

There was a shared meal that, on this occasion, I managed, and we got talking.

I blushed the whole time, asked way too many questions and talked way too much. But Mike didn't seem to mind. He told me about the jobs he had had in Deutsche Bank and I shared about my teaching in the East End. We discovered a mutual love of the mountains, Mike relaying his trips to the Lake District and I mine to Snowdonia. He told me he was the youngest, dearly loved in a family of five siblings. He described the simple home he grew up in country Victoria, Australia and the wanderlust that had brought him to the UK for seven years.

Soon after, Mike invited me to join him on a series of hiking trips before his return to Australia later that year. The first was in the Alps, the second in the Dolomites and the third in Slovenia.

I felt like I was on a honeymoon for each. We savoured the majesty of those mountains together. We walked and talked for hours each day about life, faith, the things we treasured, our hopes and dreams. He made me laugh till I cried with his gentle humour and caricatures of Australian accents.

Uninhibited, I blurted out all regarding my breakdown as a child, my failure to make it as a musician, the shame of my eating disorder and the countless relationships I'd had before becoming a Christian. I emphasised jokingly that if anyone ever needed saving when they turned up to a Christianity course, I was that person. I wanted him to know the worst so he could reject me immediately and I would not get my hopes up.

But he didn't push me away. Our friendship grew. Via email when he returned to Australia, and then in person when he invited me out there.

I remember the night we had the super awkward 'chat'. The one where you figure out whether you are officially dating. That was the night Mike asked if I would allow him to ....*hold my hand.*

I couldn't believe it. I was used to a two-week time limit for the wait period prior to sex. He was at pains to save it until we had made a mutual lifelong commitment. Mike seemed to think I was worth waiting for.

He proposed to me in a song he wrote. He sang it on a 46-degree night at Palm Beach, Sydney. He was so nervous that he sat shaking in the car for 20 minutes before agreeing to get out and sit on the dunes to watch the sun set. I couldn't for the life of me work out why, or why he had brought the guitar.

Credit to him, he sang his heart out, serenading me in front of a crowd of watery-eyed onlookers.

I cried when I said yes. I adored Mike and couldn't fathom life without him. But I felt like a fraud. He deserved so much better than me. So many girls at our church had fallen in love with Mike. That's how special he was.

I shouldn't have been the one that got to be with him. Not me with all my problems.

We returned to Wales to get married 18 months later.

*

The wedding is going to be big. Bigger than I can manage. Fireworks. 160 people. I have let Mum and Dad organise the whole thing to soften the grief they feel about me leaving the UK for good and moving to Australia to be with Mike.

But just like the night of Mike's proposal, I'm crying again. Slumped on the couch in my parent's sitting room, I look through the window and see the white marquee that awaits tomorrow's crowds. I should be happy, but I feel overwhelmed.

Dad is sitting next to me, concerned. I don't want him to think I'm not grateful for what they've done. I know they're trying to show how much they care for me. But I can't stop crying. My anxiety about the day – the attention, having to dress up, all those eyes on me, the food, everything – it is through the roof.

Dad sees my tears. He sighs, then, with deep concern says,

'Mike is a good man. He deserves better than this.'

He doesn't mean it that way, but I hear it that way. It confirms what I have always believed.

So, I walk up the aisle and say my vows, still believing all along that this man does not deserve me.

And I don't deserve him. I never will.

One day that lie will tear the whole dream to pieces.

Psych ward

We've been married one year. And my wheels are starting to fall off.

During our dating years I had pulled off life well. I looked okay on the outside. Thin but not too thin. Rigid, but still eating. Avoiding most social gatherings, but always with good excuses. In Australia I taught kids with disabilities and taught well. I did voluntary work. I was gregarious, fun, 'engaging' to talk with when I needed to be. Mike says he saw real strength in me – that was one of the reasons he married me.

But now we are living together, I can't mask so well – something I didn't even realise I had been doing.

I struggle, visibly.

Despite moving to the other side of the world, flashbacks from the past start invading my present. I cry unpredictably. I shut down and withdraw. I increase my restriction and exercise to numb the feelings. I feel anorexia tightening its ice grip on me.

Mike, in his care and concern, is bemused as to the woman he has found himself wed to. I don't understand her either. We don't fight about my behaviours. We both hate conflict and are sensitive to each other's feelings. I'm open with Mike and tell him how I'm struggling and all the ways in which I am acting out. I explain that I don't know why I am doing this. I thought my faith should have fixed me. I don't know why this is happening.

Mike is characteristically patient, gentle and compassionate with me. He supports me emotionally and financially as I begin the wild goose chase for treatment that might help. Psychologists. Psychotherapists. Psychiatrists. Psychosomatic therapy. CBT. DBT. EMDR[13]. Alternative health therapies.

I begin to piece together my past, to form a narrative of why I am the way I am. But I never find the solution. My weight plummets, so I concede to my first psychiatric admission. The first of many. Mike is relieved – he is at a loss as to how to help me and is grateful for professionals to step in.

The first time I come here I'm alarmed, scared and shocked that this is where I find myself. By the time my admissions have reached double figures the regime has become depressingly familiar.

The APU[14] doors open and lock behind me with a security bleep. From the moment I enter the ward I feel like a criminal. I'm stripped to a hospital gown for the weigh-in. I'm frisked for any harmful implement, laxatives or pills to overdose with. My bags are emptied and inspected for razors, cords, knitting needles, scissors, sewing kits - anything I might suicide with. Hot water bottles, heat packs, together with warming devices of any kind, are forbidden. Underweight as I am, my body shivers with cold.

We get a list of rules – rules to protect us from the eating disorder and the BPD and the OCD[15] and whatever else we have dragged in with us.

---

13 CBT, DBT, EMDR: Cognitive Behavioural Therapy, Dialectical Behavioural Therapy, Eye Movement Desensitization and Reprocessing. All therapeutic approaches to assist individuals dealing with complex trauma and correlating comorbidities, such as Borderline Personality Disorder, Obsessive Compulsive Disorder, Major Depressive Disorder and Anxiety.

14 APU: Acute Psychiatric Unit.

15 (BPD) Borderline Personality Disorder. (OCD) Obsessive Compulsive Disorder.

I look at the list and am swamped with anxiety. I've probably broken seven already.

No standing for unnecessary periods between meals.

Bathroom access only under supervision.

Hands on the table while you eat.

No placing serviettes on your laps.

No teaspoons to eat yoghurt with (we must eat everything with big cutlery).

No spitting.

No chewing gum.

No hot or warm drinks with meals.

No sneaking extra condiments.

No talking about weight, clothing sizes, behaviours, self-harm, trauma, suicidal thoughts.

No access to phones immediately after meals.

No unnecessary standing.

No walking.

No exercise of any kind.

On and on the list goes.

We must sign a form agreeing to every rule. That's how we show we're committed. How we promise to keep ourselves and each other safe from our illnesses.

I feel like I am back at boarding school.

Only the shame of transgressing one of these rules is infinitely worse. Breaking a rule here means you're not taking recovery seriously. You're colluding with the enemy - your illness. You're dishonest. You're letting yourself, the group, the medical team, your husband - and anyone else you are trying to get well for - down.

Mealtimes are the predictable ordeal we all know to expect. Sobbing patients around the table. Screaming, swearing, and attempts to run away. The unmentioned but known nasogastric tube in the patient's room due to non-compliance. The timer is constantly in front of us. If we don't finish the overwhelming portions of food at each sitting, we will be asked to consume supplements immediately afterward – something we all know is not worth the pain.

Our food-induced terror is overlayed by repeated and unpredictable explosions from elsewhere on the ward. One patient's psychotic episode leads to overturned tables, chairs thrown, screaming and swearing at staff. Another's detox-rage prompts main-area evacuation and seclusion to our rooms. Security guards are called in frequently.

We deal with the intolerable anxiety around what we are having to eat, and the regimented fashion in which we are eating it, by relentless recourse to PRN's[16]. Diazepam, quetiapine and temazepam become our new friends. Anything to take the edge off, to numb the flashbacks and voices that are rearing into our minds as we eat. I start smoking again. Then vaping when smoking gets banned.

Mealtimes – all six of them – are followed by hours of interminable waiting in the post-meal room where we must remain under strict observation. Standing, moving, talking on our phones, are all forbidden. We wait and wait, until such time as it is physically impossible to purge – if that is what a patient had in mind.

'Meal support' may happen during that time. It usually involves a nurse's heroic attempts to distract us in some way. A game of scrabble that no-one can bear to play. The hundredth mandala that no-one can be bothered to colour.

But if someone is in meltdown with a post meal panic attack, meal support will be needed by that person alone. They are taken next door to a room where they can vent their distress. It is supposedly soundproofed, but we can all hear the screams, cries, the suicidal exclamations, the wall-thumping, begging to go home that still permeates through to our room.

Sometimes my admission is even more confined. I am bedbound in a medical ward where a nurse has been assigned to watch me toilet, wash, eat. She makes notes as I take each mouthful. The silence is excruciating. I feel sorry for her - what a job.

But I am the offender here. I am the one that cannot be trusted.

---

16 'PRN': the acronym for the Latin pharmaceutical term 'pro re nata' which means 'as needed'. In a psych ward, this equates to medications administered as and when needed according to a patient's distress levels.

We know all of this is unavoidable. This is the only way the doctors and nurses can keep us alive from the monster that would devour us. But the pain and distress of each admission is immense. And I can only foresee one outcome when I get home.

Relapse.

Pregnant[17]

I burst into the kitchen waving the double-striped stick at Mike. It's my birthday, 2012. We've been married six years, and we've just been given the most precious gift we could hope for.

'We're pregnant!' I exclaim, breathless.

Mike is sitting peacefully at the breakfast table doing his daily sudoku puzzle. His jaw drops in incredulity for a moment, then bursts into a broad grin. He leaps up from his chair, hugs me and we twirl and cry like two teenagers.

*

Ever since we first started dating, Mike and I dreamed of having a family. We would walk along St. Kilda beach negotiating whether 3 or 4 or 5 or 6 were too many. We'd trade visions of all the things we'd do with our children, places we'd go with them, hobbies and passions we'd share with them.

Truth be told, I loved Sam years before he was conceived. Even before I met Mike.

I was 22 when I tearily asked God if He might one day grant me a son. I was praying on my knees in the tiny attic room I rented in London. My faith was new and passionate.

[17] Trigger warning: self-harm behaviours are described in this chapter.

I know I would have been just as happy with a daughter, but I'd been reading a story in the Bible about a woman called Hannah who was unable to have children. She was teased mercilessly for it by her husband's second wife, Peninnah[18], so much so that Hannah felt unable to eat.

One day, in deep anguish, Hannah took herself to the Jewish temple. Weeping, she petitioned God with silent words:

'Lord Almighty, if you will only look on your servant's misery and remember me, and not forget your servant but give her a son, then I will give him to the Lord for all the days of his life…'

When the high priest, Eli, saw the peculiar way Hannah prayed - '...only her lips were moving, and her voice was not heard...' he denounced her for mistaken drunkenness. Hannah explained the true cause of her tears and Eli softened, conferring on her, instead, a blessing:

'Go in peace and may the God of Israel grant you what you have asked of Him.'

And so, the story continues, 'in the course of time, Hannah became pregnant and gave birth to a son. She named him Samuel[19] saying, 'Because I asked the Lord for him.'

For some reason, when I read this story, I connected deeply with Hannah. Her prayer seemed to voice the cry of my own heart.

---

[18] Polygamy was still a cultural norm at the time of this story, found in the Bible, 1 Samuel 1:1-20.

[19] *Samuel* sounds like the Hebrew for *heard by God.* Story is quoted ibid, NIV.

My prayer wasn't a demand. I knew children are a gift. With my history of anorexia, I believed myself to be less deserving of a child than any other woman. Many will know that the dream of having kids can die early with this disease.

But a desire, rather than a demand, was there, deep in my heart, for Sammy.

Perhaps that is the way God brings children into this world – by planting His desire for them in the heart of two parents.

I left my petition with God that night. I was single then, yet to meet Mike. But somehow – I'm not sure quite how to explain it – I heard an oh-so-quiet, gentle whisper of grace.

The word, 'Yes'.

I held onto that word for the next 10 years.

When we started trying for a baby, Mike and I knew there were significant risks given my health. But we felt that if it was God's will, He would help us navigate through whatever lay ahead. And if it wasn't, so be it. I had never menstruated naturally, so the likelihood of success was extremely low.

But there they were, the two stripes. Only a few months after trying. Utterly miraculous. Ultrasounds in the months to come confirmed a boy. The 'Yes' whispered to me a decade ago was to come to fulfillment. Sammy was on his way.

*

Throughout the time of carrying Sam, the wonder, joy and gratitude we feel for him as he grows within me never wavers. We want him in our lives more than anything in the world.

But the task of feeding myself to feed him is harder than I ever anticipated it would be.

Starting pregnancy at a low body weight means that I must gain weight at a far greater rate than a healthy person to ensure Sam's survival. I must consume significantly larger quantities of food than the average person, when I have struggled all my life to eat a sub-average amount of nutrition.

During the first trimester morning sickness sets in, and I fail to hit nutritional targets. By month four, Sam is behind on his growth markers, and I have barely maintained, let alone gained, weight.

Mike and I agree to do whatever it takes for Sam to have the chance at life he deserves. We decide on another psychiatric admission. It will be the lengthiest I have yet experienced.

As a pregnant anorexic woman, my meal plans surpass, vastly, those of my fellow patients and are increased at a dramatically higher rate. The physical pain induced by consuming this amount of food is challenging enough. Nausea, bowel obstructions, persistent GI pains and cramping[20] are my constant and unwelcome companions.

[20] Symptoms experienced by many during any refeeding regime in eating disorder recovery. This is due to the gastroparesis (slow emptying of the digestive tract) that results from long-term starvation and disordered eating patterns. They are made particularly severe during pregnancy for an anorexic, due to the increased volume of nutritional intake required for mum and baby.

But it is the psychological torment that makes the task of nourishing Sam safely to birth seem nigh-on impossible.

As my body grows and changes, the very sensation of being in it becomes intolerable. Visual and somatic memories of sexual trauma rear their heads, intruding into my every moment. I feel as though I'm in a perpetual state of being violated, suffocated, and pressed down by the men I have been with in the past. My skin crawls as if writhing with ants. Voices of disgust and self-hatred scream in my mind. I'm saturated with a sense of shame and dirt.

My only consolation is to place my hand on my womb where Sam lies ensconced and remind myself *this is the reason* I am doing this. *He* is the reason. *I won't give up.*

I weep and howl at night, banging my head against the patient bed rail to try and get the thoughts and flashbacks out of my mind. Then I sob desperate apologies to Sam, telling him I love him, and we are going to be okay.

Sometimes the insanity is so extreme that I find myself praying to God that He might kill me, but keep Sam.

By 8 months, the psychosomatic onslaught of refeeding becomes too much. I must find a way to get rid of these thoughts, sensations and feelings.

For some reason unbeknownst to me, I've been allowed to keep my hair straighteners on the ward. One night, the final snack of the day concluded, I return to my room, turn the hair straighteners on and hear a voice whisper in my head:

'If you want this child to live, you need to be punished.'

I hesitate. It continues,

'I will not leave you alone until you harm yourself.'

Usually, I am good at telling the nurses when I have voices in my head. But on this occasion, the nurses are in handover and part of me is relieved. If this is what it's going to take to get both of us through, then I must do it, I tell myself.

Deep down I know that Sam will feel the pain. His helpless body will be flooded with a rush of adrenalin, cortisol and other chemicals triggered by sustained burning. And I know I'll never be able to forgive myself.

But I'm delirious with distress and convinced this is the only way to keep Sam alive. The voice has hijacked the truth.

'It is this or suicide – the end of both of you.' It whispers. 'If you want him to live, you have to harm.'

And so begins a new nightmare. At 35 I become addicted to self-harm.

Never one to do things by halves, I want this voice placated and placated fast. I go at the burning hard, counting ever increasing increments of time for the length of burn, the numbers of burns, and the surface area of my body that needs to be burnt.

It takes three episodes before the nurses can rail in my new behaviour. At that point, I'm in such physical pain in my arms and legs that the flashbacks, somatic sensations, and taunting voice have all been blotted out. The harming has 'worked'. I manage to eat all that is required until Sam and I reach the labour suite. Sam is born at a healthy weight.

But his body shakes uncontrollably for two weeks.

Mike, deeply disturbed by my scarred appearance when I return home, is lost as to how to help me. He expresses patient concern, disposes of hair straighteners countless times, but is unable to stop me acting out. The flashbacks continue even after Sam's birth and harming, like shooting up on meth, becomes my new drug of choice alongside anorexia.

Sam never sees me do it. But he grows up seeing my wounds.

And my wounds are to become his.

Broken cisterns

I am forty. I have tried everything. I have given it all I have got.

But nothing works.

The people helping me – a host of doctors, dieticians, psychiatrists, psychologists, social workers and case workers – said I should do all this treatment.

'If you really want to get well, you'll put yourself through this program.'

'This admission is the best thing you can do for your son. Remember the oxygen mask? You can't be there for Sam unless you take care of yourself. He deserves to have a mum that's living. You owe it to him.'

But it isn't the best thing for Sam. It hasn't been. He has PTSD now from all my hospitalisations - and so do I. I'm no healthier, no freer than I was 25 years ago.

I am such a good patient when I'm admitted.

I do everything they ask. I'm polite. I eat all the food - even though it kills me in my mind. I stick to most of the rules. Hospital nurses and psychiatrists pat me on the back saying how much progress I'm making. I watch the numbers on the scale go up every weigh day. I try to feel proud of myself.

But inside I am screaming.

I try to pretend this time round it will be different, this time I'll make it, I'll get there. But deep down I know otherwise.

When I get home, I'll have to restrict again to cope, to pull off life, to get some semblance of that clean feeling that starving gives me. The gnawing hunger – it blots out the dirt I still feel in my skin from all my flashbacks and failures. The shame hasn't gone. The self-hatred, the voices – they're still there.

We do dream boards – but I have no dreams. We do value circles – but the "values" they propose seem to me like empty buzzwords you'd find on an Insta or Facebook meme. They're wooden, flaky - I have no real passion for any of them.

We do safety plans, but I know I will never use them. When I'm in that much distress that I want to die – even though I know the immense damage it would cause Sam - squeezing a squidgy ball or taking a warm bath or distracting myself with whatever else is on that plan just won't cut it.

We do relapse prevention plans, but I know that if I've started the slippery slope to restriction, there is no-one who will be able to persuade me to turn it around. No-one will be able to convince me that living the hell I live in when I eat will be worth it.

They give me flowcharts to deal with my emotions. They look like a labyrinth before I begin. I'm meant to look them up whenever I have a feeling that hurts.

But how do I use a flowchart when the voice in my mind tells me that I deserve to be punished like no other? That if I just burn it off, the pain will go and not come back – at least until the surgery has healed? How do I think straight enough to start mapping my way through anger, self-hatred and fear like that?

They give me checklists, and I dutifully do my best, ticking my wins for 6 weeks, 12 weeks, however long. But then I start to think, to what end? I'm a ticking timebomb and it will only be a few weeks without these checklists before I must act out. I'll have no choice. The checklist isn't powerful enough.

Neither are the 'helpful' thoughts they get me to construct to challenge the thoughts in my mind. They don't tell me why those thoughts are any more 'true' than the bully in my mind that has tormented me for the last three decades.

They tell me that everyone's truth is valid and there are many 'truths': my truth, your truth, her truth, his truth. So how can a random thought plucked out of nowhere be any truer than the voice that tells me I should kill myself?

I need stronger truth. I need something with power, something my disordered neural pathways can't refute. But they can't give it to me.

Nothing works. Nothing.

Eventually the doctors start to give up on me. I get shifted to that quota of patients who, even though they're at death's door, are only admitted for a 'short' (4-week) admission. Because, crudely, what's the point of getting me up to a healthy weight if I am going to lose it as soon as I get home? I'm in the too hard basket.

'SEED' they call it. 'Severe Enduring Eating Disorder.' Code for: 'this is as good as it gets.'

One admission we are sitting watching the clock tick in the post-meal support room. A younger patient is saying how she wants to get out of here, how she is done with this shit.

Aren't we all, I think.

Then she looks at me and says 'I don't want to wind up like you, no offense.' I'm not sure what she means. Then I get it. She is 20. I am 40, still sick as a dog. She has a chance. My future is doomed.

I start to hate the word 'recovery'. The doctors and dieticians and nurses talk about it all the time, but I can never reach it. It's a horizon that lies forever beyond me. I give up on it. It's not for me and never will be.

I just have to stay alive. For Sam and Mike. Not me.

SECOND INTERLUDE - BIKE

'I think that might have been a bit too harsh.'

We are on the bike, pedalling and listening to music, the wind rushing into and around me.

He rides next to me.

I love our cycles together these days. I pinch myself that I can even do them. That I have the energy to ride just to chat with Him and let the wind blow my thoughts away – not simply to burn calories.

I love that He loves cycling with me. I throw in a thanks. Who would have imagined.... He throws me a quick knowing glance and smiles. Then looks ahead.

What do you mean?

'I mean the stuff about treatment. They were doing everything they could. They kept me alive. For all the horror of being separated from Sam during all those admissions, his life would have been infinitely worse if I had died...'

You're right. It would have been. And I have some good people in those hospitals.

I think back.

'I know. The regime was hard, but so many of them – the nurses, the docs, they had genuine compassion. They'd devoted their lives to figuring out a way to help people like me.'

He listens.

'Sometimes I think that's how You showed up for me back then. In other people's acts of random kindness. Like Kerri – that nurse that just sat with me on my bed while I bawled about being apart from Sam. She didn't try to fix it or lecture me. She just said she knew it was really hard. That meant so much.'

She's a beauty, Kerri.

He smiles – He is thinking about her. I can see it out of the corner of my eye.

'Even the psychiatrists with the shiny suits and polished shoes. The amount of study and energy and money they must have invested to try and crack this illness. To do what they do. They freaked me out - but I get that I needed them back then. I might do in the future again… I hope not, but who knows…'

We ring our bell and swoop around a young couple with their baby in a pram.

'I'm sorry. I shouldn't have said all that stuff. About how hard treatment was. How I couldn't get it to work. I guess I'm trying to make sense of so many years of trying and failing. I guess I feel mad. And I don't know where to send the anger – blame myself or them. I guess neither option is that good.'

You're right. Blame doesn't usually help.

We pedal some more. I can feel the sweat glistening on my arms.

What about you give me the anger and see what you really want to say beneath it?

He often does this. We call it the suitcase method. I talk about a feeling and unpack it. Then figure out if it's an issue I can actually do something about or if I need to handball it back to Him.

'I guess I feel grief, sadness, under the anger. For the years lost to the illness. Years with Sam and Mike I can't get back....'

He reaches out and touches me – He's a whizz at one-handed riding without falling off.

My sadness is comforted. I sigh.

'Anyway... I can't change my experiences of treatment. I probably would have died without it. And I don't know what the solution is to the myriad of challenges doctors face as they courageously attempt to help patients with eating disorders.'

I give Him the anger suitcase. And the blame one too.

'I guess what I mean is that... treatment could only ever get me so far. It showed me what the problem was – how I got sick, how sick I was, what my thinking problems were, what my dysfunctional behaviours were. It did that well. The doctors always used to marvel at the level of insight I had into my illness. But I could never get beyond that. It could never show me the way out. There was a missing piece I guess, that's all. A massive missing piece for me. Maybe not for others. But for me.'

He nods thoughtfully.

We hear two bells and a couple of road bikes overtake us. He raises his right hand to gesture a thanks.

'I don't know how to say this without sounding kind of messed up.'

What's that?

'Well… it's just that… now that we are here together, doing this… I'm kind of glad it didn't work. Me figuring it out on my own, just with the treatment, I mean. Don't get me wrong - I wish I had not put my family and everyone I know through the pain of watching me be sick for so long. Especially Sam. But I'm glad I couldn't find the answer in myself.'

Why's that?

'You know… I'm pretty darn stubborn and independent. I think if I had cracked it just with treatment you wouldn't have heard a bar from me. I wouldn't have given up. And then I wouldn't have woken up. And we wouldn't be having this conversation now.'

He pauses.

Probably best not to burden yourself with the 'what if'.

I smart a bit. He's right. Trying to formulate the reasons why things turn out the way they do and what would have happened if they didn't is a bit like playing God. And it usually ends up being offensive to someone.

'Sorry. I guess… what I'm trying to say is… thanks. Thanks for letting me not get it. Thanks for letting me collapse in a heap. For hitting ground zero. I never would have found You. I never would have found the missing piece…'

We swing over the bridge and onto the gravel track leading to the road.

Music?

Yes. Music. I hit the E.T theme tune track on my phone.

Race you!

He smiles and surges ahead.

The Turning

Ground Zero

I'm 44, sitting on the floor of my ex's house. We're house swapping so that we don't unsettle Sam. The walls are covered with Blue Tack marks from where Sam's pictures used to be. An empty space where our wedding photo used to be. Empty shelves from where Sam's toys used to be.

I'm my sickest ever.

A few years ago, in desperation, I thought maybe it was my gender identity that was the problem. Maybe that was the answer to the anorexia. Maybe the reason I couldn't stand intimacy, the reason I had all those voices, the reason I wanted to tear my skin off after sex was because I was gay, or non-binary or something.

Professionals cheer-led from the sidelines with my new discovery. Perhaps this would finally help me turn a corner. Perhaps this would get me off their books.

I didn't deserve to be with Mike in any case. I never did – not when he proposed, not when we got married, and definitely not now. He would be better off without me. If I left him, at least he wouldn't have the pain of watching me stay sick.

Covid had decimated our family. Sam's autism was newly diagnosed. The lockdowns brought extreme, dramatic episodes of anxious, distressed violence and aggression into our home. None of us felt safe. Sam was pushing his dad away. Despite Mike's incredible care and support throughout the hospitalisations, Sam felt deeply insecure from my absences and clung to me with all he had.

I couldn't fix the dynamic. I couldn't bear to see what was happening between them, between all of us. Something had to change. This will provide the circuit breaker we need, I thought. This will reduce Sam's animosity towards Mike. This will help things get better. It might even help me get better.

By this time, I'd drifted far from the faith that once united Mike and me. I was immersed in an eclectic mix of eastern and new age spirituality in my quest for healing. Separation no longer carried any sense of moral failing.

On the contrary, in the books I read and amongst the professionals I saw, it was applauded as an 'enlightened' and 'courageous' step. My primary psychiatrist not only insisted separation was best for Mike and Sam – she threatened to stop treatment altogether if I refused.

So, I left.

Me, not Mike. For all the stress caused by my illness, he never wanted to separate.

I broke his heart, completely.

We worked out a care arrangement for Sam. And I moved into a two-bedroom granny flat three kilometres away.

It's been two years now since all of that happened. But I'm not any better.

I'm worse.

I look at the wreckage around me and the awful truth dawns on me. I'm not gay or non-binary. I know some people are. But I'm not.

I'm just confused.

Sam is still distressed, still struggling.

I still love Mike. Painfully. But I've lost him. I've lost everything good that has been given to me.

And *I* did this.

I'm sitting on the floor, hugging my knees.

'I've got this all…so…wrong…' I blurt out loud, to the empty walls. 'So… so … wrong...'

I cannot name the pain of those words. Grief and regret beyond compare.

I have hit ground zero.

The Fall

I feel a Presence in the room. Palpable. Real.

I shut my eyes and see a Shepherd. He wears a rough, brown tunic. His skin is weathered and sun worn. His hair falls in thick, chin-length curls. A tall staff leans beside Him. And He's sitting on the armchair opposite me.

He sees me. Right now. Just as I am. Lost. Sick. Confused. A mess.

I can tell that He sees straight into my heart.

'I've got this all so wrong.' I repeat. Not to the empty walls this time.

I'm speaking to Him now.

I'm not sure I even know this Shepherd. He looks nothing like the postcards or the paintings I've seen. He's not white-robed or pristine and glowing. He's dusty, rough and real. Like a man who has walked miles just to sit here with me. When I look at Him, it's like staring directly into … Love itself.

And I'm blurting out these words with no idea what He will say.

Will He remind me how much I've hurt Mike and Sam? How stupid I was for thinking separation would be better for them? How much I've disgraced our families – Mike's and mine?

Will He reprimand me for all the 'wrong' religions I've tried and gods I've bowed down to?

Will He tell me how disappointed He is with me for not making better use of all that treatment and how Mike never deserved any of this? How Sam would do so much better with a different mum?

Will He lecture me about gender identity and sexual orientation and Bible verses and right and wrong theology?

Will He say, scornfully, 'I told you so!'?

I don't know.

Honestly, I don't care. I've got nothing left. The words just tumble out, like floodwaters breaking through a dam.

'I have got this all… so… wrong.' Over and over.

I bury my head in my knees. Tears. Despair.

Then … I look up again. And I don't see what I expected. I don't see judgement or disappointment or anger.

All I see are His eyes - brown, wide, deep, full of love. Full of pain.

And His arms, open.

I love you.

I sniff and pause my crying for a moment.

'Really? I… how… I don't deserve…' My voice breaks, then crumbles into sobs.

'I'm so sorry. So sorry. Please… I am so sorry... I don't know what to do… I am so sorry...'

It's okay Al. I'm here. You're safe. It's okay.

I glance at His hands. Strong hands. Open. With deep, ugly scars on them.

I hesitate for a moment, because I know what happens next. If I do this – if I surrender – everything changes. No more trying to control, fix and define myself. No more attempting to run my life and figure it all out. This moment will end it all.

Then I shut my eyes.

And I fall completely into Him.

I don't know what is going to happen or whether I will survive this illness. I don't know if I'll get Mike back and our family restored. I don't know anything.

But I feel such relief, right there, in His arms, in His wounded hands.

I feel… like I have come home.

First steps

Follow

I don't know where to go from here, this living-room moment, a ground zero and a turning point all in one.

I want to ask Him for my marriage back, only it hurts too much to hope. I want to beg that Sam will be okay, but I can't bear to consider that he might not. I want to ask to live but I don't know how to eat.

Yet beneath all these agonising longings, when I stop and listen, I find something else I want even more.

I want *Him*.

I want to go with Him, hold onto Him. To never let Him go, never be lost again, never be allowed to leave Him and do life alone again. And yet ...I have this sense that He has never left me.

He reminds me of a story I read in the past[21]. The Shepherd has died and – incomprehensibly - come back to life. He's having breakfast on a beach with His dumbfounded friends. One of His followers, Peter, has just been invited to declare his love for the Shepherd three times.

Peter does this, and the Shepherd goes on to reveal the true nature of the journey that lies ahead. A road that will be marked by suffering as Peter walks out his love for his resurrected Master.

At that moment, Peter turns to see one of the other disciples, John, following them and says to the Shepherd, 'Lord what about him?'

---

[21] John 21:15-22.

The answer he receives are the Shepherd's words to me right now.

What is that to you? You must follow me.

It's as if He's saying,

All your hopes, dreams, desires – your marriage, your son, your health – what are they to you?

You. Follow me.

It sounds hard. But it's not.

He is really saying,

I am that good, that you can entrust all these things to me. All I require is that you follow me.

I like that. I like it so much, because it's simple, not complicated like my life.

So… I let it all go.

All those hopes, desperate wishes, fears, dreads. Mike. Sam. Family disgrace. Anorexia. I put them all in His hands like precious jewels. And I look up into His eyes.

'Okay,' I whisper. 'I will follow…I don't know what to do, but I will follow.'

I don't know what will happen.

I don't know if I'll get Mike back.

If Sam will be okay.

If I'll ever beat this illness.

If Mike's family and friends will forgive me.

I don't know how to begin cleaning up the mess I'm in.

But I trust those eyes.

I trust Him.

I choose to follow.

And He smiles.

Cut Loose

I need to walk away.

From all the voices, opinions, professionals, therapies, and programs. All the things I've been told I should be doing.

I am on a disability support pension, and people say I need these things, and maybe there was a time when they were right.

But in this moment, I need something else. I need stillness. I need Him.

It's time to put everything down - the books, the self-help material, the Dharma texts, the meditation guides, the psychology manuals, worksheets and podcasts. Even the appointments.

I know the professionals will be worried. They'll probably think it is another of my BPD episodes[22], my acts of self-sabotage. They might even call CATT[23]. But I don't care.

I just need everyone except Him out the room right now. Like all the wailing voices in Jairus' house when they thought his little girl had died. The Shepherd came, and the first thing He did was get all the voices out the room.

---

22 BPD: Borderline Personality Disorder. A BPD episode refers to an intense emotional reaction or crisis triggered by stress, perceived abandonment or interpersonal conflicts. Impulsive behaviour and decisions can be one symptomatic feature of a BPD episode.

23 CATT stands for Crisis Assessment and Treatment Team. These teams are responsible for assessing individuals experiencing psychiatric crises and providing short-term interventions as an alternative to hospitalization.

The next thing He did was raise her to life[24].

So, I cancel all my appointments.

It's not because all those incredible, dedicated professionals helping me are bad. It's because *I've* been completely confused while I've been seeing them. And I've drawn them into my confusion. They've listened to my words so patiently and compassionately, as though 'my truth' is the holy grail, even when that truth has changed like a chameleon depending on my thoughts, feelings and physical health at any given moment. They've reassured me repeatedly that I can believe in myself, trust myself, find my recovery in my own strength, because I know what is best for me.

But I don't have a clue what's best for me. I've never had a clue. I don't trust myself at all. I have gotten myself completely lost.

But when I look at Him, right into His eyes, I know in my bones that He does know what's best. He knows the way ahead better than I could ever figure out. He can cut through my confusion.

I just want to listen to Him right now. One voice. That's all I want.

So, I clear my phone diary in a series of phone messages left after hours so that no-one picks up to ask me what's going on.

And then I ask Him what to do next.

In all the time I have been sick my weight has never been this low. I could have a heart attack tomorrow. I don't want to die – Sam needs me.

What now?

---

24 A story of healing found in three of the four Gospels of the Bible. Matthew 9:18-26, Mark 5:21-43 and Luke 8:40-56.

Eat My word

I close my eyes and see Him in a desert. He is talking with a dark, shadowy figure.

The Shepherd is tired, starving, depleted – just like I feel now. He's hunched on the ground, surrounded by dust and stones, His clothes thread-worn and His face pale.

The Black hovers close around Him, whispering mockingly in His ear.

'Feed yourself. Turn these stones into bread. You know you can do it. All it will take is one word. Do it yourself. Feed yourself.' His words are taunting, laced with scorn.

The Shepherd sighs. He knows this voice well. Then, weakly, but firmly, He replies,

Man does not live by bread alone, but by every word that comes from the mouth of God.

And the Black vanishes, leaving only the howling wind, dry sand. And stones[25].

I don't understand. He's telling me something. I ask Him to say it again.

This time He looks directly at me.

If you want to be able to eat food again, you need to eat My word.

---

[25] Matthew 4:1-11, Luke 4:1-13.

'What?'

He repeats it, slower, emphatically.

If you want to be able to eat food again, you must eat My word.

I pause. I sigh.

He's inviting me to read the Bible. Again.

I'm filled with fear. That book has offended me so often in the past. I've been enraged when it has been used to abuse and subjugate others. It has terrified me with pictures of a God I feel I could never trust. At times it has seemed to condemn everything about me - my opinions, my decisions, my identities, my behaviours – everything.

His gaze penetrates my thoughts.

I know.

But the invitation remains.

I can help. If you like.

He's right. I need help. I can't understand this book. My thinking is black-and-white, judgmental and rigid. I'm incapable of reading it without wielding it violently against myself and then running a mile.

But I don't have the energy, the heart, or the mental capacity right now to read all the books I can find on how to understand the Bible, how to interpret it, the exegesis, the hermeneutics[26]. I'm broken. I'm weak. I've nothing left to embark on that kind of intellectual journey.

'I'm so tired… I don't have the energy… I don't know how or where to begin…'

He smiles, compassionately.

Simply. One bite at a time.

'But what do You mean? Old Testament? New Testament? I don't know… I've tried it so many times. I'm afraid I won't understand and then I won't hear You and I won't believe You're real, and I'll lose this feeling I have of You right now... and …I'll be on my own again…'

I can show you where to begin.

And I can show you how to understand.

I realise the times I've been most offended by the Bible are the times I've tried to figure it out on my own. Or the times I wasn't happy to sit with a question, a mystery, a paradox. In my impatience and desire to make it all wrap up neat and tidy, I would arrive at some wooden message that was life-sapping rather than life-giving. That condemned and scared me. Or made me feel smug and one-up on someone else.

A message that pointed away from love, not towards it.

---

[26] Biblical exegesis is the critical analysis and interpretation of a biblical text to understand its original meaning in its historical, literary and cultural context. Biblical hermeneutics is the broader theory and methodology of interpreting scripture, including a variety of approaches such as literal, allegorical, moral and anagogical interpretations.

'Okay. I see. I'm sorry. I've always tried to work it out myself. I'm a bit like that. Sorry.'

I know. It's okay. You want answers. I have all the answers in the world. But I know the ones you are ready for, and the ones that need to wait.

I look at Him, dusty with dirt. He is playing with the desert sand, with that subtle, soft smile.

I think I can trust Him and wait for the answers. I would rather wait His answers than come up with my own.

'So where do I begin?' I ask, willingly, this time.

Wherever you like.

And so, dazed and delirious from hunger, I open the book and start reading.

I go to the Gospels[27] because I feel safest with the Shepherd. I find the things He says, the stories He tells, and I copy them out. I shut my eyes and imagine myself in them.

I don't really understand what I'm reading or what it means for me right here, right now. There are no lightning-bolt revelations. But I feed it into my brain anyway.

When I'm not writing I listen to an audio Bible app I find on play store[28]. I get a version with a voice that doesn't irritate me. I listen when I'm

---

[27] Gospels: the first four books of the New Testament that detail the life of Jesus.

[28] YouVersion Bible App and Audio. A free download with most versions of the Bible and many in audio version format.

walking, doing the washing, vacuuming, getting Sam's dinner, going to sleep.

I don't care that it doesn't make sense, I just want it in my brain. I want my neural pathways rewired with something truer, more powerful than the voices that never shut up in my head.

I look up key words, emotions, topics, anything I can think of, in Bible search engines. I spend hours copying out what I find while Sam is at school or having his screen time. I write and write and write.

Slowly, something changes.

I realise that the passages that used to offend, scare and condemn me, I can now just sit with. I can give them to the Shepherd and say 'I don't understand this,' or 'This freaks me out,' or 'This would hurt my friend, or those people and I'm worried about that – can You hold this bit for now?'

And He nods, smiles willingly and takes them for me. I am happy to trust Him with those bits because He's good and kind, and He's helping me.

As I keep saturating myself in His word, I realise that He's building up a new 'Truth' bank in me. The words might not make sense, but I trust Him when He says they are Truth. And I discover that the Truths in this bank can help me do things I never thought I could – if I'm willing to believe they are Truth.

I look at the food in front of me at a mealtime and think 'I can't'. I ask for a Word, and He reminds me that the battle is His not mine, there is no fighting and muscling through required, all I need to do is hold onto Him[29] and see what happens.

I'm filled with waves of dread as I finish a meal, waiting for the skin-ripping self-hatred to set in. I ask Him to help, and He reminds me that He has not given me a spirit of fear but of power, love and a sound mind[30].

Each time He calls a verse to my mind from my growing subconscious 'Truth bank', I speak it out, because I remember Him saying in one of the bits I listen to:

So is my word that goes out from my mouth: It will not return to me empty but will accomplish what I desire and achieve the purpose for which I sent it[31].

I figure that the only mouth He has to use right now is my mouth. So, I say the words in the empty kitchen trusting that I'm sowing seeds of Truth that will break a chain and yield a new area of freedom.

Sometimes I speak it very weakly, trembling, nauseous, tired as I approach the next thing to eat. But I know that doesn't matter. He is proud of me for saying it, for daring to believe that His spoken word has power.

As I do this, day in day out, a new hope starts to grow in me. It's very small, but it's there, like a flickering flame.

---

[29] Exodus 14:14, 2 Chronicles 20:15.

[30] 2 Timothy 1:7, King James Version (KJV)

[31] Isaiah 55:11.

I start to realise that it's not the food that makes me feel terrible when I eat. It's the *lies I believe* about the food, about myself, Him, other people, or anything else in my life – that hurt me.

Each time He puts a Truth from His Word into my mind I don't question it. I can't afford to do that right now. My life depends on it. I stand on it. I hang onto it like I used to hang onto diazepam.

Slowly these words become an anchor, a rock, a shield more powerful than the ED thoughts or the psych tools, strategies and PRN's I had relied on to get that food into my body.

I begin to see that anorexia, the thing I'd hated most in my life, and carried the deepest shame about, has become a springboard for His Truth. For every lie it throws at me, He swaps it for a Truth. And when I feel like I can't believe the Truth, I ask Him for the faith I need. Always, always it comes – even if it's as small as a mustard seed. He gives me just enough to believe what I need to eat the next mouthful.

As weeks pass, I discover the Bible is not the terrorist manifesto I thought it was.

It's all about Him. His love. His relentless rescue.

And He is everything I need to know about me.

Change my want to

'I need You to change my 'want to.'

It's a month after my living-room moment. I've been eating His word, seeing little shifts, having tiny wins – an extra spoon of rice here, an additional sprinkling of nuts there. Hope is rising.

But I've hit an impasse.

I'm standing at Mike's kitchen bench. It's his turn to care for Sam in our current care arrangement, so Mike is staying at the granny flat I'm renting. I hold a measuring spoon in my hand, debating whether to add a teaspoon of oil to my dinner.

My hand quivers, pushed and pulled by the tension in my heart.

Will I, or won't I? Do I really want more? Am I ready for this? Do I want to turn the ship around or don't I?

I can't work it out – I am so used to going in the 'Don't eat that', 'Less not more', 'No not safe' direction. But I don't know if I want the new direction enough to overcome the fear.

He sees me trembling, frozen in indecision at whether to make this tiny increase. Nigel, the family cat, meows and curls his way around my ankles.

'I need to *want* this.' I say to Him.

Health. Recovery. Putting on weight. Getting better. I need to want it so bad. Because refeeding is hard. I know – I've done it that many times. I need to want healing enough to push through that pain. The backlash. The tears. The body sensations, dysmorphia, self-hatred. The hell it always has been.

'And right now, I don't know if I want it. I should. I've asked You to help me eat. I'm reading Your Word. I'm getting Your Truth. Yet right now, in this moment, I don't know if I want it enough. I'm scared.'

Nigel keeps rubbing at my leg. He must be hungry.

'I need You to change my 'want to.''

I don't have to explain what I'm saying. He knows.

He's watched this tug of war play out in my heart time and time again. He's seen me sabotage and relapse repeatedly. It's as if He has been waiting for this moment – the moment where I ask Him to change my will, to bend it to His.

Every time I have tried treatment, I've wound up worse than I started. Yet I never let myself stop and face the awful truth. That, for all the good intentions in the world, deep down inside a screaming part of me *didn't want to get well.*

I didn't want people to smile and say, 'Gosh, you're looking better!' 'You're looking so well!' 'You look like you have put on a bit of weight – well done!'

I couldn't bear the thought. I didn't want them to applaud me for eating. Being thin, looking like death has been my way, my best – or perhaps worst - way, of saying,

'I still hurt.'

'Things have happened in my life that hurt, and *I want people to know.*'

'I am *not* okay …and I refuse to let people think I am.'

This part of me is angry, furious. 'I'm damned if they are going to think I am okay!' it rages. 'I am *not* over it – the trauma, the past, that moment, whatever. I'm not over the fact that you left me there, that you did that to me, said that to me, took that from me. That you screamed at us, worked us like slaves in those practice rooms…'

And on and on. So much toxic raging anger.

This part of me doesn't want to – no, *refuses* to – grow up.

Even at 44.

It's still crying out for the missing parts of a childhood lost to hothouse music schools, insane teachers and unpredictable family explosions. Still crying out for a home that had vanished by the time I was finally sent back - too sick to do anything and too late for it to matter.

This part of me refuses to step into a woman's body that might invite unwanted intimacy the way it always seemed to.

This is the part of me that always sabotages treatment - always doubles down the restriction the moment I get home from hospital, always increases the exercise, always resorts to hundreds upon hundreds of third degree burns to blot out the voices and say to a world out there:

I.

STILL.

HURT.

It is a storm-tossed, disconsolate, untameable beast inside of me that refuses, *refuses* to get well.

'How will I ever do this?!' I let the spoon and the oil fall to the floor, my head on my knees, rocking back and forth like I often do.

'What is *wrong* with me?! I need You to change my 'want to'. *Please*.'

Nigel purrs and nuzzles my cheek.

It's okay Al. I can do that.

'How on earth?' I moan. 'I'm a self-saboteur in disguise....'

He reaches me with the cat's touch for a moment longer. Then whispers,

By My Spirit.

I don't know what He's trying to tell me. I'm tired. I feel stupid I could even imagine I might get well on my own. I'm angry with myself.

He speaks again.

Not by might nor by power, but by my Spirit.[32]

---

[32] Zechariah 4:6.

I take a breath and lift Nigel onto my lap. He pads and claws and pads and claws then runs away. I think he's still confused by Mike and I house-swapping every two weeks.

'You mean, Your Spirit can …change my 'want to'?'

Yes.

He repeats a verse I've heard in my obsessive audio-Bible listening.

For it is God who works in you, both to will and to work for His good pleasure.[33]

I turn it over. God …works in me….to will…. and to work … for His good pleasure…

'I guess getting well would be part of His…'good pleasure?"

Yes.

'And willing and working to that end would be…. Pretty much the same as … Him changing my 'want to'?'

Yes.

Suddenly, I see.

I want His Spirit. I want Him so bad.

He could make me *want* to get well – completely and truly want, through and through, to get well, to go forward not backward. And He could give me the strength to *do* the things I need to do get well. I would no

---

[33] Philippians 2:13, (KJV, NIV).

longer be in danger of my own self-sabotage. I would no longer be that kamikaze pilot in disguise.

But now I'm completely confused.

Who is this Spirit? Is it the Shepherd? Or is it Someone else? And from memory there's another person in this Divine mix – a Father – I haven't begun to talk with Him – am I getting this all wrong? After all my spiritual meanderings I should know this stuff – I've wrestled with the Trinity[34] over and over and never got close to understanding it…

And do I have His Spirit or don't I?

There was that time 20 years ago when a bunch of people prayed for me to be baptised in the Holy Spirit … it was a bit freaky that… I had to pull off speaking in tongues and I did, but I'm not sure I was being genuine and so, was it all real or not …?

Or maybe decades later when I got confirmed Catholic and the Priest anointed me with oil – was that it? Oh – but did I lose it after that – when I wandered off onto a million other paths of belief and spirituality, or when I separated from Mike?

Do I need someone to baptise me again? Or do I need to go to confession again?

I'm stressing out. It's getting complicated. Too complicated.

He interrupts my thinking.

---

[34] The Trinity – one of the most mysterious tenets of the Christian faith. The understanding that God is three persons but one God, each fully God, distinct but existing in perfect unity and relationship.

You already have Him.

'Really?!! I'm not sure… that sounds a bit dodgy, a bit too easy, too good to be true ... I don't want to get this wrong again. I don't want to get lost….'

An image of a pilot light comes into my mind. The small blue flame on one of those large gas wall heaters they have in some older houses in Melbourne. When it gets cold you press this button – you push it quite hard until something clicks and …whoosh! The pilot light bursts into flame, and the heater blasts out warmth.

'Are You saying that Your Spirit is in me, like that pilot light?'

It is what gave you your first breath[35].

I process.

'So ... what is the button bit? How do I let it ignite? How do I fan it into flame?"

You did it the moment you gave up. The moment you stopped trying to do life on your own. The moment you fell into My arms[36].

And every moment you do the same.

I'm worried. Can I really trust what He is saying?

'I... I'm sorry, I think it would help me if I could be baptised in the Holy Spirit…again. I know I have, like, in a million different ways, a million

[35] Genesis 2:7.

[36] Acts 2:38.

times before but… just to be sure. I'm paranoid. I just need to know. Could You make that happen?'

I'm talking about an event embraced by many Christian traditions. An event that signifies an outpouring of His Spirit, an increased capacity to walk the Royal Road of Love and a deeper sense of His presence and transformation.

He's silent. He gives a gentle, understanding nod.

I've no idea how He's going to pull this one off. I've not yet gone back to church – I'm too embarrassed after separating from Mike. Who would baptise me with the Holy Spirit? But I've asked Him now, so I leave it with Him.

I stand up. It's early days on this path, and I'm so thin I still get muscle burn moving from sit to stand. I manage it all the same, using the bench to help pull my body weight. I pick up the spoon and pour the extra measure of oil again.

For now, I will go with the pilot light thing and try acting 'as if'. 'As if' I have a power greater than myself in me, willing me to get well and giving me the strength to do it.

I tip the oil into the bowl.

I feel a spark of wonder – that I just added a teaspoon of oil when, a moment ago, I was paralysed. Wonder that I really might have His Spirit.

But I want to be sure. I have OCD, remember. I need tangibles…a definitive event I can recall every time I doubt it.

I can see Him standing close. Arms folded, leaning against the corner of the bench, watching me pour.

He's smiling again – a kind of playful smile – like He knows something I don't.

*

A few days pass and I'm at a community project. It's run by the church that Mike still goes to. I've cringed at the thought of going back to this church because of the public nature of my blunders. But on this day, I shelve my pride and go to the project. I need to be with people that know the Shepherd. Even if I say nothing, I just need to be with them.

I'm sitting quietly at a table where a bunch of senior ladies are doing some kind of craft activity. It's totally not my thing – I got crafted out in hospital. But I'm glad I'm not alone.

Next to me sits an older gentleman I've never met. His name is Bob. He doesn't know me or my story. His energy feels a bit intense, which kind of freaks me out. Out of the blue – no chit chat or pleasantries - he turns to me and asks,

'Would you like to be baptised in the Holy Spirit?'

Bob's cut to the chase, and I can't believe it. Normally I would run a mile. But today I don't care if I'm afraid. I say,

'Yes… er… yes, very much.'

He pulls out a tiny tract that he walks me through. It's the kind of leaflet that I would have reeled against in the past with plenty of objections and offense taken. The whole encounter is that kind of thing.

But I don't care. I want to be sure I've got His Spirit, so I say yes, and I let Bob roll.

The tract looks simple, but it's trying to explain something quite mysterious. There are weird diagrams to help me stay focused. I hear that I have this Father, or 'Abba[37]', who made me, cares for me and wants to bring me home. Apparently, He is kind. Apparently, He is Love, too. He was behind my whole Shepherd encounter, so I think I can trust Him, even if – after all these years - I still don't really know Him that well.

I have the Shepherd who died for me – I still don't quite understand the why, though I'm blown away that He would do such a thing. I can invite Him into my heart and my life, to take over and run the show from now. A bit like I did at ground zero – only this time it's witnessed. It's official, I tell myself.

I get to receive His Spirit. A connecting line to my real, Creator Father and the Shepherd, that can help me see things the way They do, receive Their love, and give Their love, better.

Apparently, if I've seen the Shepherd I've seen my heavenly Father. And if I love the Shepherd and follow His words, a Divine Threesome - the Shepherd, my Father, and His Spirit – will come make their home in my heart[38].

---

37 'Abba' - an Aramaic word that means "father". It's a term of affection that conveys intimacy and a close relationship.

38 John 14:9, 23.

Maybe I'm overthinking this, but to me it's triple confusing. In all my theologising and spiritual seeking over the decades, I've never really understood it.

The Shepherd I can get my head around. Having His Spirit come to help me I can understand too. Having a loving Dad in heaven who made me and wants me home makes sense as well.

The three of them all being One but distinct.... the mystery the Early Fathers of the church called 'the Trinity[39]' ...bamboozles me.

I do my best. I play with it in my mind. And there is something kind of beautiful about it - a divine dance. Three beings, intricately connected, interwoven, devoted to one another with a love so abundant and overwhelming that it can't be contained. It overflows – pouring out ceaselessly.

An endless, ever-giving, ever-creating source of Love. It's beautiful... and utterly baffling.

So, I hold onto the Shepherd for now.

Bob asks if I would like to say sorry to this beautiful God, who has all the love in the cosmos for me, for trying to do life on my own terms for so long. He invites me to let go, hand the reins of my life over and receive His Spirit. I don't mind that I've already said sorry to the Shepherd the night He met me in the living room – and countless times since. I say

[39] The first recorded use of the term 'Trinity' is often attributed to the early Christian theologian Tertullian, around the late 2nd to early 3rd century AD to describe the concept of one God in three persons, Father, Son and Holy Spirit. It is a concept rooted in scripture, though the exact term does not appear in the Bible.

yes. A lot. Bob says this prayer, I say Amen, and that's it. We've finished the pamphlet.

No bolts of lightning. No bells and whistles. No ecstatic experiences.

But I know it's for real now, because I prayed those things with Bob observing and received the Holy Spirit with him laying hands on me to confirm it. I've got an eyewitness. No doubts now. That's good enough for my OCD brain.

Maybe I didn't need to do this, maybe I did. I'm just grateful the Shepherd has given me this meeting without me doing anything to engineer it. If He says I have His Spirit right now and I have someone who witnessed it as proof, then I really can start acting as if.

Something changes in me after that day. It's small and gradual. But it's undeniable.

I realise I don't want this raging anger and bitterness anymore. The old desire to make people see and 'pay' for my pain has gone. I can see that any offense I hold onto will only impede the flow of His Love. Love that I need to breathe and bathe in daily to live. I don't want that.

I want Him to help me forgive and forgive and forgive and never stop forgiving, whatever the injustice, however hard that might seem. I want to be a conduit for His love, not a plug; to see anyone I ever felt wounded by through His eyes, not mine.

I'm a slow learner at this. I falter often. But when I do capture a glimpse of them in this way, I see vulnerability, brokenness, pain, and beauty all rolled into one. I see they are no different to me and thinking of them makes me weep.

When the old anger spikes again, I talk about it with this new Counsellor of mine, His Spirit. It's like having triage[40] on tap – but a good triage, with the best advice. I let the anger out, cry, swear if I need to. He always listens, understands, validates. Nothing surprises or shocks Him. He has known my wounds all along.

Very often He shows me the lie that is really hurting me, rather than the person themselves. I renounce that lie. I give it back to Him to dispose of. Always He has a better Truth to exchange for it.

If I still have feelings that sting, I imagine the Shepherd right in front of me and offload them like a bag of stones at His feet. I tell Him I can't deal with this anger, or hatred, or bitterness or whatever it is and can He please take it for me. I might have to do it innumerable times, but always He carries my burden.

As the anger shifts, a new desire awakens in me.

I realise I want to live, to be free, to be healthy and whole.

I dare to believe there is a purpose for my life. Even at 44, with a broken marriage, a troubled child and a mountain to climb in my health.

And the purpose is so simple.

It is to live loved. Loved by Him. And then to let that love flow – just like it does between the Divine Threesome that I can't get my head around. Pass it on. To everyone He has ever placed, and ever will place, in my path.

---

[40] The number a person is directed to call when they are in an acute mental health crisis.

I see that I can fulfil that purpose every moment of my life, right here, right now, no matter what my struggle, or health status.

Daily, I start asking Him,

'What step do You want me to take today?'

Or,

'What new freedom do You want to give me?'

His response is always gentle. It might be an extra mouthful, or an extra snack. It could be taking a walk instead of doing a workout. Or resting when I eat rather than getting up to reheat my food 10000 times. We're not stuck for ideas – He and I – I've done that much treatment I know the nuts and bolts of what it will take.

But it's His leading this time, not mine, that guides me. And He never asks me to do something He doesn't give me the strength to do. Even though the refeeding process is hard, it doesn't feel like I'm pushing water uphill anymore. Or climbing a sand dune that is forever taking me down.

And when I'm panicking, He doesn't tell me to toughen up, try harder, 'do it if you really love Me' or that kind of thing. He's not pushy or hard on me. He just takes me by the hand, one baby step at a time.

As the months pass something very strange happens.

I'm excited to see my weight go up and disappointed if it's dropped or stayed the same. I'm glad when people say I look well, that change is happening, and they can see it. I'm happy my cheeks are chubbier, and I don't mind saying it.

This amazes me. So much that I cry a lot. Good tears. Too many, Sam says, and I know, I try not to be too emotional for him. But good tears all the same.

The wild beast inside of me is starting to be consoled. His Spirit is doing the thing I never could do myself.

He is changing my want to.

THIRD INTERLUDE – POKÉMON

'Where do we go from here?'

We're sitting on the couch next to Sam playing Pokémon Scarlet[41]. Currently we're hunting for a Titan (an extra-large, powerful type of Pokémon encountered in the game's storyline). I have no idea where the destination flag on my map has gone.

He laughs at the pun.

'You know what I mean! Not the Titan… I mean the story. Where do we go from here? It wasn't like it was all plain sailing from that point onward. Like ...I started reading Your word and believing I had Your Spirit in my heart and then suddenly ..Ta daa! …I could eat anything and never had another ED thought again.'

Of course not. Where would the growth in that be?

Meowscarada – the ace on my current team of Pokémon – faints. I divert to a Pokémon centre to heal up. (It's a kind of servo and hospital for Pokémon all rolled into one.)

'But who wants to hear about two years of learning to eat again?'

Some might. And... what kind of story are we telling?

---

41 Pokémon: a gaming franchise created by Nintendo, Game Freak and Creatures. The game centres around fictional creatures (Pokémon) that trainers can catch, battle and evolve. Pokémon Scarlet was released by Nintendo in 2022, as part of the ninth generation of Pokémon games.

'Okay. Yeah... I know… a love story. Not a recovery manifesto. But recovery is kind of the raw material here. And it's all such a muddle. It's not like a straight sequence of events. A straight journey up.'

Is Love ever like that?

'No. Sometimes it's all over the place I guess.'

My Pokémon are healed. He nudges me to get moving. I go back to 'grinding' (defeating Pokémon after Pokémon after Pokémon to gain 'XP' (experience points)). I'm being assaulted by hordes of Paldean Tauros[42]. They're driving me nuts.

'I still don't know where to go next. I don't know how to string it altogether.'

How about stepping stones?

'What do You mean?'

Think about it. Think about the stepping stones.

I do. Walking with Him has been a series of steps. The step of dealing with increases. The step of dealing with weight. Body image. Body sensations. Self-harm urges. Suicidal thoughts. Each one has been a step. One I might have to learn repeatedly. Faltering steps usually, rather than giant strides. Sometimes we have stepped sideways. Sometimes forward. Sometimes backwards.

It's been like learning to dance, with Him guiding the steps each way.

---

42 Paldean Tauros: bull-like Pokémon that roam the game's East and South Provinces.

'I guess 'stepping stones' is kind of nice. Tells it like a journey. With You. I love that journey.'

He smiles. We've escaped the pack of Tauros. He points to the flag that is showing up North on our map – in the opposite direction I am travelling.

I reroute.

I do too.

Stepping Stones

Grace stone

I hold the leaflet in my hand.

It was lying stuck in the bottom of my letter box with a snail track over it. A picture of a bunch of women running with marathon vests on. There's a yellow daffodil at the bottom.

I skim it and see it's an invitation for a fundraiser. I feel a pang of inadequacy – I should be doing more things like that. More things to help people with illnesses like cancer.

'I'm sorry.'

Is there something you want to say?

'I'm embarrassed to say it.' Silly really – I know He knows everything I'm going to say before I've even thought it.

'I feel ashamed because I'm… I'm … jealous.'

Jealous of who?

'Of people with cancer.'

I can't believe I just said that. I am so ashamed. I have lost some of my closest friends to that brutal disease. I wouldn't wish it on my worst enemy.

Do you want to say a bit more?

'I just… I just feel like if you have cancer – you are – like – some kind of hero… or MS or MND or any other illness out there…. Any illness other than anorexia... I know they are terrible, terrible illnesses. But people cheer you on. They run fun runs for you. Make coloured ribbons for you. Throw morning teas for you.'

I am mortified at the anger rising in me.

'I mean – if you are a mum with cancer, it's a tragedy and people tell you how brave you are fighting this illness for your family. They say how terrible it is for the family – but at no point do they blame the mum. At no point do they say: 'Well if you really care for your child you'll beat this illness. You'll quit doing this silly cancer thing.' They don't remind mums with cancer what a trial they're putting their families through and the burden they're placing on their partners.'

I scrunch the leaflet up, angry and ashamed that I am angry, and put it in the recycling bin.

'I'm sorry. I shouldn't feel like this. I can't believe I'm talking like this.'

This is something important that needs healing. It is good that you are talking about it.

I could handle having a chronic life-threatening illness in itself; I could handle the voices, the exhaustion, the muscle burn, the anxiety, the warped body sensations and dysmorphia - if it was just that.

But it's the stigma. The shame of this illness. That's what I can't handle.

Do you want to explain?

'That feeling I have that this is all my fault. All my fault. Always has been. Everything is all my fault.'

We walk down the drive that leads to the granny flat I'm renting with Sam. I unlock the door, and it swings open. A waft of damp blows over me. The flat is riddled with mould, and I haven't worked out how to get rid of it.

Who says it is all your fault?

'You know. That time years ago when a nurse at the APU told me that anorexia was different from all the other illnesses on the ward there. It was something we can control, unlike the other patients, who couldn't help having schizophrenia or psychosis or bipolar.'

You know that that wasn't Truth being spoken to you back then.

I sigh. I do know. At that time the psych ward was being run by a particularly archaic registrar whose old-school thinking on eating disorders, whilst notorious, trickled down to unassuming nurses on the floor.

'But even if it is a 'disease', even if I didn't ask for it – what about all the half-brained things I've done because of that illness? The times I've lied to pretend I've eaten when I haven't. The priority I have given compulsions and exercise over things that really matter in life. The harming. The family gatherings I've avoided, year in year out. The relationships I've shut down. The marks it's made on Sam. The husband I have pushed away. That's my fault. Surely.'

I throw the shopping bags on the table. We have half an hour before school pickup.

I sit down, head in hands pressing hard on the frown above my nose – something I always do when I'm stressed, like I'm trying to crush the thought itself. Back when we were together, Mike would spot me doing what he called the 'squash'. He'd lean over and gently smooth my frown with his thumb, a gesture of love and concern.

I miss him.

I pause.

No blame.

I pretend I can't hear Him.

He pulls up a chair opposite me, puts His arm around my shoulder, and gently lifts my chin up. I let Him look into my eyes.

No. Blame.

Suddenly, we are somewhere else, far away from the granny flat and its smell of damp mould which set in since the rain came this winter.

It is a court, in front of a temple in Jerusalem, 2000 years ago. I'm sitting directly behind Him as He sits down, ready to teach a crowd of people hungry for His words.

Without warning, they storm in – a cluster of stern-faced religious teachers, their eyes sharp with certainty, their brows furrowed by years bent over sacred scrolls. Men carved by study and judgment with minds set like stone.

They drag with them a woman, her hair tangled, garments dishevelled, face pale with fear. She is thrown to the floor and lands with a crunch, gravel grinding at the feet of the Shepherd.

She's been caught cheating on her husband.

Awkward in our day. Lethal in hers.

She is summoned to stand. Her guilt and shame merit full display.

One teacher looks provocatively at the Shepherd, names the woman's crime and reminds Him that punishment is death by stoning – so what is He going to say?

But He says nothing. Not at first.

Instead, He bends down and starts writing in the dust with His finger. No rush. No intimidation. As if He's scribbling the parts of her story they've never cared to read.

Still, they press Him.

'Well, what do you say? What do you say?'.

They want to trap Him in His words, snare Him with law and blame.

Finally, He stands up and calmly meets their challenge:

Whoever has a clean record, throw the first stone.

He stoops down again, slowly, and continues writing.

Silence. Eyes shift. Throats clear. An awkward cough. The older men shuffle away first, one at a time, then the younger. They leave the Shepherd on His own with the woman, still standing, and me.

He is the one remaining. That would make Him the one with the clean record. The only one with the 'right' to throw the stone.

But He doesn't throw any stones. Instead, He straightens up, turns to her and asks softly,

Woman, where are they? Has no one condemned you?

'No one, sir.' She replies.

Then neither do I condemn you.

She turns and looks with disbelief into His eyes.

Go now and leave this life of sin[43].

I don't smart at those words. I know that 'sin' just means the hell she was living - a life where she was trying to do it alone, survive alone, pleasing a bunch of guys that didn't care for her the way He does. A life without Him.

She came in a shackled woman. In six words He sets her free. To begin again. To live.

He brings me back to the flat. Where the woman was, I am sitting, and He is holding my hands, holding them tight. Like her, I lift my eyes of disbelief up to His.

Alys. I don't blame you. I don't condemn you.

Go now, leave this life you've been living. Be free.

For a moment I let myself imagine what it would be like to trust these words. I imagine a life where I no longer carried guilt and shame - whether for an illness I never chose, or the mistakes I really did make. I imagine what that would feel like. What I could do.

I could be kind to myself when I am struggling with eating.

43 John 8:1-11.

I could be gentle with myself when I slip up.

I could forgive myself for the past.

I could say sorry freely and not care what people did with that.

I could let go and start over.

I could have hope.

I could change.

It is nearly time for school pickup. I hurriedly put the shopping away and grab my keys. I'm nervous. Sam is struggling at school, and I've no idea how he will be when he gets home today. If he's doing it tough, he might have a melt-down and I know I'll blame myself again like I always do.

Alys. No blame.

I've got you. And I've got Sam.

It's going to be okay.

As I drive, I chew on His words.

Thirty years battling this illness showed me that guilt and shame never cured anyone. Never helped me quit the crazy stuff I was doing. Never stopped me starving.

But grace opens a different path.

Grace can set me free.

Love Potion

I've got three meal increases to do this week. Three to get the weight gain we need. It's dinner time and today I'm going to smash out the first. I want this now. The pilot light is ignited, and the flame is burning strong.

But I'm caught in another moment of kitchen freeze.

Here goes my brain. Abridged version.

'Okay. Here it is (surveying meal complete with increase). But is this increase really necessary? And should I really do it today? Is today a good day to try more? What if the backlash is terrible – if the voices give me hell afterwards? Then I'll be useless for Sam.... I've got to be good for Sam! What if what I've chosen is wrong? What if it gives me nausea? Maybe I should change it for something else ... but what do I change it for? No... I'll stay with it but...did I measure it right? What if I put in too much? Maybe I should remeasure everything just to be sure .... it might have changed size... that means it might feel different – awful even! What about the dish? Is it the usual dish? The usual spoon? It might look different in the usual dish – then what?! Oh what the frick is the point of all of this... this is so goddamn stupid! Why can't I just do this? Why can't I be normal?'

My neck and shoulders feel like they're going to explode. I put the bowl of food down and slump, defeated, on the bench stool.

'This is too hard. I should just eat rice crackers...'

I've got nowhere to go with this.

Weakly, I mutter His name. My best effort at asking for help.

His response is instant. And, in my mind, totally inappropriate.

I love you.

What?! Right now?! In this state of utter insanity?

He whispers again. But even more surprising…

I love you, My darling[44].

'Seriously… that is cringe! Fine to say that kind of stuff in Your book to beautiful queens and brides and the like. But me?! Look at me! I'm a complete fruit loop right now!'

But I do!

I try to stay with His words, aware that I just unashamedly knocked back a divine gesture of affection. A vulnerable one.

'How can You love me like this? And how can You call me Your 'darling'?'

I've never been good with terms of endearment. Even from Mike when we were together.

'I deserve a kick up the ass – not kindness! I should just muscle up, push through the fear and get on with it!'

And how has that worked in the past?

Point taken.

There is no fear in love, but perfect love drives out fear[45].

---

44 Song of Solomon 4:7.

45 1 John 4:18.

I don't know a definition for perfect love. But looking at Him right now, with those scarred hands, I think He comes pretty close.

I drop the pushback. I breathe. I accept. That right here - amid a kitchen freeze moment, going round and round in anorexic circles, taking forever to get the freaking food on the table - *He loves me.*

And I let go into that love. I let Him hold me in the craziness. I fall back into His arms again.

Somehow, choosing to receive His love in that moment unlocks my mental paralysis. I see the food and the increase for what it is. The nourishment I need right now. The step I need to take today.

I serve it. And I eat it.

Love becomes my remedy to heal the fear that paralyses. Receiving His. And giving mine.

Brilliantly, I can be entirely proactive in taking this medicine. I can have 'loving time' with Him. Some call it worship. It's intimate stuff. The closed-door bedroom of my relationship with Him. The time where I invite His Spirit to open my eyes to His love and my heart to reciprocating mine, whether by speaking, singing, drawing, or simply thinking it out.

This two-way love flow carries me through the fear that paralyses before a meal. It protects me from the backlash afterwards.

Kitchen freezes may continue to happen. But I have an antidote now.

A love potion to thaw them out.

Meal Support

I've started laying another place at the table. I feel stupid doing it. Ridiculous even.

But meals are lonely right now. Sam is unable to eat with me. He has ARFID[46] and is highly distressed by exposure to a plethora of foods. He needs to have his meal solo and then retreat to his room while I eat mine. Meals aren't the warm family experience I hear others talk about.

I raise it with the Shepherd one evening.

'I feel lonely. Sad. Sitting here, eating this food, with Sam doing his own thing. Mike and I still apart.'

I know. It's hard.

Pause.

What about you set a place for Me?

?!

I baulk.

'Wouldn't that be the ultimate sign of crazy? Like seriously, my faith is childish enough already – the oversimplified way I rely on You, talk to You in the shops, ask You what to eat. But laying an empty place? Sam will think I've completely lost it…'

---

46 ARFID: Avoidant / Restrictive Food Intake Disorder. A condition that is common in the autistic community, related to sensory processing challenges.

Childish? Or childlike?

I am quite okay with childlike.

'I guess so… I…'

My voice trails off.

I throw caution to the wind and put a place mat out. I leave the cutlery – that's a bit much for now. I thank Him for the food I have in front of me, daunting as it is. Then we start our meal together.

This becomes a new pattern for me. Laying a place for Him.

In hospital they called it 'meal support' – having someone sit with you while you eat, make sure you get the whole lot in, try and distract you from the distress you're feeling.

It didn't always work for me. Distraction quizzes were overwhelming - too much stimulus on top of the food. Medical companionship felt like scrutiny. It just made me ultra-anxious.

But the aim was good. To not eat alone. To have someone stand with you against the eating disorder. In that sense, I miss it.

From this evening on, the Shepherd brings a new kind of meal support.

Sometimes we talk. Surface level talk.

'The autumn colours are beautiful today. You're amazing what You do with colour.'

He smiles.

Well... we've been practising a while now.

Very often I spew out something I'm worried about. Usually Sam, poor kid.

'I am so concerned about him. I can't seem to help him balance his gaming with other stuff – stuff I know would lift him. He's so down. I don't know what to do. It's all my fault. I should do better.'

It's okay. One step at a time. He is healing too. We can help him broaden. You're not doing this alone.

Sometimes it's the food itself that is troubling.

'I just feel like I can't do this today. It looks so much. So overwhelming.'

I know it feels that way. Try one mouthful at a time. Take breaths. We have all the time in the world. Ask Me to help you see the food the way it really is – the way I see it. That might help.

So, I do. And it does. For a moment I see it as medicine, strength, a pathway to life. That glimpse gives me the strength to take another mouthful.

Maybe I'm tempted to get up and down and engage in behaviours. Like repeatedly reheating the meal I've prepared – that is one of my worst. So exhausting.

How about you give that urge to Me right now. You can rest. It is good enough as it is. It'll be fine if you don't reheat it.

As time progresses doing meal support with Him, a new topic emerges. I'm embarrassed that it took me as long as it did to raise it.

'So… how are You doing?'

There's a lot going on in the world right now. Ukraine. Israel. Even in my local community. The family at school whose dad has cancer. That friend I know who's so isolated. My uncle who is in his last days, severely depressed. And that's just the stuff I can think of.

The Shepherd must have a lot on His mind.

Thanks for asking.

He brings to my mind another friend, Denise, who is escaping from domestic violence. She's in a bad way with her mental health.

'Your heart is aching for Denise… I can see it.'

Yes.

'I wish I could do something.'

He pauses.

I feel guilty. I can't go rescue people these days. My hands are quite tied caring for Sam with his special needs.

But I realise I could pray. For Denise. And the plethora of other issues that have popped into my mind and that I know are on His too.

'I don't really understand how it works, prayer. Me praying for Denise when You already know she's going through a tough time. I've never understood it.'

Prayer isn't a reminder of My 'to do' list. If that is what you mean.

'No. That would be pretty dumb.'

I take another mouthful.

'So how does it work?'

I see an image of a giant web. It's a strange image. There are people attached to every portion of the web. Beneath the web there is darkness. Above it, light. I see myself in the web, holding onto its threads and realise that when I move my arms, others are affected. If I reach up, lifting my portion of the web up, a person next to me is lifted too. They become bathed in light.

It's as if He is saying that when I pray for someone, I'm lifting that person up into His light. I'm allowing His light to flow into their situation.

I still don't really understand, but I go with it.

When He shares something that His heart is aching for, I shut my eyes, and lift my arms towards Him, pulling up that person or situation with me. Sometimes I do it in a request – a practical entreaty for some resolution. Very often I'm not sure what that is, so I just ask for His will to be done and His kingdom to come, in that person's life[47].

His meal support becomes more than Him comforting and supporting me alone, much as I cherish that. It becomes a time when He tells me of the things on His heart too. A time where I get to support others as well.

He gives me a real purpose sitting there, chugging through the breakfast or lunch or dinner I find so hard. As I eat, I can take my place in that web

[47] Words taken from the Lord's prayer. Matthew 6:9-13.

and lift up someone on His heart. I can offer up the very act of eating that meal – with all its pain and difficulty - in the process. Like a love offering.

It's as if I am saying,

'I really don't know what I can say or do to help this person You are telling me about, or this country, or situation. But I am offering You the meal I'm eating right now – with all the difficult thoughts and feelings it gives me. I'm asking if You might take that offering and use it in some way to help that person. If You might use my act of eating this food to do Your will in their life.[48]'

Many will think I am bonkers. But I don't want to waste a moment of this journey. There can be so much pain in eating. I don't want to waste that pain. If I can use it for someone else, that's what I will do.

He is giving me meal support with a difference – for more than just me.

[48] The idea of offering up suffering to help others is taught within the Catholic church, and is rooted in Paul's words, Colossians 1:24.

Weight – Identifying the conundrum.

It's a Thursday morning. For some reason, my OCD brain has insisted that we do this ritual on the day it always took place during my hospital admissions and on all the day programs I attended.

I look down at the scales in front of me and take a deep breath.

I'm transported back 3 years.

*

Thursday is 'weigh day' on the EDP[49]. It goes something like this.

Excruciatingly awkward silence as six patients wait (excuse the pun) in the centre's wait room (and again. Sorry.) We scroll our phones, break the silence with an occasional cough, take it in turns to use the toilet – obligatory before weigh-in.

Nobody knows whether to mention the inevitable ritual that awaits.

Footsteps thump down the corridor and a jangle of keys is followed by the door opening.

'Hi everybody. Come on through and grab a seat,' says the clinician. She's nice. A bit too nice for today, perhaps.

We shuffle in and find our favourite spot. I'm not sure why, but we all seem to need to sit in the same place for weigh group.

[49] EDP: Outpatient Eating Disorder Program.

Awkward silence number two as the clinician waits for everyone to put phones away and get kind-of comfortable.

'How is everyone doing?'

No response.

'Jeanie, how are you?'

'Good.'

'How are you feeling about today?'

'Shit.'

'Feeling a bit anxious about the weigh-in huh?'

'Just shit.'

I think shit is a good answer. It's honest after all.

'How about you Kath?' And so, starts the creeping circle of death. We all share one by one how we are feeling shit – or some such equivalent.

'Right, well, let's all fill in our weigh charts. Has everyone got one?'

We pull out our proformas. 'Anybody need a pen?'

Nope. Armed and ready to go.

I look at the sheet. Ug. I hate it. Here are the questions:

My weight last weigh day: [.........]

What I need to have gained to meet the program weight restoration requirements: [……….]

What this means my weight will be: [……….]

A healthy weight for me is: [……….]

What I feel about my weight being [……….]

If my weight is not [……….] I will need to go up a meal plan. This means I will start meal plan [……….] today.

We scribble away.

'Great, everybody finished?'

A few nods. One whisper 'yes'. Jeanie is scrolling her phone.

'Jeanie…' the clinician whispers.

Jeanie looks up, rolls her eyes and puts her phone away.

'Okay, let's hear what everyone has put down.'

The creeping death begins again. Different direction this time so that kind of helps. We read out in a slightly AI tone of voice our script, gaps filled in.

Jeanie starts crying.

'Jeanie is there something you want to share?'

She sniffs, swears under her breath and says,

'No. I just f***ing hate this shit.'

‘I know. Weigh day is a really tough day for everyone,’ replies the clinician with genuine compassion. ‘But this is about reducing your anxiety and obsessional thinking about weight. This is about helping you take steps forward in your recovery. That’s something you want isn’t it Jeanie?’

No response. I am feeling Jeanie’s pain.

The group format creeps on at a snail pace… individual recitation of each person’s weigh sheet. Then a painstakingly slow queue for the changing spot behind the slightly flimsy privacy screen. Another queue at the locked weigh-room door in our starchy hospital gowns for our turn to be weighed. Then the weigh itself with its slightly awkward silence from the weighing nurse. Then waiting to get dressed again behind the privacy screen. Then a return to the couches and... you got it, filling in and sharing the second part of our weigh sheet. About what our weight has done and what we are feeling and what is going to happen now.

It’s tiring even writing it out.

I worked out that if you total the number of hours we spend in weigh group - anticipating how shit we will feel about our weight, writing it down, sharing it, getting undressed, getting weighed, writing down how shit we really do feel about our weight and sharing that, oh… plus the bonus panic attacks in response to the impending meal increase that’s going to happen in response to our weight - for a 3-month block on program, that would amount to 24 hours solid thinking about, writing about, talking about and angsting about .. our weight.

So, weigh group is about reducing our obsession with weight.

Got it.

*

Weight. That terrifying number on the scale. It evoked in me the extreme fear it did every other patient I journeyed with in and out of hospital.

From the day I started restricting at the age of 14, the need to control and reduce that number on the scale was my all-consuming focus. Initially the eating disorder trained me to believe that a number that did anything other than go down, and down by a sizeable amount each day, was equivalent to me being fat, lazy, and not trying hard enough for this new set of restrictive rules I had placed upon myself.

I used that number to turn the instinct for survival that is wired into every human brain into a drive to starve, get less and disappear. A drive that was so strong it could overrule my body's inbuilt hunger cues however loudly they screamed.

As time went on, weight became a conundrum that was deep, complex and much harder to shift than simply telling myself 'up' is the new 'down' and 'healthy' the new 'thin'.

It had five functions – five stakes that drove my hope of recovery firmly into the ground:

First, low body weight was a means of holding onto being a child. A way of not growing up. Of hanging out for a dream snuffed out – a dream that I could be the kid I never was.

Second, low body weight was a perfect solution to the terror of having a woman's body. It meant I could avoid stepping into that body – and all the expectations and vulnerabilities I perceived around it.

Third, low body weight was a means of getting help and rescue – when nothing else seemed to work.

Fourth, low body weight was a means of disappearing and shrinking from a world I thought I was too much for.

And fifth, low body weight was a means of creating some semblance of control in a world that felt completely out of control.

So, no surprises, like most folk with an ED, I dreaded weigh days, weigh groups, weigh anything. I found it torturous if my weight randomly fluctuated at home without me knowing how or why. I was mortified and thrown into a state of panic if it crept up by so much as 100g.

Yet here I stand in front of a scale, on a self-appointed weigh day at home, with a completely different mindset.

I want to see my weight go up. I get a thrill from that number doing something that for decades I couldn't cope with at all. I'm nervous - not that I might have gained, but that, after all the hard work of eating, I might not have gained enough.

What has happened? What were the missing pieces?

Weight – Finding the missing pieces.

Where did the missing pieces come from?

Conversation after conversation with Him. Every time I stepped on that scale. And every day after it. Walking with Him. Cleaning with Him. Shopping with Him. Driving with Him. Waiting for Sam at the school gates with Him. Falling asleep in my bed with Him.

He was - and still is - my Divine therapist for the weight conundrum. And the missing pieces came from our therapy sessions.

But let's skin this rabbit in a typically autistic way. Detailed. Methodical. Thorough. We'll do a problem, then the missing piece, one by one.

Here we go.

Gaining weight problem #1: The fear of growing up.

So, increase in body weight represented …. having an adult body.

And being an adult meant I had to let go of being a child.

Sounds kind of obvious. But at 42, part of me couldn't let go of the fact that I was still homesick from school, still pining to go home and play with my toys and do kid things rather than slogging away in a practice room.

Having an adult body was, to me, the final admission that my childhood, complete with its magic as well as its wounds, was gone for good.

No.

More than that.

That the child herself was gone for good.

And that was embarrassingly painful.

Missing piece #1: Permission to be a child.... forever.

He explained that the child part of me that wasn't ready for an adult's body .... wait for it.... *didn't actually have to grow up.*

She could stay a child forever. He had a home for her in His heart, and she could find her place in it – daily.

I know. It sounds like I'm finding excuses to hold on to the egocentric demands of a toddler.

But I'm not. That's the kind of childish that He wants me to grow beyond. The 'We played the pipe for You and You did not dance; we sang a sad song, and You did not cry...[50]' kind of childish. The type that demands of Him: 'Do the thing I want You to do, when I want, the way I want!'

He wasn't endorsing that.

But the child in me – and I guess in everyone – that's blinded enough by love to trust Him no matter what, that wonders and plays with no sense of heavy duty or rush, sees His magic in everything, who simply delights in the life He has given and in the One who gives it...

That child – He has all the time in the world for.

---

[50] Words spoken in exasperation by Jesus to those listening to Him in Matthew 11:17.

That child He adores.

That's the child He says will make it into the Kingdom of Heaven[51]. It's the child of whom He spoke when He told the crowd at Jairus' house,

She isn't dead – she's just asleep.

The one who He went on to summon,

Little girl, get up![52].

And I discovered He was right.

She was still there, still alive and well. Just asleep for a time. He was inviting her to wake up and get up. He was calling her out to play.

Not so much by doing another round of inner child work or endless fun kid activities. A glut of schema therapy[53] and craft sessions in hospitals and day programs, coupled with a boy that hates paint and sticky things, beat that one out of me.

But more by seeing the world in a childlike way.

Finding a lens of wonder for everything. Realising that the wardrobe door is still open, and I can step through it at any time[54]. That the Lion really was bounding next to me on my bike today, looking at me with eyes filled with delight and joy as we raced. There really were angels in

---

51 Matthew 18:3.

52 Mark 5:39.

53 Schema therapy: a type of psychotherapy that helps individuals understand and change long-standing patterns of thinking, feeling and behaving often rooted in childhood experiences.

54 A reference to C.S.Lewis' novel, The Lion, The Witch and The Wardrobe (1950).

the garden yesterday afternoon. This world really *is* more than what we see, touch, feel and smell.

He let the child in me come on an adventure with Him and assured her she would never have to go back to school again, or pull herself together and grow up, or quit crying and practise harder.

We could take care of this kid part of me – so no need to worry anymore about the adult part stepping into an adult body.

Gaining weight problem #2: Fear of having a woman's body.

Gaining weight meant inhabiting a woman's body. And being a woman represented vulnerability, together with a plethora of unwanted sexual experiences.

And I just plain did not want to make myself available for that.

Ever. Again.

Missing piece #2: Finding safety in a woman's body.

He showed me it was okay to have boundaries around my body. It was okay to say – and insist on – 'No'.

When I was experiencing intrusive flashbacks involving sexual trauma of some kind, the Shepherd would swoop in like a fiercely protective older brother. He would intercept the other party with loving firmness, then transport me from the situation to a place of cleansing, safety and security.

In those moments, I felt the incredible power of a Champion fighting for me - of Him declaring,

Hands off! She's My treasure and you have no right to do what you're doing!

I saw Him obliterate the darkness that told me I was not worth protecting or saying no for. There is nothing quite like it – the moment you realise you are worth rescuing and defending.

He told me that I am the King's daughter[55].

And in His Kingdom, no one messes with royalty.

That gave me the confidence to say no – to sex in the future if ever I felt I couldn't manage it (Mike would never have forced it on me – but the ghosts in my mind did), and to hugs in the present if they make me uncomfortable.

He helped me feel safe again. Safe enough to let my body grow.

Gaining weight problem #3: A faulty cry for help.

A painfully low body weight was my way of screaming to the world that I was still hurting. I needed to be sick, sicker than all the rest to attract the comfort, care and help that I seemed to relentlessly crave. Even if that help came in forms – like many well-intended treatment programs - that were a complete nightmare.

Missing piece #3: An eternal Source of rescue, help and validation.

He showed me He would never turn away from me if I had internal pain I needed to talk about. Even if it was something we had spoken of innumerable times. He would validate me forever if that was what I needed.

---

[55] Psalm 45:10-13, 1 John 3:1.

His Spirit was and is a Counsellor[56] within me, always there to unburden pain and guide me through it, without need for a sick body to communicate it to the world. He would never exclaim in exasperation, 'For goodness' sake – this again?! You should be over it by now – why can't you move on?!'

My pains and struggles – momentary or lifelong – will always be legitimate, worthy of listening to, caring for and honouring in His sight. So, I no longer needed to act out my emotional pain in a way that got others to rescue me. I had, and have, an eternal Source of rescue in Him.

That didn't mean I couldn't ask others for help. It just meant that I didn't need a malnourished body to do so. I wasn't a lost girl in a boarding school crying out for someone to take me home anymore – I was a grown adult, walking with and leaning on Him, with access to whatever support and help He saw most beneficial to give me. All I needed to do was ask – in a functional, rather than self-destructive way.

Gaining weight problem #4: The need to disappear.

An ever decreasing, or dangerously low body weight, assured me that I wasn't taking up too much space in this world. That I wasn't being too loud, or clever, or annoying. It made me feel like I was slowly disappearing. I was getting out of everybody's way.

And the converse – the number going up – represented the opposite. That I was going to be too much, in the way, too loud, too clever, larger than life – and with that came a shame and embarrassment I couldn't shake.

---

[56] John 14:26, Isaiah 9:6.

Missing piece #4: Permission to take up space.

This was a simple but life-changing missing piece.

Every time I opened to an encounter with Him and allowed myself to be exposed to the radiance of His love, I realised that it *just might be safe* for me to grow. That I wasn't too much in His eyes. That I didn't have to be doing a million acts of service for Him or others to deserve my place on this planet.

Encounter could be through a conversation with Him in the shops, or a moment sitting somewhere beautiful and gazing at His workmanship, savouring Him in a verse from His book, or simply imagining Him right next to me.

There were and are infinite ways I can bathe in Him.

And each time I do, I realise it is safe for me to stop diminishing myself. He is okay with me taking up His time and space. The glow of compassion, grace and love radiating from Him and His words tell me that.

He would remind me that in His Father's house there are many rooms – one for each of us. And that none of us will have to earn our place there. We will be kids come home, for all eternity. And one day He will come to get us for a school holiday – the good kind - that will never end[57].

Gaining weight problem #5: The need to control.

Low body weight was for me the litmus test of control.

So long as I could control what that number on the scale was doing – namely, make it go down – then I at least had control of something in my

[57] John 14:2-4.

world. Controlling my weight was the drug that softened the feeling of being completely 'out of control' in both my external environment and my internal emotional and sensory worlds.

It was a fake lifejacket I discovered as a kid but still clung to decades on in my middle age.

Missing piece #5: The ability to let go.

This is the piece I leant and still lean on the most... the miraculous ability He gave me to simply surrender the whole darn weight thing to the One who designed me in the first place.

On days where ED thoughts would catch me unawares, suddenly wobbling at the prospect of being a healthy BMI and what that looks like, I would find myself throwing the whole issue back on Him, saying,

'You made me. You designed me. You know what this body was meant to look like. That it's a vessel for Your purposes not mine. And if I'm freaking out at that number right now, I'm just going to trust that You know what You're doing better than me. I spent my life trying to control my body weight and it didn't get me to a crash hot space. So, I'm giving it to You. You take care of it.'

There's a Saint that says it more simply:

'Lord. I surrender myself to You. Please take care of everything.[58]'

---

[58] A simplified version of the Surrender prayer, St. Alphonsus of Maria de Liguori.

When I lose sight of all the other missing pieces to help me chill out about my weight, surrendering myself and my anxieties about it to Him seems to be the fastest route to peace.

I just throw it all back at His feet.

That's the moment He opens my eyes to see things a bit clearer.

That His love is a greater measure of my worth than the earth's gravitational pull on my body ever could be.

Body image

It's 6 am and I'm standing bleary-eyed in the bathroom.

I sigh.

It's time to take off my clothes and get in the shower. Should be fairly straightforward. But this morning, like so many, I'm struggling with it.

I don't want to see the mirror. I don't want to look down as I take my pyjama bottoms off. And I don't want to look anywhere as I wash my body. I can't bear to see anything. Any glimpse of myself and a thousand monsters roar at me from my skin, limbs and flesh.

So, I scrunch my eyes and try and do each of the above without having to look.

I almost pull it off, feeling my way into the shower, until I realise, I'm not much good at shaving my armpits blindfolded. I acquiesce to the inevitable and catch a snapshot of this body of mine that, today, I can't stand.

'Oh God, why am I like this? Why does this have to be so freaking hard?'

I'm humiliated by this part of the illness. Six months in and I'm still completely confused about the way I see my body.

On one level I'm ashamed of still being thin (we're only a third of the way with weight restoration). I can't bear my gauntness and bony protrusions. I hide in hoodies. I make jokes about it to friends when really it cuts me to the core. I want people to say I'm looking better, well-er, healthier.

On another level, I catch images of distorted curves and bulges that I've been hell bent on getting rid of for the past 30 years and cower. I still feel that crushing need for continual reassurance from someone, anyone, that putting on weight doesn't mean I'm horribly fat.

'So stupid. I hate it. I'm embarrassed to even say I feel this way to You.'

It's a weird thing, but I've got used to the fact that He is with me even in the shower.

What's to be embarrassed about? I know you've suffered with this for decades.

'It's so freaking self-preoccupied, self-obsessed, to have these thoughts, this dread of seeing this body of mine. Like I fit this stereotype people have that anyone with anorexia is just trying to look like the photoshopped models you see on Insta.'

I know it's so much more than that. I know how cruel it is.

I'm grateful for His compassion. I always used to fear He would ridicule me for body dysmorphia, or roll His eyes, or chide me for not getting that my body is the temple of the Holy Spirit[59] so, hey presto, I should love it.

I turn the shower off and go back to scrunching my eyes. I can see the towel on the floor and if I shut them now and bend down at the right angle, I can grab it and wrap it around myself without having to see my skin and legs and stomach and everything else.

---

[59] 1 Corinthians 6:19.

'I just… these parts of me… these limbs... these bits…'

I can't put it into words. And I realise I don't have to.

He knows.

That they still carry the sensations, the emotions, the memories of the time I let this guy or that guy do a hundred shameful things to 'get his oats', as one family member once explained. Or the time that dorm-mate prodded me to highlight the chubbiness in my thighs. Or the time that waiter kept jumping on me and kissing me in the empty kitchen when I was doing silver-service waitressing as a student.

The body keeps the score, one writer said[60]. It sure does.

And for that reason, I need it hard, I need it firm, I need it impermeable, and I need it rigid. Curves, softness, roundness are totally *not* okay.

Enter the body dysmorphia.

I quickly grab my clothes and put them on. I'm relieved as I pull today's hoodie over my stomach and hips. Concealed for another day. We can open our eyes now.

'Seriously, I'm meant to be in recovery. People write about finding a new acceptance, love of their body. But look at me… I can't stand to look at it. I'm constantly tensing my muscles because I can't bear to be in it.'

There is silence. Then the slow but tangible sense of … embrace. His gentle embrace.

---

[60] Bessel van der Kolk M.D. The Body Keeps the Score: Brain, Mind, and Body in the healing of Trauma (2015).

I don't know quite how that helps… but it does.

As if He's reminding me of words I once read in His book,

Underneath are the everlasting arms…[61]

Arms that hold and contain me in the torment of the dysmorphia. They cocoon me in His love – a love that shelters me from my warped body image better than my hoodies ever could do.

Sometimes when you're in distress, being held is more helpful than words.

But in the holding, words do come, words for which I can prise open my clenched heart to receive.

I see you through and through – though you can't bear to see yourself. And I love you.

The door of my heart creaks open.

I made you and know every part of your being. And I love you.

The opening widens a little more.

You may want to hide from yourself right now. But none of you is hidden from me. And I love you[62].

A little more again.

---

61 Deuteronomy 33:27. An expansion of this phrase reads 'The eternal God is your refuge, and underneath are the everlasting arms.'

62 Words drawn from Psalm 139, Genesis 16:13.

He brings a song to mind that, ironically, I first heard years prior whilst languishing in admission number four of umpteen. He sings it over me.

'Cause all of me
Loves all of you
Love your curves and all your edges
All your perfect imperfections
Give your all to me
I'll give my all to you....[63]

I stay with it.

I let that truth wash over the insatiable rules and standards of the ED. I remind myself, my Maker knows how my body is meant to look. And whatever that is today, He is okay with it. I choose to trust His eyes right now, His eyes of love, so much kinder than the eyes of the world or an ED.

The tension that has put my dysmorphic body into a state of living rigor mortis starts to ease. I start to melt.

Now I am ready. Ready for His final whisper.

Look up child.

I lift my eyes from the downward perspective of my body to the upward image of His face. Rugged. Pained with compassion. Real. With eyes that are dark, brown, infinite. Looking right at me.

---

[63] John Legend's song, 'All of me' (2013).

And in that moment, I see a reflection of myself that is truer than any I might get from an earthly mirror.

It is the reflection of Love, unconditional Love. I see what I really look like to Him – and it is nothing like what the ED is throwing at me.

I see the image of the beloved.

I realise that my eyes were never created for looking down at myself – they were created for gazing up at Him. And every time the dysmorphic storm hits, it is in that space that I find my peace[64].

---

64 Isaiah 26:3.

Exercise and learning to rest

It is an exercise break day.

I've been advised that I need them by a personal trainer who's helping me build up my strength. Not just a daily cut back of my frenetic levels of physical activity. I need days where I take a break from exercise altogether. It's a day where I am supposed to lie in. No extra walks. No frantic vacuuming.

A day of rest.

I'm guessing a 'normal' person would relish the idea. Setting the alarm for half an hour later than usual. Getting up knowing no physical effort is required before the first meal of the day.

And I'm telling myself that it will be like that for me too, soon hopefully. It'll be great – to have a rest day, yeah?

But right now, I feel like a hamster on a leash.

I wake up way before my alarm goes off and lie in bed, nervously twitching. Voices in my head chatter away.

'If you did it right now it wouldn't be too late – then you will feel just fine for the day...'

'What are you thinking? You are going to be a nightmare mum if you don't just go and do what you always do!'

'Who are you kidding thinking you can do a day without exercise?'

And on and on.

The voices have a point. I've been compulsively exercising for years. When I first became sick it was early morning runs, in the freezing cold, dark, on the moor near school. Torture. Then I got too weak for that, so it became compulsive walks. Later, the runs returned. Then a hybrid of 'yoga' and 'Pilates' that constituted an intense workout.

I even tried to kid myself my own brand of Tai Chi was a holistic 'spiritual' thing, not real exercise at all – whilst working up a considerable sweat. Then YouTube came into our life, and I found all manner of instantly accessible routines to drive myself through.

Hospital tried to beat the exercise urge out of all of us. Doctors insisted on bed rest, no standing, no moving as we weight restored. But it seemed to make the drive to exercise even worse.

I would work out compulsively and guiltily in the middle of the night, hoping the nurses didn't spot my nocturnal 120 salutations to the sun. As soon as I got home from admissions, I would launch into relentless and excessive physical activity to make up for the torture of attempting to sit still for three months.

Then came Covid. Months and months of extensive lockdowns, confined to home for hours on end with Sam's heartbreaking explosions and distress. The urge to get out, get moving, do something, anything, to shake the anxiety was irresistible.

So here I am at 530 am, pinned between the sheets, clenching my fists to refrain from a flurry of compensatory star jumps.

'Ugh. This is so stupid. I'm meant to enjoy having a sleep in. But I'm not sleeping. And I'm not enjoying it. Really? Do we have to do this?'

A car drives by outside. I hear a Rosella chirp. Then silence.

The Lord is my shepherd[65].

It's almost like He is humming over me while He says it.

'I know... I know. Sorry... I know You are my Shepherd. You're guiding this whole process. Help me trust in You more. Sorry...'

He makes me lie down in green pastures[66].

I chew it over. *Makes me…* It's not even that He's giving me permission to rest. He wants me to. It's His will.

'So…this is Your will… difficult as it may feel.'

I hear a creak in the ceiling.

'But green pastures? I'm not feeling it…. What are the green pastures?'

You might be surprised, but there are blessings to be found in taking a break. In pausing[67].

I try to imagine what they might be as I lie here counting the minutes before I can get up and do something at least. Even if it's cleaning the bath.

---

65 Psalm 23:1.
66 Psalm 23:2.
67 Matthew 11:28-30.

Strike that. I can't clean the bath at 6.30am. That seriously is insane...

Even though I walk through the darkest valley, I will fear no evil, for you are with me;

Your rod and your staff they comfort me[68].

'Ok.'

I try and hold that. It feels like a dark valley refraining from any compulsive behaviour. The voices in my head. The accusations. The urges. The threat that I've made a terrible mistake, and I will pay for it later in the day. I'll regret it, just you see.

What if I were to believe He could protect me from those thoughts? What if I were to trust His words in this moment?

My shoulders relax a little. I feel a little more secure.

You prepare a table before me in the presence of my enemies[69].

What if He was at the table at breakfast, in the face of all the thoughts that tell me I don't deserve to eat because I haven't worked out? Perhaps that would be enough – to know He'll deal with those objectors. And prepare nourishment for me all the same.

The alarm vibrates. We're all systems go. I swing my legs out of bed and head to the kitchen to prepare breakfast for Sam and me. It's a school day and we need to start the whole morning regime with lots – and I mean lots - of time.

---

[68] Psalm 23:4.

[69] Psalm 23:5.

'It's the hardest of Your commands You know.' I put Sam's Weetbix in his bowl. The maple syrup in its usual place. Meds and lemonade to wash them down. Milk out.

Which one?

'The sabbath rest one.'

Tell Me more.

'I feel like I'd rather stick pins in my eyes than… than… *stop*. Do nothing. Be still. I just … I just can't stand resting. I'm sorry...'

I can't remember when I ever could rest. I can't remember a time when stopping and resting didn't incur a barrage of self-inflicted judgement for being non-productive or lazy. It's made me an exhausting person to be around.

It's not meant to be a punishment.

I stop and reflect. That's exactly how I've considered the fourth commandment[70]. For some a petty kill-joy rule. For me, a sadist insistence that I can't keep running from myself and my feelings.

'Sorry. You're right. That's exactly how I've seen it. So… why did You make it a law… to … rest?'

Rest is My time for you to heal[71].

Rest? Healing time?!

---

[70] Referring to the Ten Commandments, found in Exodus 20:1-17.

[71] Leviticus 25:8-38, Proverbs 14:30 (Amplified Bible, (AMP)).

'Ok. That's different. I just think of it as another 'should' in my life. *Should* have a rest day from exercise. *Should* have a break from cleaning. *Should* take some time off work. Should … should… should. Sorry.'

I'm getting my breakfast together now. No kitchen freeze today. Phew.

Now I think about it, His words make sense. When I'm not exercising – or running around doing a million other things – my guard is down. My feelings bubble up.

Which is what makes me want to jump straight back on the hamster wheel.

But apparently this stopping thing… it's healing time…

How can I touch your wounds if you don't take time to stop and be still with me. If you don't lie down in the green pastures?

Imagine that. Personal trainers talk about rest being muscle repair time. He suggests it's heart repair time.

Which means, for one day, letting the feelings surface rather than running from them. Holding His hand as I feel them. And, like a dog being trained to sit, learning to 'stay…stay….*staaaay*…'

So, what's behind the exercise urge this morning, Al?

I pause, breathe and get with my feeling while I head to the shower. Breakfasts are good to go.

'Fear.'

Nerve jangling fear. Often is. Sam's disability plan got slashed three days ago. I've no idea how to spread the support workers without giving the impression that someone has abandoned him, given up on him. I don't know how to break it to him.

I know. It is scary for you. It feels unfair. It's hard.

'I just don't know what to do. I never know what to do. I always run out of ideas when I should be able to fix it.'

I know what He's going to say. I guess I just need to hear it … a lot these days.

You don't have to fix it. That's not your job.

'I know. I just wish…. I could. I can't bear to see him let down.'

I will never let him down[72].

I hold those words while I wash myself.

The Lord is my Shepherd. I lack nothing.

Lack nothing. Lack nothing.

'You'll provide... right...'

Always. Maybe not the way you imagine. But always.

I relax a little and open my eyes a slit while I put my clothes on.

'I just need to… trust more. Trust more. I should trust more.'

---

72 Deuteronomy 31:8 (and countless other verses.)

Not should. You're allowed to. I give you the freedom. To trust me.

The morning progresses and it's not long before I lose sight of what He has just said.

I am sipping my coffee and scrolling through Google for reassurance. I punch into my phone, uncontrollably, 'How many rest days are okay?' then 'How much exercise should you do on a rest day?', followed quickly by 'Will I gain weight if I don't exercise for one day?'.

I can't believe myself. Well actually... that's just it. I can. That is what I am like.

Al.

He whispers gently.

I pause the scrolling, feeling sprung.

Under whose authority would you come right now? Under whose protection? Mine? Or Google?

His reprimand is gentle... but outstandingly appropriate. Why would I put my trust in a search engine when I have my Maker telling me what I really need right now?

'I'm so stupid. I am sorry.'

Not stupid. You're learning. I expect you to forget at times. But you have an exemption card.

'Exemption card?'

From all the standards and rules and recommendations you might find out there. Or in your mind.

I like the idea – an exemption card that I could wave at the demands of my ED, my OCD. The media's impossible standards. The expectations of the past.

It's My Blood.

An image of His hand, agonisingly driven through with a nail, springs into my mind.

To some it probably seems gruesome to be contemplating that right now. But I'm grateful for Him placing it there. I know what He is saying. He gave something that was enough to exempt me from every recommendation, standard, judgement, expectation thrown at me from within or without.

He gave His blood.

I am not a theologian, and I don't understand how the cross works. I get tied up in knots trying to work it out. I just know that He gave His body, His blood. He gave them for me. And they are precious. Very costly. They pay the price. They make me His[73].

It exempts me from my eating disorder's rules.

It exempts me from having to exercise today.

It buys me freedom.

He is showing me that today, exercise or no exercise, I am enough.

---

[73] 1 Peter 1:18-19.

Because His blood is … He is… enough.

I feel gratitude. Deep gratitude.

Rest. Healing time. Exemption card. Enough.

I think today will be okay after all.

Identity

The sweetest command He ever gave me was dying to self.

If any man will come after me, let him deny himself[74].

He says it many times. I need to hear it often.

I'm looking out the window of the granny flat I share with Sam at the small garden plot that sprawls beneath. The lavender is out of control for want of a gardener better than me. As I smell the wafts of its fragrance on the summer breeze, I watch a cabbage white butterfly perch on one of the spikes, its wings poised whilst resting before another flight.

They might be cliched in recovery memes… but I still love butterflies. The way they epitomise freedom springing from a chrysalis. Of life bursting from death.

I think they called it 'identity disturbance' - the professionals working with me to combat my borderline personality disorder. I've been a classic case. A chameleon. Always switching from one identity to another in a desperate attempt to feel a stable sense of self, to feel at peace and okay in my own skin.

If I could just work it out – *who I really am* – then maybe I would be able to nourish, grow, this thing called 'me'. Then just maybe I can get well.

I know I'm not alone. You only need to jump onto Insta, TikTok or Facebook to see the amount of effort most of the world puts

---

[74] Matthew 16:24 (KJV).

into determining and marketing who they are. Self-propelled self-determination is pretty much a pandemic.

But I was a particularly embarrassing case of it.

I never really believed it when my DBT team said I had an unstable sense of self. I thought they were being mean, not taking me seriously, rejecting the latest version of 'me' that I'd come up with. They weren't accepting me for who I really was, or thought I was, at any given moment. I took offense to it.

But golly did I switch and switch around. I tried everything to figure it out.

Maybe I'm Buddhist. Maybe I'm a free spirit, untethered by religion. Maybe I'm the person that goes to this kind of church or that kind of church. Maybe I'm the good girl. Maybe I'm the bad girl. A teacher. A massage therapist. Your friend. No longer your friend. Social. In hiding. Loud and opinionated. The one who rocks the boat. Quiet and placid. The one who keeps the peace.

It's got to be here, I told myself, somewhere in all these types and characters I created – the 'me' that is the key to unlocking it all and freeing me from this illness.

The damage…

The damage of not knowing who the heck you are. To those who love you, who commit to one version of you, only to find you have shelved that and are trying something new…. again.

It's been several years now since the marriage equality debate came out in Australia. I was in the throes of self-harm, severe neutropenia[75] and a merry go round of hospitalisations for starvation. I felt like I was willing to do anything to stop this nightmare, to be a better mum for Sam.

I like to think I was not alone in getting the majority of my 'feedback' for my ever-changing sense of self from social media at that time. I became incensed by the insensitivity of posts that advocated against marriage equality and gender diversity using terror tactics and offensive arguments. I cheered and felt passionately for the Rainbow community, the injustices it had been subjected to over the decades and all it was going through during this debate.

But as I scrolled and responded day in day out to the debate, in true borderline style, I found myself asking a whole new set of questions - about who *I* really was in all of this.

'Maybe that is me too.... I have so many painful memories of sexual intimacy - maybe I was never meant to be with a guy. Maybe the reason I have such difficulty being touched is that .... I am gay. Maybe that is why I can't cope with sex when I weight restore. There was that time I felt a sense of attraction to a girl at school and, terrified, buried it ... I never much liked wearing dresses – too many people laughing at me.... Maybe I wasn't ever meant to be a girl in a girl's skin. Maybe the Rainbow community could be my tribe, maybe this is the 'me' I've been searching for all along.'

---

[75] Neutropenia: a blood disorder where a person has a low count of neutrophils in their blood. Neutrophils are a type of white blood cell that play a crucial role in fighting off infections. The condition is common amongst those experiencing anorexia and makes self-injury and its correlating risk of infection particularly dangerous.

Maybe this will fix it.

Mental health professionals congratulated me on the braveness of my new self-discovery - though I had never actually had a same-sex relationship. As my weight continued to stalemate at a dangerous level, the new question in therapy was, what am I going to do about it? Do I really care about my husband and my son? Because if I do, I need to be true about my gender identity and orientation and start living it. I owe honesty to my soon to be ex-husband. And I owe authenticity to my son.

Sam needs to have a mum/parent who stays around, who doesn't suicide from this illness, and coming out is the only way I can guarantee him this. What a great example it will be to him if his mum finally steps into the shoes she/they were always meant to wear.

So that is what I did. I came out. On Facebook. Public.

And our family came crashing down.

I broke Mike's heart. A husband who had walked with me for 16 years through thick and thin.

Two years later, the last and most disastrous of my attempts at self-determination executed, there I lay on the living room floor of my ex's, the sickest I ever had been, despairing and suicidal, with my family in shreds.

Yet no more convinced that I was gay or non-binary than I had thought I was Buddhist or a rain-forest-scientist-to-be.

Though an imposter, I had received generosity, love and acceptance from the Rainbow Community during my time of confusion. I was given a brief window into the world of pain many of its members go through. For these things, I am deeply grateful.

But where some within that community may get it right, I had got it completely wrong. It was only the Shepherd's vast forgiving love that enabled me to name it as such. To finally give up the fight to try and figure out myself by myself.

I looked at Him, gazing into my soul from the living room armchair in His rough Shepherd's clothing, and blurted out,

'I have absolutely no idea who I am. Still. And I quit trying to work it out.'

'I have no idea how to begin to clean up this mess. I have no idea if I can ever restore my family.'

I sobbed as I spoke those words. For a long time.

'But I can see You are a Shepherd.' I continued. 'And Shepherds lead sheep, and lambs, and I think… well… I think if it is okay for now, I would be happy just to be a sheep. You can take all the other identities and labels. I will just be a sheep if that is okay. You lead. I follow. The rest I leave to You.'

He seemed okay with that. So that's what we did.

He showed me a different path. A path of looking up and out at Him, rather than down and in at me. A path of letting go - of labels, opinions, views, anything I'd latched on to define me - rather than holding on.

He was kind. Gentle. He had a whole lot more grace and forgiveness for my messed-up identity than I ever gave myself.

The day I met Him in the living room I'd vowed to myself that I would never forgive myself for the damage I had caused. He pulled me up on that one. Showed me there was a reason I had been the way I had been and maybe it wasn't all my fault. Trauma creates a fractured sense of self, and a kid naturally goes to whatever source of feedback they can find to give them a sense of who they truly are. When the feedback is unstable and insecure the sense of self that emerges is the same.

Apology and reparation were needed, yes. But they were only possible if I gave myself some grace and quit self-flagellating.

He invited me to shelve all the faulty sources of feedback I had relied on to tell me who I was. Social media, other people's ideas of me and who I should be, books, podcasts, even well-intended therapy material.

Then replace it with His feedback.

His words. His love. His touch. His gaze. Stable, solid, enduring feedback that makes for a stable, solid, enduring sense of self.

He taught me what being a woman really looked like. Real basic stuff. I'm sure lots of people would roll their eyes at it – it was stuff from His book that I used to think was dated or chauvinistic.

Now when I read it, it seems quite beautiful.

His kind of girl is humble. Loving. Gentle. Doesn't stress about dressing up fancy. Is willing to trust those that lead her. Has strength – the real kind. Is innovative. Brave. Imaginative[76].

[76] Proverbs 31:10-31, 1 Peter 3:3-4, Ephesians 5:21-33, Philippians 2:1-4, 1 Corinthians 13:4-8.

Being a woman didn't sound that bad after all.

If I had an identity crisis moment, a 'Who am I and what do I do in this situation?' kind of moment, the answer was always clear.

Look up. Look at Him. Be like Him.

I was made, wired, to be in His image.

Have this mind among yourselves, which is yours in him, who,

Though he was in the form of God, did not count equality with God a thing to be grasped,

But emptied himself, by taking the form of a servant, being born in the likeness of men.

And being found in human form, he humbled himself by becoming obedient to the point of death, even death on a cross[77].

Have His mindset. Who emptied Himself. Made Himself nothing[78]. Became a servant. Humbled Himself. By becoming obedient. Even to death. On a cross.

Might sound morbid to some. But I love this.

Because it tells me I can let go. I don't have to cling to this 'me' I've been creating and defending and recreating and taking offense for all my life. So much work and effort. I can let it all go.

---

77 Philippians 2: 5-8, English Standard Version (ESV).

78 'Made himself nothing' is the translation of the same passage, v7, NIV version.

Thank goodness. What a relief.

The Buddhists arrived at emptiness as the answer to the suffering that results from self. Imperfect as my understanding may have been, Buddhist 'emptiness' seemed to have me winding up in a place of nothingness. Of extinction. Like a candle being snuffed out.

But He didn't call me to extinction. He called me to *self-emptying*. And self-emptying doesn't mean nothingness. It means potential. Like the space in a vessel that is waiting to be filled. Filled with Him.

What does that look like? Do I find some new form of self-flagellation? Quit life and look miserable all the time?

No. Just serve, He says. Look for His will – right here, in the way things are unfolding right now. Say to Him, 'Here I am for You … What is it You desire of me – in this moment? What is the path of love You have in mind for me here?'

Then ….

Yield.

Yield to love in all the little things, the unnoticed things, as well as the large.

He gave me an imagination. I'm grateful for that because, true to my autism, I'm a visual kind of girl. So, I am not ashamed to ask Him for pictures of Himself daily. Hourly even.

I take whatever He gives. A Lion. His Shepherd brown eyes. A Lamb. Pure radiant light. Whatever He is today, the more I look at Him, the more I discover that the need to define anything about myself has ceased to be of any importance at all.

He is my Creator. A tree doesn't need to spend weeks and weeks figuring out what kind of tree it is – it just grows. So, I figure I don't need to worry about what kind of human being I am. He loves me. I am His child. And …. That is about all I need to know.

The chrysalis breaks. The butterfly flies.

Months passed on with me walking along this road. Self-emptying – at least to the best of my wobbly ability - in place of self-determination.

Surprisingly – or perhaps not - I was able to nourish this new person better than all the previous ones I had fabricated for myself. Day by day I grew. I took up space. I became more solid and stable – emotionally, in my 'self', as well as physically.

And with a heart shattered by multiple rejections, Mike witnessed this transformation. Miraculously, or perhaps insanely, he was given the courage to trust it and forgive.

And our family came back together.

A new family, with a mum who, after 46 years lost and searching, had finally come home to who she really was.

What about Mike and Sam?

I've been told that many reading this book will, by now, be asking a lot of questions about Mike and Sam.

How on earth did they cope throughout the years of my illness? Why did Mike take me back after I had so publicly rejected him? How did all this impact Sam?

Try as I might, I can't seem to give a balanced answer. I drop the grace stone when it comes to Mike, Sam and I way too easily.

With Mike, I still feel as I did on my wedding night – that I never deserved him with all his goodness and he never deserved me with all my mess. I can only speculate on the hell I put him through, and I can't possibly justify why he took me back.

As for Sam, I'm not sure I will ever stop blaming myself for his struggles. When people ask me how he is doing, the best I can give them, beneath stifled tears, is that he has no fingernails - he chewed them off years ago with anxiety - and it's rare that he has a bedtime where he doesn't tell me he wants to 'go home' – his code words for ending his life.

So, you see, it is very painful to answer those questions.

But they are fair to ask.

Sam? I'm afraid you will need to wait until he is old enough to tell his own story, if ever he chooses to do so. I pray I have the grace to hold that story and honour it, however painful it may be to hear.

Mike? I would not trust myself to speak on his behalf and he has not had an opportunity to sit down and write his own account. So, my best alternative was to scribble on a Post-it note the questions I guessed many might want to ask him. Being the deeply thoughtful man he is, he took the note away to reflect on before responding. A week later he kindly allowed me to record a conversation over dinner where he answered them to the best of his ability.

Ever the master of understatement, you may find his responses difficult to believe. Mike is one of the gentlest people I know, and his manner of communication reflects this.

But they are his answers, not mine, and hopefully they satiate people's curiosity better than my own self-flagellation would.

So here they are, unabridged version.

*

Me: 'Did you know about, and were you worried about, my eating disorder before we got married?'

Mike: 'Yes to both. I was worried. I went to a counsellor to talk about it – to work out whether I was resourced to support you in it and prepared to take that on. It was a big issue. I had a lot of anxiety about it. '

Mike pauses.

'That said, I think neither you nor I knew the depth of the problem at that point, including the trauma you had experienced in your earlier years. And whilst you struggled with eating, you appeared to be doing reasonably well. That fact, combined with talking the whole thing through with friends as well, plus praying a lot about it, helped me to move beyond my fear and make the decision to marry you. And once I took that step, I had a strong sense of comfort and peace about it. I sensed that God was behind us being married despite your health issues. I never looked back after that.'

These last words are indicative of two of Mike's most beautiful qualities: his faithfulness and tenacity. Granted, he can take time to make a decision (not such a bad thing when it comes to marriage) and he may experience anxiety and vacillation in that process. But once Mike decides - on anything - he is solid as a rock. It's true in his friendships, no matter how draining or 'needy' the other party might be. It's evident in his work as a business analyst which, he shares, can make for tedious labour. It shines through his faith: steady and constant despite the wrestles and questions he expresses so honestly at times. And, of course, it is most visible in his role as a husband and father. As this story attests, no matter the pain of a commitment, Mike sticks with it through thick and thin.

Me: 'What was it like for you seeing me get sicker during our married years?'

Mike: 'It was hard to watch somebody I love suffering. It was perplexing. I questioned whether I was supportive enough, or there was something I had failed to do or say that would have helped you climb out of the hole you seemed to have fallen into. And the cyclical nature of it was difficult. Early on I thought the hospitalisations were a good idea - they were almost a relief, because I felt I couldn't help you. I saw you losing weight and looking unwell and I didn't know what to do. But as time went on, it became clear that treatment was a double-edged sword - I didn't know whether any admission was going to help or harm you further. Particularly after the Belvere[79] incident.'

Mike is referring to one hospitalisation where a nurse reminded me how much I was damaging Sam by being admitted. I was so distressed, I overdosed that night (I broke out of the ward, which had minimal security, got myself to a local pharmacist and downed a stash of over-the-counter meds in the public toilets nearby). I realised what a dumb move this was, so fessed up to the medical team the next morning, asking for help to process the nurse's statements better. They discharged me immediately, saying I was too unstable for treatment. Mike was summoned to drive me straight to Emergency at a separate hospital to neutralise the medications I had ingested, before being sent home.

This, after he had gone to painstaking ends to persuade me an admission was the best thing I could do for Sam right now.

Me: 'It must have been so incredibly frustrating for you – not just that occasion, but seeing me go into hospital, come out and relapse over and over again. And seeing the impact on Sam too.'

Mike: 'I think more than anything I felt bewildered about how to help you. But I also loved you and wanted to see you in a place where you could thrive. I saw so much potential in you, so many talents and qualities. So, I guess, yes, it was frustrating to see how much the illness was holding you back.'

Me: 'What about the strain on you – when I was in hospital and you had to look after Sam? How did you cope with that?'

---

[79] Name of hospital has been changed.

Mike: 'I don't remember it being a huge strain. I remember being tired because there was a constant rhythm I needed to fall into. But I had a lot of support from our church and my family. In fact, I fondly remember those times I got to spend with Sam and the connection I had with him. It was a rich time. We had a lot of fun. Sometimes I worried about whether I was giving Sam enough support to deal with your absence, because I had to work during the day and he was in daycare. But despite that, I don't remember it being a strain in a parenting sense.'

Me: 'What was the hardest aspect of it all?'

Mike: 'I can't name one. But probably the pendulum swings. The way you would make very clear statements in one direction – particularly about spirituality and faith – and then suddenly there would be a very different perspective. One minute you were saying you would never veer from our Christian beliefs, and then the next moment you would throw it in and go down the Buddhist path. And you were often unaware of what you had said previously. The faith element was hard because I wanted to walk with you in that – like we had when we first met.'

Me: 'What about the identity thing – me saying I was gay, non-binary? That must have been incredibly painful.'

Mike: 'Yes ... of course it was hard. But beneath the rejection, rightly or wrongly, I had a sense deep down that it wasn't true. I rolled it into the same pendulum-swinging confusion. I saw it as part of the whole gamut of your mental health struggles.'

Me: 'Did you ever want to leave me – did you ever think you had had enough?'

Mike: 'No. I always held onto the fact that I loved you. I saw your beauty, and I always hoped you would get to a place where you might have some kind of freedom. I held onto that hope - and I wanted to stick with my commitment. I never wanted to leave you, though there were times I wanted to sole parent, mainly because of the way Sam would push me away and cling to you when you were around. But that was his insecurity - a separate thing to us. I wanted to maintain what we had.'

Me: 'Why did you take me back after all I put you through?'

Mike: 'For all the reasons I have given. When you first came and spoke through what happened with you and the Shepherd in the living room, and you gave your apology and all of that I wanted to see a consistent change for a decent period before I was willing to trust it. Because I didn't feel I could cope with another rejection or severing.'

Mike is referring to the impact of my torturous 'identity-switching' already discussed in the previous chapter. One minute I was gay, non-binary, and separating was necessary. The next minute I had got it all wrong and wanted to reunite. This happened on multiple occasions, breaking Mike's heart repeatedly. Needing to see consistent, stable change was essential for his own healing.

Mike: 'And I didn't think it would have been good for Sam if you had switched again. He needed stability too. But me taking you back – ultimately, I did see that change, and then it just came back to knowing your beauty and qualities as a woman. I had already made that decision to be with you eighteen years ago. I don't think it ever stopped. I remember walking in the Dandenongs[80] and praying that you would see the beauty

80 Hills in the eastern suburbs of Melbourne.

in what we had. I guess your living-room moment was the culmination of those prayers.'

*

I ran out of questions at that point. Maybe there are more you would have had me ask, but that was as much as I could manage, so I hope it's enough for you, the curious reader for now.

More than that, I hope it encourages you that no prayer for another is ever wasted. Particularly those we love, including those who have betrayed us, who are lost in a place of dark confusion.

I know many people have prayed for me over the years. But in my heart, I feel it was Mike's prayers, his especially, that woke me up that fateful evening when I encountered the Shepherd.

It is perhaps the most romantic thing, the most courageous thing, Mike has ever done for me. To keep praying for me, keep fighting for me, for us, even when I had given up.

And for that, I will be forever grateful.

FOURTH INTERLUDE – AWAKENING

'It's all about waking up, isn't it?'

I'm walking through the car park to Coles armed with empty bags, on the hunt for something – anything - to vary Sam's dinner tonight and stop him food jagging[81] on chicken fingers.

Go on.

'I'm always wondering what this life is about. Why You placed us here. Why You give us the number of years You give us. Then I thought about the living-room night – when I saw You for the first time – well the first time in ages. I think I woke up that night. I woke up to Love. I woke up to You.'

You did. It was beautiful. And every time since.

'So we're put here to wake up? To wake up to Love[82]?'

That's one part of it.

'But it doesn't stop there does it!'

No. That's just the beginning.

---

81 Food jagging: where an individual has a particular food that he/she prefers to eat, cooked or prepared in the exact same way each day. Eventually it results in that food no longer being tolerable to the person, and therefore their diet becoming even more restricted. It's a common phenomenon for individuals experiencing ARFID.

82 References to waking up can be found in Revelation 3:2; 1 Thessalonians 5:5-6; Ephesians 5:14; Isaiah 52:1, 60:1; 1 Corinthians 15:34 (KJV).

I dodge a car reversing and head for the pedestrian crossing. I'm trying to resist the urge to jay walk these days.

'Of course... how could anyone wake up and not want to wake up others? How could you wake up to discover Love is right there, right in front of you, and let somebody else stay asleep in a dream that is ...maybe terrible?'

He nods and smiles slightly.

'So You wake us up so we can wake up others ...'

I feel excited. The meaning of life might be simpler than I thought... But I'm cautious too. I don't want to be inventing my own religion.

'When I was practising Buddhism waking up took a lot of work. A lot of meditating. Dharma reading. Chanting. A lot of insight and concentration. It was hard.'

It was, for you.

I reflect. I wasn't a very good Buddhist.

'But You... You are saying that a person wakes up when they encounter Love – like when I encountered You in the living room... or maybe when Saul encountered You on the road to Damascus[83]... or Thomas when he touched Your wounds[84]... they all encountered Love. And they woke up. Something – everything - changed for them.'

We're through the doors now and heading for the freezer aisle.

---

83 Acts 9.

84 John 20:24-27.

'So.... if I want to help someone else wake up, I just need to love them. Love them awake.'

You're getting close.

Suddenly, I remember a story I read in a newsfeed years ago. It was about a mother whose premature baby was stillborn. She was given time with the child to say goodbye. So, she lay with her baby, at first weeping, but then singing to him, stroking his tiny limbs, holding him and loving him. And slowly, miraculously, the child took a breath. He opened his eyes. He came back to life.

The power of love.

'I couldn't possibly love the way You loved me back to life. You are amazing. I am so...empty...run dry half the time. I get so cranky and irritable with people. Inside at least.'

I don't expect you to. I only ever ask you to love with the Love I give you.

We pause the conversation while I deliberate between chicken fingers (nope – need something different), chicken dinosaurs, chicken nuggets, chicken tenders, chicken kievs (garlic – can't do that one). I throw caution to the wind and go with the nuggets this time.

'But I know it's about loving You too. In fact, ... I think I can only love others when I fall more and more in love with You...'

Quite right. The two are inseparable[85].

---

[85] Matthew 22:36-40.

'Yet… my love for You can be so lacking. So empty too. I'm sorry. I wish I could love You more.'

You are empty only when you forget to be filled. I am ever ready to pour My love into you. For you to pour it back out to me[86]*. It is a never-ending flow. Loving back and forth. It's what I made you for.*

I pause. A divine exchange. So that's what worship is. Not something I do with my own effort. Something that is given.

And in it, we are both filled with delight[87]*.*

He looks at me and smiles. I smile back.

We're heading home now.

It's all about waking up. Waking up to Love.

---

[86] 1 John 4:19, Ephesians 5:18, Psalm 62:8, Matthew 22:37.

[87] Psalm 37:4, Psalm 147:11. Reference also the entire book of the Song of Songs which, whilst describing the nature of marital love, has been interpreted by some as an allusion to a divine romance between Creator and creature too.

Crash

'Alys... you're in relapse. We need to admit you.'

Two CATT[88] team nurses are sitting opposite me at my kitchen table in our new home.

I hadn't planned on this visit. I mean, who would, at 6pm on a Friday evening, last day of the school term?! Sam is completely burnt out and it's the witching hour.

But they've called and left a message while I'm running Sam's bath and cooking his dinner simultaneously, and they've assumed that no pickup from me means go ahead for them.

So here they are. Nurse 1 is taking notes; Nurse 2 has that 'we-need-to-go-in-hard' kind of look on her face. I wonder if she's been waiting for this all day.

I'm unable to contain the panic and begin sobbing uncontrollably.

'You don't understand,' I gasp. 'I got well – I did it on my own – I don't need an admission; I just needed some help with my anxiety. This isn't what it looks like…'

The more I talk, the deeper the hole I dig for myself.

They don't believe me. It's my eating disorder talking they say. Not me. I don't exist, apparently.

[88] CATT: Crisis Assessment Treatment Team.

'What are you currently eating each day?'

How long have they got? I hold my breath and list my current meal plan. 3 meals, 3 snacks. It takes about 5 minutes to describe every portion, every amount, because Nurse 1 is scribbling as I talk, getting me to repeat everything at least twice.

I finish the description and Nurse 2 looks over her glasses with suspicion.

'But are you *really* eating that much?'

I press my stress spot between my eyes.

'Yes...*yes!*'

I launch my desperate attempt at an explanation, knowing by her look that I'm on a losing battle here. She is not going to believe me.

'I'm eating everything I just said, but it's not as much as I was eating before, because I can't with the nausea and the cramping! I know I need more but I can't get it into me – I just end up retching over the toilet! Please, you've got to believe me – ask my husband! I just need to take this medication that the GP prescribed for the anxiety and maybe that will help. I didn't need for you guys to come over – it was just the family support worker that suggested it because I couldn't get in with a psychiatrist for some meds. But my GP has given me the Amitriptyline, and I just need to start it, and then maybe the nausea will go down and I can go back to increasing my diet.'

I stop to take a breath.

Nurse 2 takes the box of tablets away from me.

Sam bursts into the room -

'Mum, Mum who are they? What's happening?' He is spiralling rapidly into panic. 'Why are you crying Mum? Why are you crying?'

'It's okay buddy,' I quake, face blotchy as. 'They're just checking up on a few things, they will be gone soon.'

Sam starts a barrage of questions, 'Are they going to take you to hospital, don't go to hospital, I don't want you to go to hospital!'

Hysteria and melt down are imminent.

Nurse 2 waits for a pause in Sam's words, which never comes, then in her best authoritarian voice, fires at me,

'We don't want you to take these tablets. Do you realise that if you take an overdose of this medication you will die? For certain. This is the one medication where, if you are suicidal, it will kill you if you overdose. Period.'

In front of Sam.

'Are you going to die Mum? Are you going to die? Please don't kill yourself please don't kill yourself.' He begins to howl. I grab him close.

'It's okay buddy, I am not going to die. I am not going to kill myself. It is okay.'

I turn to them,

'I am not suicidal! Do I look suicidal? I have a child to care for! Why would you say that in front of my son? I need you guys to go – please.

This is not helping. Sam can't handle this. We have just got him to a place of stability. This will take him weeks to get over.'

By now Sam's distress has gone through the roof. He is screaming, punching walls, swearing. Out of control.

They see they have hit an impasse. Both nurses agree to exit the house and confer with the duty registrar on the phone in their car as to my fate - a voluntary or involuntary admission. Bail is granted and I'm told that I must check myself in to the hospital ED the next morning for emergency physical review.

It's Good Friday. Our first Easter back as a family.

What the heck had happened? How did I get to this place?

*

Nine months prior, weeks after Mike and I made the decision to reconcile and come back together, Sam's emotional struggles began to increase exponentially. I told myself it was my fault: the fallout from all my hospitalisations, my identity confusion, my separation from Mike.

And the daily challenges for a child living with an autistic brain in a neurotypical world[89].

But the straw that broke the camel's back was the loss of Sam's school principal. His was the class whose teacher needed to step in to the vacant

[89] A vast topic that I felt unable to address in detail in this book. But any parent of a child with special needs will have a sense of what I mean here, and for those who have not had this experience, maybe ask someone you know who has. I'm sure they will so appreciate their child's story, and their own, being heard.

principal role, leaving Sam and his classmates with a series of substitute teachers. The turnover was intolerable for Sam, and an extended period of school refusal began.

Sam and I were still living separate from Mike while we waited for a home we could all move back into. Frozen with anxiety, Sam could not leave our two-roomed granny flat, so neither could I. It was lockdown all over again, but this time we could see the rest of the world carry on with its life happily outside our living room window.

Sam became increasingly distressed, dysregulated, unsafe in his behaviours and, ultimately, suicidal. Many nights I would try desperately to console him as he sobbed in his bed, begging me to tell him how he could kill himself. He was only nine.

The stress, predictably, took its toll.

I did not harm, but I tortured myself internally with self-blame as I watched Sam's distress, powerless to do anything to make things better for him. I couldn't sleep. I was constantly nauseous – not just when I ate but in between meals too. If I did get to sleep, I would wake multiple times in the nights with nightmares and unbearable stomach cramps, heaving over the toilet. I was convinced that, God forbid, if Sam ever did suicide, it would be on me, 100%, after all I had put him through.

After a honeymoon period of 'breakthrough' and recovery, eating had become, once again, an ordeal. Only this time it was not because of classic anorexia – it was because of stress.

Within four months, I watched the weight gain that I'd never dreamed possible slip through my fingers, kilo by kilo. I found myself back at the bottom of the pit, horribly gaunt, wracked with waves of nausea even after we had got Sam back into a regular school routine and settled ourselves into our new home. Sam's outbursts and distress continued, and my nervous system refused to recover.

The onslaught in my mind was relentless.

'This is all your fault you idiot. Told you so. You were stupid to even believe you could recover. Look at you. You're pathetic. You never deserved to be back with Mike. You think you can make this family whole? Ha – think again. Nothing has changed – you're just kidding yourself. This whole Shepherd thing is a hoax.'

And on and on, day in, day out.

*

'What the f*** Lord?!'

It's late Saturday morning, the day after the CATT team debacle. Miraculously I have been able to convince the hospital doctors that an admission is not what I or my fragile family unit need right now.

I'm sitting alone at the dinner table after lunch, my feet pushing into the ground in an effort to stop the room spinning. Mike and Sam have gone ahead to Bendigo to see family. I'll catch them up shortly.

'What the f***?!'

He is giving me that holding space – He often does it when I swear. I guess He knows what's coming.

'I've failed You. Completely failed You. I am a failure.'

What makes you think that?

'Look at me! I'm a freaking mess! I'm as underweight as I was a year ago. I need to go back on meds. I need to see a psych again. I've lost everything I gained. What kind of story is that for You? What kind of testimony?!'

I am furious – I don't know with who or what. Myself. Nurse 2. Reality. Him. I don't know. I am just mad.

'I don't know why I even bothered thinking I could get well. It's just like they said it would be – when I apologised to everyone – they said they would only believe the change when they saw it. And here I am, just the same old. Just proving I could never do it. What the f***.'

Tears. Again.

I don't think you realise how much you have changed.

'What do You mean? I'm skinny as a rake again. Terrified of food because I want to puke all the time. Seeing a psych because I can't stop crying after Sam's meltdowns. So freaking pathetic.'

He can handle the pushback.

Look at how far you have come, Al. Look how different your thinking is.

I pause letting another nausea wave pass. I could faintly appreciate that my mind still wanted to eat, get strong, put on weight. It was my body that couldn't handle it. I guess that was something.

Medications aren't a failure. Seeing a psych is not a failure.

'Yes, it is!' I shoot back.

'I promised You I would do this journey without either. I never wanted to go back to mental health professionals. I don't trust myself not to get confused and destroy my family all over again. I vowed I would never do it. I wanted to show people that You were enough. That I could do this just with You. No meds. No psychs. No nothing. But I failed.'

Did I ask you to do any of that?

I stay with that for a few breaths. I guess not.

I quite like using others to do My miracles. And I have some good psychs out there.

He was right. Jeremy, the psychologist I had started seeing, was gentle. Kind. Not thrashing at me in an attempt to thrash my eating disorder. It had been a relief to start unpacking why I kept disintegrating every time Sam had a meltdown. To process the turmoil and upheaval of the past three years.

'But I was so passionate for You before the nausea and the stomach pains. I was so on fire for You when I worshipped. I sang my heart out. Prayed my heart out. Spoke Your Truth out with this boldness and command and …. Now I can't do any of it. I can't do anything. It's the best I can do to just breathe out Your Name."

That's good enough for me[90].

Pause. The room spins again, and another wave of nausea rolls through my body.

'I just feel like I am never going to get there. Get back to where I was. Let alone beyond it.'

---

[90] Psalm 51:17.

You know, I am far more interested in the journey than the destination.

Pause.

I love you as much 'un-recovered' as recovered. My love for you is not contingent on whether you have a perfect recovery.

Longer pause.

I am not bothered about the strength of your arms and legs. Just the shape of your heart[91].

He takes a breath.

I can work good from this, Al[92]. *Trust me.*

Something in me stings. I push back.

'It hurts to even consider that. I can't hope for anything right now. It is too painful.'

For a moment, I can feel His arm around my shoulder.

Al, sometimes you try too hard.

'Isn't that what You want? Us to try our very best to please You… isn't that us showing we love You?'

I don't need you to try and impress me. I know you love me. You don't have to prove it to me.

---

[91] 1 Samuel 16:7, Psalm 147:10-11.

[92] Romans 8:28.

The scene of Him standing on the beach with Peter flashes back into my mind once again. The Shepherd has risen from the dead. Peter is a broken man. He asks Peter to reaffirm his love for his Master. Three pledges of love, to replace three moments of gut-wrenching betrayal[93].

Maybe the request is not to reassure the Shepherd. Maybe it is to reassure Peter.

All I want you to do right now is let Me carry you.

Be carried? Like a limp, helpless rag?

I blurt out, insensitively, 'But I don't want to be carried! *I* want to do this for You. *I* want to win this, get myself well...*I* want to show You.... show everyone... *I*...'

My voice trails off. I can hear what I am saying. The angry, childish me railing again.

We need to let go of that, Al.

Let Me carry you.

I sigh. The nausea has paused enough for me to wash my dishes. Grab my bags. Lock the house and get in the car.

Let Me carry you[94].

I've no idea what that will look like. But it's all I've got for now.

---

93 John 21:15-17, Matthew 26:75.

94 Isaiah 46:3-4, Isaiah 41:10, Exodus 19:4.

Body sensations

I hit the play icon on YouTube. The faint sound of strings grows to a slightly nauseating harmonised chord reverberating on my phone. I think it's meant to be relaxing but I swear it's synthesised, and that irks me.

The voice begins.

'Today I will guide you through a brief body scan practice to connect your body and mind, relieve any stress you might be feeling and promote an overall sense of relaxation and wellbeing.'

Optimistic.

'Begin by finding a comfortable upright seated position in a chair or on the floor, allowing your hands to rest in your lap or on your thighs.'

Seated… why seated? I'm dog tired… And scratch the resting your hands on my lap and thighs. I do not want to feel either.

I curl into a semi-foetal position on the couch. I'm not sure that qualifies, quite. Oh well.

'Next, bring your attention to your body with your eyes closed or, if it's more comfortable maintain a soft gaze with your eyes partially open but not focused on any particular object.'

Partially open? Nope, that looks weird… Truth be known, I would quite like to sleep for the next ten minutes.

'Take a moment to bring awareness to how you are feeling.'

Arghh. That's the whole reason I'm doing this! I don't want to feel how I am feeling!

I grit my teeth and hang in there for the next statement.

'Unclench your jaw, soften any tension between your eyebrows.'

'That's it, I'm done! ' I exclaim out loud in frustration. 'Why am I even trying this? 45 seconds into a ten-minute body scan and I can't get past my eyebrows. What was I thinking?!'

It's ten minutes before school pickup, and I am trying to quell the nausea and find some peace in my own skin.

Some call it interoceptive difficulties. Others interoception OCD. Most acknowledge it as a symptom of trauma and the cognitive distortions that accompany an eating disorder. Many of my friends in ED treatments described it as 'feeling fat'.

I have coined the term, the 'yuck' feeling. The feeling that I literally can't bear to be in my own body. Like every signal I get from it, whether 'painful' or 'neutral', 'pleasant' or 'unpleasant', feels completely distracting and intolerable. It makes me grumpy, irritable, preoccupied - everything I don't want to be.

For thirty years or so, hunger solved the 'yuck' feeling. The constant gnawing ache in my stomach seemed to wash out all the other body sensations. I ramped that up a notch further with harming. I preferred the feeling of multiple third degree burns than the normal sensations of having a body.

But right now, I'm not harming. And I'm not hungry - I am eating a sizeable amount each day to put weight on again. If anything, I am nauseous. The 'relief' of feeling hunger is a long way off.

So I have to feel my body sensations, nausea included. I have to be in my body.

That's why I thought I should try a body scan. They used to get us to do them in DBT for distress tolerance and I thought I should be proactive and give it another go.

But I can't do it. It is just making the sensations jar even more.

I slam my hand on the phone and pause the meditation.

'Ug. I can't do this. I wish I didn't even have a body. If this is how it's going to be every day for the rest of my life without starving and harming, I don't think I can do it. Why can't I be normal?'

It's one of my slightly self-pitiful rants with Him. He listens, patiently.

I find myself wishing that when I die, I don't get a resurrected body. I want to be floating around like some ethereal spirit – like the angels. That would be grand.

I sense His frown. He paid a lot for my resurrected body[95].

'I'm sorry. That was insensitive.'

Obviously, not having a body – now or then – is not an option. He made me in His image – body and all. He even deigned to come to this world

95 I Corinthians 15:35-58.

in a human body Himself. Clearly having a body wasn't an accident for me or for Him.

I sigh. I just have a few minutes before I must move my body (ug. more body sensations) and go and get Sam.

'Why is it like this? Why do You even give us a body? Why can't I get these body scans and sitting meditations and mindfulness exercises to 'work'? How comes half the world seems to enjoy getting things like massages and having baths and…'

I trail off.

Can I say something?

'Yes, sorry. Sorry to complain like that...'

It's okay. But Al, your body is not a vehicle for self-gratification. It is a vessel for love[96]*.*

I smart. Self-gratification?! Isn't starving and harming yourself the very opposite of self-gratification? Isn't it self-punishment?

I let His words sit for a moment.

Then I feel very small.

I can see that both those behaviours are still a form of self-gratification. Their aim is to push away one kind of feeling and pull towards me another. They are grasping behaviours – no less than scrolling too much or retail therapy or eating or drinking too much.

---

96 1 Corinthians 6:19-20.

My hatred of body sensations is entirely because I want to feel a certain way in my body, and I can't. I am still seeing my body as a way of pleasing myself.

I feel ashamed.

'I'm sorry. I hadn't seen it that way.'

It's okay. There are reasons why you use it that way. And you're not alone.

I reflect on my survival instinct wired from past experiences in my life. But I figure it goes deeper than that.

It does, for each person. It is because you forget often the One who fulfils all your desires[97]*. You forget Me. You forget My love.*

I glance at Him as we get in the car to go to school and see the scar on His right hand.

You operate out of fear, thinking that the only way you can find peace is by using your body to get what you want. But remember, perfect love casts out fear[98].

I let it sink in while I wait for a gap in the traffic.

What if that were true? If all this hating of my body sensations was because I'm simply seeing my body as a means of feeling good, feeling okay? What if I saw it differently - if everything my body can do, and everything it feels, was for the sole purpose of loving Him?

---

97 Psalm 37:4.

98 1 John 4:18.

Would that change my focus? My obsessing over sensations I can't stand?

'Is that what You mean?' I ask Him.

You're close.

'So what would it look like – using my body, whatever it is feeling like, for love of You - practically speaking?'

When you make a cup of tea, make it for love of Me. When you prepare a meal you are dreading, prepare it with love for Me. When you weed the garden, weed it for love of Me. When you breathe in the spring air, breathe it for love of Me. When you respond to Sam in his distress with kindness and patience, do it for love of Me. When you give Mike a hug, do it for love of Me[99].

'Hang on a second… Mike wants me to give him affection because I love Mike! I don't think he would feel happy knowing I only did it because I loved You?! Could be a bit of a turn-off…. if You know what I mean... And Sam too – he wants to feel loved because he's him. Not just because I love You...'

If you truly love Me, you can't but help love those whom I place in your path. I adore every creature I have made. So your love for Me has to be expressed in love for others. Without loving others, it is not true love for Me[100]*.'*

We reverse out the drive.

---

99 1 Corinthians 10:31.

100 Matthew 22:34-37, Luke 10:25-37.

Using my body for the love of Him. Responding to its signals and using it for that alone. I imagine what that might look like as I drive from home to school. Let's try it out, I think.

Seeing other drivers on the road, there is a pang in my heart as I sense His love for each one of them. Love that's deep and strong like it is for me. I say a quick prayer for them. Something small, insignificant because I don't know – I don't know what they need right now. So, I just blurt out 'Let them know Your love...' and imagine lifting them up in that giant human web He showed me a while back – the one where we are all lifting each other up into the light.

The cars stop at a red light. I thank Him for the traffic lights – imagine if we didn't have them? We'd all have car crashes and get really mad at each other... I thank Him for the people that figured out how to build traffic lights. I feel a bit childish, but I do it anyway. Then I realise it's nice to pause, to stop, even if the cars are banking up and I don't want to be late for Sam. So, I thank Him for the moment of stopping.

I swing onto the main road that leads towards Sam's school. I feel the warmth of the steering wheel beneath my grip and realise I am so fortunate – to be able to hold a steering wheel, turn a car, have this freedom. I think of all the guys with cerebral palsy I used to work with when I was a teacher and a support worker. And people who don't have enough money for a car. Or who have agoraphobia and can't leave their house. All these people - they could never do this. But here am I, holding a wheel, driving. So, I thank Him.

I pick up Sam and he's burnt out. I can tell. He is quiet, nonverbal. I am anxious. I don't know what is coming or whether I will get my work done this afternoon. I'm thinking about myself as much as Sam.

We swing into the garage, and I know I have a choice. I can ask Sam if there is anything he needs in a rushed, 'hope-there-isn't' kind of way whilst getting his bag, getting out the car and reminding him that I have work to do.

Or I can give him his promised 'car time', something we began months ago when he started going back to school. The time where we sit in the car in the garage for as long as it takes so he can get everything about the day off his chest.

It can take a while.

Lots of nonverbal communication, yes and no questions in signs to help him piece the day together. Then lots of swear words. Lots of me trying, and often failing, not to fix everything. I'm still feeling my way with it.

I know which one is the love choice.

So, we spend the next 30 minutes in the garage.

As long as I focus on these things – the present task in hand, the present moment, the present person with me – *for love of Him*, my mind is off the body sensations that I can't stand.

The function of my body has ceased to be to please myself. It has become to love Him – however imperfectly I try and follow through.

'It's all well and good though,' I say to Him later after car time has finished and Sam is having some couch time to recuperate.

'But how do I do all of that when I still drag my body around like a mouldy rag, when I still have that overwhelming aversion to it? When, for all the effort of doing things for love of You, I still have that chalk-scraping feeling of being in my body? How do I keep that up?'

It won't be forever Al. It's a wound. The legacy of an illness, of some difficult experiences. And one day that legacy will be gone. Healed completely[101].

I have a picture of myself running through streams and meadows and climbing trees like I used to as a 7-year-old, with no thought whatsoever for my body – only a sheer delight in living. What I would do to feel that way again.

For now, let Me help you live this life in your body.

He brings to my mind a verse I've always loved.

The life I now live in the body, I live by faith in Him who gave Himself for me[102].

I have a sense that when I can't tolerate being in this skin, I can let Him do it for me. I can drop into Him and let Him live through my body while I hide in, and find my peace in, Him[103].

Maybe it is me doing mental leapfrogs with a Bible verse, but it helps.

My laptop is open, ready to go. I have one last question before I get back to work.

'I'm worried that I might try to do things for love of You, but in a stressed-out kind of way. Where I am trying hard, always trying - boil the kettle

---

[101] Revelation 22:1-2.
[102] Galatians 2:20.
[103] Psalm 32:7, Ephesians 2:14.

for love, say a kind word for love, try, try, try, push, push, push. I don't think I have it in me to be operating from love all the time. Even if You are helping me tolerate my body for now. What do I do about that? What if I just don't have enough love in me, or I am not feeling it?'

He repeats words He has had to say to me often.

I never expect you to give what I haven't already given you. I never expect you to love without giving you the love to do so.

I feel stupid. I feel like I need to be reminded all the time. But I ask all the same.

'Show me that love – I know I know it, but show me right now that love, so that I can use this body to love the way You want. Please...'

I wait for a moment. Then pictures flash before my eyes.

A cross.

Nails.

Crown of thorns.

Lashes from a whip.

Spear wound in the side.

Sweat. Tears. Darkness. Abandonment.

I see a love that is more than the memes you find on Facebook, or pretty cards you buy at Hallmark.

It is a love that costs. Costs more than I ever could imagine. And it is given to me – everyone in fact – but right now, to me.

It's the love that brought my family back together, that is helping me pick myself up after the crash and keep moving forward. But deeper still, it's the love that has awakened me to Him – that calls me His own and that will one day take me home.

That is the love my body responds to when I do the dishes, when we do car time, when I hug Mike, when I write these words.

My body. A vessel for His love.

Maybe I can do that body scan after all.

Increase days

Here we are again. Another increase day. Post-crash. A second crawl up the mountain.

And this time round, it's lost its thrill. The novelty of wanting to gain weight and wanting to look healthy has worn off. It's just plain hard work. With the heartache and stress of Sam's current challenges, increases mean one - or all - of three possibilities:

More nausea. More stomach cramps. Less sleep.

I'm back to dreading increase days as much as I did in hospital.

I stand at the eternal kitchen bench preparing dinner for the umpteenth time. Kitchen freeze, once again, is approaching fast:

'Will this extra teaspoon of LSA have me up all night on the puke-wave rollercoaster? Will that extra rice shaft my day – and the next three – with GI symptoms? Can I bear to put this food into me? Is this even worth it?'

I know, as always, the problem I have with food is not the food itself. Right now, it is anxiety. My vagus nerve is in overdrive and for the life of me I can't get it to calm down. At least, not enough to stop freaking out about everything I eat again.

I take a deep breath and load up the new amounts of everything into my bowl. Breathe.

Then a howl. Something has gone wrong with Sam.

'What is it darl?'

I'm trying to sound, be, feel calm.

'Oh no oh no OH NO!' The words crescendo and escalate in their pitch to an explosion of swear words.

'F*** my life!'

He pushes his tray of food away and storms off, thumping the walls as he goes.

I look at the tray to work it out. Chicken fingers, check. Popcorn, check. Drink, ch… got it. He has spilt a small amount of lemonade to the corner of his plate, and I think it might have touched his food.

'It's okay love.' I say, trying to hide my desperation. 'It's okay. We can clear it up. I can fix the food. It's okay.'

I grab the cloth to salvage the food. It took 25 minutes of precision cooking with the air fryer to get it exactly right. Sam is howling next door. I stick the food back in the air fryer to dry off any moisture and get it the correct temperature again.

If I get it wrong the meal will be a write-off and the evening could be hard. Potentially three hours of hard.

I go to Sam, who is curled up on the couch under his blue blanket, still howling. I'm reassuring him, telling him I have fixed everything, the food will be fine, it is okay. Now he is apologising profusely and cursing himself. I try to reassure him about that too. It breaks my heart when he does this. I understand. But it still breaks my heart.

It takes ten minutes to get him back to the table. Thankfully he is still able to eat his dinner. Rescue mission achieved. Mike heroically distracts him with hangman. I think we're good. We might be calm now.

I return to the kitchen bench. The increase is still sitting in my bowl. The nausea has set in before I've even started eating. My mind dissociates and I'm completely overwhelmed.

'I can't do this. Seriously I can't do this. This is too hard!'

Eyes on me, Al. You've got this.

'I feel sick before I've even started to eat. I want to give up, I can't do this.'

A picture of a storm-tossed fishing boat in a turbulent lake flashes across my mind.

There's one man in the boat who has dropped what he is doing and is looking out to the sea. His friends are trying to sail the thing, which is buffeted by wind. There's fear in their eyes, but the man looking out to sea – he is watching in astonishment.

I follow the man's line of sight.

A figure is visible a few hundred yards away. It's standing on, and walking through, the waves. The person shouts some words to the man who is looking from the boat, and, insanely, the guy raises his leg over the hull and jumps out. To his amazement he can stand, and he starts to walk towards the figure, laughing in disbelief[104].

[104] Matthew 14:22-33.

Now I am that man. I am standing on waves that are sweeping over and around me, my eyes fixed on the figure. For a moment I panic and start to sink.

Courage! It is I![105]

I reorient myself away from the waves and towards Him.

Eyes on Me Al, eyes on me.

I take one faltering step after another. Closer. Closer. Now I can touch Him. I grab His hand and fall on Him.

We are back in the kitchen.

'I need Your peace… I know the nausea... it's anxiety. And when Sam blows off, it's not his fault, but I get it twofold. I need Your peace... please can I have Your peace.'

I have read a lot of things about peace in His book. How if you are thankful, you will receive His peace. How He breathed His peace on His disciples in the upper room. How His peace is a fruit of His Spirit[106]. But I can't for the life of me imagine having a warm fuzzy peaceful feeling right now – much as I desperately want it.

I don't just give you peace, Al. I am your peace[107].

'What does that mean – in this moment?! How do I make that work when I need to sit and eat this meal and I have no idea if Sam is going to

[105] Matthew 14:22-32.

[106] Philippians 4:4-7, John 14:27, John 20:21-22, Galatians 5:22.

[107] Ephesians 2:14.

get upset again, let alone how I'm going to cope with the backlash from this increase.'

Eyes on me.

'So I just hold You in my mind?'

Yes. Then, surrender.

'Surrender – surrender what? I can't walk away from my child right now! I can't give up trying to eat this meal! What do I surrender?'

Every single thought that comes into your mind[108].

I think about it. Mike and Sam are in full flow with the hangman game. Things are looking okay.

'But I have to think to function…. If I sign off thinking I won't be able to do what I need to do for my family. That's why I've got to quit this dissociating...'

I'm confused.

Every thought you get, hand it over to Me. If it's good to keep, I'll hand it back. If it's harmful, I'll take care of it. You, fix your eyes on Me.

I think of the waves around the boat. What if they were my thoughts – stormy, intimidating waves. If I fixate on them, I sink. But if I look at Him, the waves just roll past, and I stay afloat.

Get a thought. Let it roll past. Eyes on Him.

---

[108] 2 Corinthians 10:5.

I get a flashback of Sam's distress, just then.

Let it roll. Eyes on Me.

I think I must fix everything that goes wrong for Sam. I have to rescue. Always.

Let it roll. Eyes on Me.

I start obsessing about what this food is going to make me feel like. I imagine the voices, the self-loathing, the nausea.

Let it roll. Eyes on Me.

I start asking if I really need to do this increase today, with all this stress.

Let it roll. Eyes on Me.

I notice that each time I do this, I bypass a nausea wave, just slightly.

'So now what – do I keep doing this?'

Yes. Then, when there is a lull, ask Me for the next right thing to do.

No thought. That must be the lull. 'Okay, what do I do now?' Mike's food is ready. Mine is ready.

Cutlery.

I lay it out.

'Now what?'

Glasses.

I lay them out.

Sit.

Meals are on the table for Mike and I. Hangman is still going. I sit.

Breathe.

I breathe.

I look at Mike and Sam and am reminded how much I love both.

Keep that one.

'Love you Sam,' I say croakily. He doesn't respond, but I'm glad I said it all the same.

'Love you babe,' I whisper to Mike. We grab hands, say grace and I eat. One mouthful at a time.

You've got this Al. You're doing great. Eyes on Me. One step at a time.

This will be how we roll for the next six months, one increase day after another. Things are turbulent at home. And increases are turbulent inside.

But He is my Peace. Not a feeling, a Person. And a Truth.

My Peace.

Flashbacks and Trauma

It is 3am and I just woke up panting. I'm soaked in sweat.

I try to work out what the dream was but it's already fading into my subconscious. Somewhere in the mental soup is the clatter of a boarding school dining room. A crescendo of banging doors as the housemaster screams 'Fire alarm! Get up! Fire alarm! Get up!' A practice room with a teacher yelling hysterically 'Do it again, do it again, do it again!' as I stare at frozen fingers that won't work.

I think that was when I woke up with a jolt. My fingers were stuck to the keys, and she was heading straight towards me with a broom.

Strange. Even in the freakiest of school music lessons, I don't think anyone wielded a broom at me. Maybe it just felt that way.

My flashbacks feel hard. They aren't just visual. They are auditory, body-felt, coursing through every part of me. Especially those involving sexual trauma.

And it's not just night-time that they show up. They intrude on my day as a frantic three- or seven- or eighteen-year-old acting out in my own skin, in place of the grown woman I'm meant to be.

Embarrassing.

Anorexia numbed the flashbacks. Self-harm seared them away too. Every time I went through refeeding and refrained from self-harm they would come back with a vengeance. So, no surprises they make themselves known now.

Someone once told me that trauma begets trauma. It kind of sucks. Like the cracked vase that's been repaired, you have a propensity for getting shattered all over again at the drop of a pin.

I never truly realised, until I started to get well, that anorexia, BPD, OCD – in fact the whole smorgasbord of mental health illnesses I've had - have created their own trauma album.

The flashbacks of waking up every morning wondering if you will make it through today without a heart attack and your kid finding you collapsed on the floor. Of nights imprisoned in my bathroom wondering how many more burns it would take to quell the voice in my head. Flashbacks of meals in wards where there is a cacophony of human suffering and distress. Of intimidating ward rounds and panic-inducing weigh days. Of Sam screaming on the phone begging me to come home but I can't comfort him because the nurse says it's no phones during after-meal supervision.

These days it's not just the re-runs of my younger years or the illness from which I'm recovering. I get parenting flashbacks, separation flashbacks, Covid flashbacks, yesterday's meltdown flashbacks, meal increase flashbacks.

Even good memories spark off a chain reaction of painful 'opposite memory' flashbacks. Like my brain is anxious I might forget the hard times, so better pop one in as a reminder. My psychologist calls it 'backdraft[109].'

---

[109] Backdraft: a term used in trauma-based therapy that refers to the emotional flare-up that can occur when someone starts to experience healing in the context of trauma recovery. It can take place when the person is opening up to a safe listener, practicing self-compassion, or when they are being exposed to positive, healing life experiences. Instead of immediate relief, painful emotions, memories, or sensations may rush back in.

The past constantly intrudes on my present. It's exhausting. I feel like I'm going crazy. And tonight is no exception.

I'd like to say that after my 3 am wakeup I go on to have a long deep and meaningful with the Shepherd about the stew of memories that has me in sweats. But I don't. I'm dog tired. So, I spend the next three hours drifting in and out of semi consciousness hoping I might still get some semblance of sleep.

I wake up to Saturday and Mike is around, so I take a chance to go someplace on my own where I can try and snap myself out of flashback-brain.

I head for the river, sit on the bank throwing leaves into an eddy and start talking.

'I suck at this trauma stuff.'

Go on.

'Aren't I meant to be a new creation? 'The old is gone the new has come.[110]' Isn't that what You said? But I seem to have days where I live in my past – and I don't even want to.'

I find a flat stone and try to skim it. Fail.

'I know You can rewire my brain. And I know You can rewire my memories. But they still pop up like whack-a-moles as if all the talking them through with You has been for nothing.'

I let the sound of the river soothe me. Water can be so healing.

---

[110] 2 Corinthians 5:17.

It's true, He has begun healing some of my flashbacks through a kind of rewiring. In the months before the crash, when Mike and I were still house-swapping and I had some time away from Sam, the Shepherd gave me the rare gift of time to bring painful memories to Him. One by one, I would invite Him into them. Without fail, He would enter each flashback and transform it.

Here are a few examples:

'Hold everyone together': He swooped in, gently prised me out of Mum's hold, whisked me away from the family argument and took me to this super-safe little cottage on a cliff where I could drink cocoa and read stories in His arms. Each time I started to worry about whether Mum and Dad would be upset or whether I needed to go back to take care of everyone, He would gently reassure me:

It's okay Al. I'll take care of them. They'll be okay. You can stay here. You don't need to go anywhere.

'Bathroom': The moment I am howling on my own in the school bathroom I look up to find that He is right behind me, inviting me to climb into His lap. I do that, He rocks me and sings to me until I fall asleep. Then He takes me away to that super-safe cottage on the cliff.

'Do it again': He bursts into the practice room and says a word of comfort to my stressed-out piano teacher that makes her shoulders drop. Then lovingly explains that I'm wanted somewhere else right now. He picks me up and tells me I don't need to worry about the practice - He never intended me to be doing all that work. Then back to the super-safe cottage again. (I like that place… in case you hadn't noticed.)

I hold onto these rewired memories with all I've got. When each original flashback comes up, I go straight to the rewired one. I do this religiously to try and allow the new memory to take hold. And I find some peace and relief in His arms.

But once Mike and I were together again I didn't have the luxury of a few hours to myself where I could let the Shepherd do that kind of work. And after the crash I was so completely burnt out from the whole recovery-fall-start-all-over process, I simply didn't have the energy to go back into my memories and do a rewiring session with Him. There were too many. They popped up everywhere, all the time.

It was too much.

What do you think My greatest desire is for you when you experience a flashback?

His question snaps me out of another moment of dissociation. I jump at the thing I want most - for me.

'That the memories would go away? Never to come back again? That I would be completely healed of CPTSD[111] and be able to walk in the face of any event totally untriggered by anything?'

That is something I could do. But it's not My greatest desire for you.

I'm disappointed. But slightly relieved, because it wasn't happening anyway.

'So what is it that You want most when I get these symptoms?'

---

[111] CPTSD: Complex Post-Traumatic Stress Disorder. Distinct from PTSD in that it is caused by repeated or long-term trauma, rather than one isolated event.

I want you to encounter Me. I want you to trust Me. I want you to take refuge in Me.

I remember a verse I love:

...the Father of mercies and God of all comfort, who comforts us in all our afflictions, so that we can comfort those who are in any affliction, with the comfort with which we ourselves are comforted by God.[112]

There is no sweeter comfort than the comfort you receive when you're wounded...

I think about how I used to love Bandaids as a child. So much that I would wear them even if I didn't need them. Bandaids to me represented love and comfort. Whenever I hurt myself and somebody had to put one on my graze or cut or whatever it was, their love and care felt so much more tender than if I'd not tripped and fallen at all.

Whenever you get a flashback, I give you an opportunity to receive My comfort.

I realise that without any painful memories I might not come to Him at all. I might just mosey on my way content and self-sufficient, never encountering a Love like His.

I wouldn't want that these days. Me doing life on my own is not a pretty sight.

Perhaps letting Him step into my flashbacks doesn't always need to take three hours of prayer ministry. Perhaps it could be in a ...flash.

---

[112] 2 Corinthians 1:3-5 (ESV).

'I never saw it like that. I don't think I have even thanked You for all the times You've done that – comforted me when I am rattled by flashbacks. I didn't …appreciate… the tenderness... the Love. I'm sorry...'

You're learning.

He's gentle in His reprimand.

Perhaps one day you might even see your flashbacks and painful memories as gifts.

Treasures, I think. Like the pearl in the oyster.

I try again with another stone. I get two skims. Win.

'But what about the times when they're just too overwhelming. Too painful to even invite You into them. Like the Sam flashbacks.'

I don't know whether it's part of the special needs parenting thing, but I find I can't allow myself to think of any memory of Sam at the moment. They all juxtapose against the many images I have of his distress. Of his pain.

Mike treasures photos, memories. I must be the only parent that can't look at them at all.

He interrupts my line of thought.

Think of that stone you just threw. Think of the river.

I do.

Imagine the stone is the memory. The river is My love.

I look around me. I'm surrounded by stones. All shapes and sizes. Some sharp, some smooth. Some look like junk. Others like glass. Some very old. Others… new… in so far as any stone is new.

Memories.

When you can't bear a memory that enters your mind – just throw the stone into My river. Into My Love.

I pick up a mottled, grey sandy kind of stone. Yesterday's moment at school comes to mind. I came to pick Sam up early to find him in floods of tears, screaming, surrounded by a bemused group of friends. My stomach drops as I remember the pain of finding him like that. In so much distress. I couldn't fix it. I couldn't make the pain go away for him. I can't bear to think of it.

Just throw it to Me. Let My Love take care of it.

I throw and watch the stone plop gently into the waves of the river's flow. I know it's still there, sinking to the bottom of the river. But the river holds that stone in its stream, in its flow. Just like His Love.

The memory is not forgotten. Just taken care of.

'Is that what You mean when You say 'Forget the former things' and 'Do not dwell on the past' in Your book?[113]'

Those verses worry me, because when I hear them, I wind up feeling guilty about the flashbacks. Like I should have dealt with all that stuff by now. I shouldn't be thinking of it anymore. I should be over it.

---

[113] Isaiah 43:18.

It is. But not in the manner that you're thinking. I know your flashbacks are a wound. They're not your fault. You can't control them. There is no judgement, no condemnation from Me for experiencing them.

Only compassion.

That helps. I feel like I can let myself off the hook a little for getting triggered so easily.

'So what do You mean by those words?'

Read it again. Read wide.

I get the passage up on my phone and read both verses. 'Forget the former things; do not dwell on the past. *See, I am doing a new thing! Now it springs up; do you not perceive it*?[114]'

Each time you throw a stone into the river, your hands are empty for something new that I want to give you – right here, right now.

His words remind me of a moment I had at the swimming pool with Sam and Mike three days ago. It was the first time we'd gone swimming together as a family since Covid. It was the first time I had gone swimming with them, healthy. Not shivering with cold. Not drunk with fatigue.

A flashback of earlier years of sickness came into my mind as soon as we got there. Of being unable to lift Sam up and throw him around like he wanted, like other parents were doing with their 7-year-olds. Of counting the minutes till we could get out because I was so tired and cold.

---

[114] Isaiah 43:19.

I felt a wave of sadness and grief. I couldn't deal with the memory, it was too painful, so I did just what the Shepherd was saying right now – I handballed it to Him. Let Him take care of it.

Then I came back to the present. I realised I was warm, not cold. I had energy, not fatigue. Sam was laughing, happy because I could wrestle with him in the water. We had a family hug – 'a sandwich hug' Sam said with glee – one I never dreamed possible a year ago. It was a beautiful moment.

See, I am doing a new thing....

Every moment begins anew. Every moment He is doing a new thing.

I watch the sun rays sparkle on the river surface and feel His smile.

'So if I can't deal with a memory, if it's too painful to process, if I don't have the energy for inviting You into it and rewiring it and all... it is okay if I just hand it back to You for now. And then let You open my eyes to what I have right here, in this moment?'

Yes.

I reflect on His words.

I want you to encounter Me. I want you to trust Me. I want you to take refuge in Me.

'Oh....' I take in a deep breath and exhale.

'Where do I encounter You? Back here - in the Present... Right now.'

Him, the same yesterday, today and forever[115]. With me always. No matter the ripples of the past in my brain and body.

He smiles again and nods.

I throw another stone. I realise the pain of the past may be with me for a little while yet.

But He is ever Present. In that I find my refuge.

[115] Hebrews 13:8.

Self-Harm[116]

Some days I feel like someone who has been rescued from a serial killer. I guess I am.

I stand in the bathroom looking at my hair straighteners. Sam is good to go to school. We have five minutes, enough time for me to tame the bird's nest of a hairstyle I wake up with each morning.

But they still make me shudder, these straighteners.

I switch them on, waiting for the red bars to hit the correct temperature – for the correct purpose - and I'm transported back to when it all began. This, the cruellest of the Black's lies. The most sadistic of its compulsions.

'You deserve to be punished.' it had taunted me as I fought to feed Sam and I, six months pregnant.

'The only way you will ever be able to tolerate being in this body of yours is if you harm,' it continued when body sensations and flashbacks of past trauma intruded relentlessly into my mind throughout the time I carried Sam, and then beyond.

'Burn and the pain will make you feel clean – just like starving does. The memories will go away.'

The voice knew my weak points. It knew my shame. And it promised a lethal remedy.

---

[116] Please note, trigger warning for this chapter. It contains explicit references to self-harm.

I tried to muffle it with diazepam. Ignore it with distraction. Override it with affirmations. Dob it in with the nurses when they were available.

But none of these were powerful enough. I had cracked back then and unleashed a new behaviour that was as impossible to reign in as anorexia.

Five bars are red. Good to go.

'Oh God… the harm… the harm it would have caused Sam…' I whisper to Him, as I think about it. I can't bear it.

You can let it go, Al. It is done. It is forgiven. I am doing a new thing.

I sigh and start hair-ironing.

The moment I began to harm it felt both horrendous and a relief.

Horrendous, because it was never enough. The lie that I deserved to be punished morphed with my brain's OCD wiring. Numbers were the game. Last time the temperature was X degrees, contact was for Y seconds and the number of times performed was Z. So this time it has to be X + 10, Y + 10, Z + 10…and … you get the gist.

Never could it be the same as the previous occasion. Always it had to be more. By the time Sam was 18 months, a harming episode was only good enough if it necessitated surgery, grafting, IV antibiotics and the works. As long as I was on oxycodone for pain and immobilised in bandages the need to punish abated. As soon as the pain went and the grafts took, the pressure was on to punish again.

Harder and harder and harder.

But – insanely – harming brought relief. Because it blotted everything else out. The dysmorphia. The intrusive voices. Emotional pain. Body sensations. Flashbacks. Shame. Everything gone. Seared away by the burn. For a time. Then all returned, laced with a new layer of guilt and shame from the act itself.

Sam never saw me harm, but he saw my scars.

A bemused three-year-old, he cried on Christmas day begging me to come home when I was bedbound healing from surgeries. He asked over and over why was I always in hospital, why did I always have bandages and tubi-grips on my arms and legs, why couldn't I just be like other mums?

The lie told me something terrible would happen to Sam if I didn't harm.

The truth was that something terrible did – *because* I harmed. Each episode threw a sledgehammer at his own sense of security and safety that leaves its mark to this day.

I snap myself out of ruminating. Hair is straight, device put away.

'Ready to go love?' Sam nods, shuts his iPad and checks the locks. He always checks the locks. Every door, every window. He can't leave the house unless everything is locked.

The journey to school is quiet. Often is. I know he's working himself up to mask up, step out, pull the day off, like he always does. I pull in at the school gates and tell him I love him. Usually, he puts a quiet thumbs up in acknowledgement as he gets out the car. Today he's picked up on my energy. He pauses and turns to me.

‘Will you be safe mum?’

My heart aches. I squeeze his shoulder.

‘I will be buddy. I’m safe. We’re safe. I love you.’

I drive home in a daze. Too much reflection. Too much remembering.

‘How did You get me out of it? How did You rescue me? I swear I would have lost my limbs if I’d have kept going…’

The Shepherd has taken Sam’s place in the passenger seat and looks at me with a gentle smile.

‘I remember – when I saw You in the living room I had just healed up from another episode, another surgery. It was that time when the urges would start all over again. But then I saw You and… and everything changed.’

You thought you had to deal with it on your own. But no-one could fight that voice on their own.

It helps to hear that. I felt such a failure for not beating it. That I was weak. But I couldn’t explain to people what it was like not to harm. To sit with everything I was running from. To endure the punishing voice day in day out. To hear its threats to Sam.

‘I guess… I needed someone to rescue me. But no human could. I tried so hard with DBT and kept failing… I think I was beyond help... Even the professionals got tired of me... So how…?’

Trust.

I turn the corner into our street.

Trust. Yes. I remember that. Those early months of walking with Him. I didn't have any other option. Nothing had worked. I'd walked away from all the doctors. All I had left was to throw myself on Him. And as He scooped me up in His arms everything – the self-harm monster included - seemed to recede into a place of complete insignificance when compared with Him.

The longer I let Him carry me, feed me, talk with me, care for me, the more I had a sense that I was in the hands of Someone far more powerful than the Black's lies. He was stronger than the threats I used to cower beneath. I began to trust that if I didn't obey an urge, if my accuser really did try to come and 'get me' - or Sam, like it threatened – it would be utterly powerless in the face of His love.

That trust enabled me to walk week by week, then month by month, and eventually year by year, without harming.

'It is good to be carried by You....'

You didn't always think that.

I blush, remembering my outburst after the crash. He is not wrong.

'But... the self-harm train tracks in my brain... they can still kick in sometimes... and You've helped with that too. It's like You kicked the liar out – the one that told me I had to do it. But there is that broken part of me that still thinks that way at times. That still wants to punish myself... when I see Sam suffer and I can't fix it. When life is stressful. Even if someone gives me a compliment. The train tracks are still there – I still get the urges...'

Remember Jacob's hip?

Jacob… a guy in the Old Testament that woke up one night in a fisticuff with an angel. He won the fight but carried a limp for the rest of his life[117].

'I guess I still have the self-harm limp.'

Does it push you away from or towards Me?

'Towards. I only feel safe from those urges when …I am hiding in You.'

Exactly.

I'm back in the house now, picking up after the morning rush. Dishes away. Housework to be done. I launch into my usual flurry of vacuuming and tidying before work starts. It's online admin work. Nothing glamorous. My mind ever whirring, I unpack what hiding in Him really means when it comes to residual self-harm urges.

Staying with pain comes to mind. That is one part of it. When I harm, I think that I'm not going to tolerate whatever life is throwing at me unless I act out. So, I trade emotional pain that I can't control for physical pain that, I tell myself, I can.

But the truth is that even if I *feel* like I can't cope with the emotional or psychological pain of something going on in my life, He can. And I am in Him. And in Him I can weather the storm.

Whatever is going on around me may feel as though it is going to rip me to shreds – whether that be body sensations, dysmorphia, flashbacks or just plain old life. But, when the urges to harm come, if I just cling to

---

[117] Genesis 32:22-32.

Him so tight, put my head against His chest, and hold on knowing that He has got me, that storm will pass, and we will be okay.

I smile, thinking of the number of times He instructs His kids to … stand[118]. Not be flash heroes thrashing and fighting and doing somersaults and all. Just stand. Or perhaps, in my case, stay – in His arms when pain is whirling around like a tornado.

Years ago, there was a poster up in our post-meal room in the ED unit that I looked at for hours. It read H.O.P.E.

Hold On Pain Ends.

I used to think it was a fluffy cliché. But with Him, I have found it to be true. And every time I cling and hold on to Him, breathe Him in through the pain, through the urge, feel the anger, the anxiety, or whatever it is the harming would do away with, I come out the other end of the tunnel with a sweeter, deeper intimacy with Him than I ever had before I entered it.

Staying with the pain. I never used to be able to do that. But with Him, I can now.

Downstairs is done. Upstairs can wait till tomorrow. I start packing the vacuum away.

'But to hide in You with the urges… ' I say trying to disentangle a cord spaghetti. '...It means I have to let You deal with the punishment drive too. I had to quit trying to satisfy the beast…'

I'm glad you did.

---

[118] Examples abound, but include 1 Corinthians 16:13, Ephesians 6:11, James 4:7, Matthew 24:13.

Machine away, I wipe the table and sit down for a moment. My work laptop is ready and waiting.

'Commonsense was never enough to defuse those thoughts. You know the ones I mean … Somebody hurts and I deserve to be punished. My friend gets cancer, I deserve to be punished. Sam has a tough day at school, and I deserve to be punished. Russia invades the Ukraine, and I deserve to be punished. And on and on…'

Well, lies don't always take kindly to commonsense.

'But for some reason, I couldn't even get Your best Bible verses to do it either. You know, the ones about being forgiven, having no condemnation… there are so many. But they still didn't stop the punishment drive. I needed something stronger than that even….'

I know.

I start thumbing a leaflet I left on the table a few days ago. It's on how to pray the rosary. It helps me pray when I am all out of words. And sometimes I just need a Mother to pray with.

The leaflet falls open on the sorrowful mysteries[119]. I think about how many times I have walked the block meditating on those mysteries. Sitting with Him in Gethsemane and putting my arm weakly around Him as He sweats tears of blood before His execution. Burying my head in Mary as she watches His scourging at the pillar because I'm still too squeamish and can't look. Touching His forehead to try and comfort

[119] The Sorrowful Mysteries are one of the four sets of mysteries in the Rosary, a form of prayer in the Catholic tradition. They focus on the passion and suffering of Jesus Christ before His crucifixion.

Him as it bleeds with the piercings of a hundred mocking thorns. Trying pitifully to help Him as He drags His cross to Calvary in blood and sweat and tears. Standing speechless with Mary at the foot of His cross, seeing the blood seep from His hands and feet, His side punctured with a spear.

They are agonising images.

I used to think I could never meditate on the Passion. Perhaps doing it with Mary has made it possible. But every time I do, I hear Him say,

It is finished. Enough. It is done[120].

And nothing, nothing can tell me that any more punishment is needed now. He has taken all the Black could throw at mankind, let alone me. He has paid the price. He has ransomed me from my serial killer. He has set me free.

I close the leaflet.

'Thanks…seems so little to say…'

He is quiet.

I reflect on Sam's question in the car. 'Are you safe mum?'

I never used to be able to give an honest answer. But today, with His wounds to protect me, not mine, I can.

[120] John 19:30.

FIFTH INTERLUDE – DEJA VU

I saw Nurse 2 the other day. In the parking lot. At Coles.

I am rushing to get the shopping before school pickup. I go for the ten-minute short stay area – the strip by the kerb for cars-in-a-rush, like me.

Someone has parked right in the middle. They've left a gap between themselves and the other person in front of them. So there isn't much space for me. Maybe not enough at all.

I can't be late for Sam. If I look for another spot, I'll be late. I've worked out exactly how many minutes I have to get Sam's pretzels and not be late.

Everything goes south if I arrive at school late.

I mutter 'Great.' under my breath and inch about as close as I possibly can to the middle cars-in-a-rush spot without bumping them. The driver is still in the car, and I'm wondering, 'Why don't they see me and move forward? Seriously?!'

Then the door swings open and I hunch low in my seat because I can tell from the way they get out they're super-rushed. Like they are on a mission impossible, the kind of mission that makes you swear at someone parking too close to your bumper.

They turn and face directly towards me and that is when I see who it is. It is Nurse 2.

For a moment, I freeze in terror, thinking she is going to recognise me as well, pull out her clipboard and phone and arrange for another emergency admission. But she looks right through me. She doesn't recognise me at all.

Which gives me a chance to take a longer look at her.

Anxious eyes. Crumpled frown. Locked jaw. Tense shoulders.

She slams the door of the car and heads straight for the Coles entrance, her entire body leaning forward as though her head making it to the shops first will speed the job up.

Something in me softens towards her. She looks how I feel, often.

She has a name you know.

His words startle me. They remind me I am not alone.

'I know. I'm sorry.'

I remember the name.

Natalie.

Why don't you try imagining what her day might have been like today?

I let myself spin out random possibilities as I get out the car and head for the pretzel aisle.

Maybe she just clocked off from the shift from hell. Or maybe she is rushing to a shift from hell, grabbing some food before she gets there because she didn't get time to make anything at home.

Maybe she's going home to a partner who loves her – or a partner who's mad at her.

Maybe she doesn't have a partner at all, maybe she separated, and she is lonely, desperately lonely, but trying to fill the hole with work, stress, life.

Maybe she has kids, and she's rushing to school pickup like me, only exhausted after a day's work. Or maybe she doesn't, and she wished she did.

You don't know, do you, Al? You don't know what any person is carrying. When you draw your own conclusions. When you look at them with your eyes only.

I feel small.

I hadn't forgiven Natalie about the CATT team debacle nine months ago. I told myself I had, but I still had bitterness and resentment floating around. Especially when I think about what that visit did to Sam.

'I'm sorry. I know, You're right. She is just someone trying to survive – like me. Trying to get through another day. She might not even know You are with her. She might be trying to do this all on her own.'

I shudder for a moment, remembering how awful that feels.

He lets me stew on that while I find the only pretzel brand Sam eats.

She has another name too.

'As well as Natalie?'

Yes. As do you.

I think on it as I swipe the pretzels through the scanner and head back to the cars-in-a-rush parking lot.

I look at the strip. Natalie's car has gone already.

We call her 'Loved'.

Perfectionism

Christmas. It was meant to be perfect. The pressure was on.

I've been sourcing Sam's presents for months. We (well, I) have planned a perfect, quiet day for him – a bit lonely for us, but perfect for him because he finds family gatherings overwhelming. I've got the perfect food that won't set off Sam's ARFID too bad and will still make Mike feel special and loved. Sam's favourite Christmas lights are up. Christmas Eve went smoothly – we even managed to sleep through the night…

So, it should all go perfect – right?

Wrong.

It goes okay to start. Everything I have got him looks like it has hit gold (I know, it's not all about the presents but... for Sam… still… it kind of is…). I take photos of him with a big grin, thumbs up, 'Thanks Mum!' That kind of thing. Not for Facebook – I know our Christmas won't compete with that – but just to help me see I got something right.

Then something breaks. It's the new gyroscope.

Sam is so excited by it, he spins it high, and it falls to the floor. The axle bends and it won't spin any more. He disintegrates. Like any kid, to a point, but for Sam, who's 11 now, it's harder. He can't grasp that it might take time, but we can fix it. He sees in black and white, and the white has just turned black, very black.

I try to console him with the promise that we'll replace it tomorrow in the sales. It doesn't help.

We take him out kayaking in the afternoon to get his mind off it, to still feel like we've done something enjoyable as a family, to get a memory to treasure, another photo.

But there are no photos. It is too hot for Sam. The beach tent is broke. He can't stand the feel of the sand. There's a hole in the kayak. He spirals. And it continues, not just for one day but three.

Amid his distress he blurts out,

'This has been the *worst Christmas ever*!'

Over and over and over. I can't get it out of my head.

I go into emotion coach mode and arm myself with all the skills I'm told to use in my parenting-for-autism classes. I try to validate. I try to listen. I try to gently reassure him that sometimes our feelings don't come to the party for Christmas and even all the gifts in the world won't fill the hole in our soul – but there is Someone that will – and on and on.

But none of it helps. I'm saying too much as usual, trying too hard. God, I wish I would just shut up sometimes.

It's day 4 that I crack. Maybe it was the Facebook photos other friends shared of their Christmas that I stupidly scrolled through. Or all these ridiculous hopes I had that this Christmas would be something special, something different to mark us being together. Or maybe it's that Mike got the wrong brand of Sam's rice crackers at the supermarket last night.

Whatever it is that breaks my camel's back, I cry, and I cry, and I cry. I can't stop. Sam is worried and asks me why I'm crying, and I try to explain calmly that I'm struggling with Christmas too but don't worry buddy I'm okay... Then lose it and end up crying more and then swearing at myself.

Which makes Sam even more worried and more dysregulated.

The next morning, I get Sam's breakfast, and I cry. I drop the dustpan on the floor, and I cry. The kettle's unplugged and I cry. I sit at my meal contemplating another nutritional mountain and I cry and swear and cry and swear.

I've totally failed the perfect parent bar, again. And if I'm not perfect, I don't deserve…. Fill in the dots, but pretty much anything goes.

Mike suggests I take a walk with Him. So, I do.

'I'm such a freaking idiot.' I sob as we walk along George St. My perfectionism is in full ruthless flow.

'I can't even talk to You after acting like that.' I exclaim, in fury with myself. 'Crying all the freaking time, swearing at myself in front of Sam. I shouldn't be having this conversation with You. I'm a shit parent. Completely worthless, useless.'

Alys.

It's the Mary moment[121].

I gasp trying to calm down. Trying to trust the compassion in His voice.

You know you can always come to Me and talk to Me.

---

[121] John 20:11-17, specifically verse 16.

I know what He is saying. I know it's true. I just don't feel it right now.

I have objections.

'Even if I can come to You, because Your blood washes me and You have forgiven me for the last forty minutes', or four days' worth of mistakes – and the rest of it, how can I accept Your forgiveness when I can't guarantee I'll make the exact same mistake when Sam has his next meltdown?'

I take my glasses off and wipe my eyes angrily.

'Because I'm all out of juice right now as a parent and all I ever seem to do is cry. And swear. How can I say I'll do better next time when I know this is the best I've got? And my best isn't perfect – so it can't be any good.'

He gives me some time in case there is anything else I might want to add. I think I'm done.

Perfect?

'I thought You said we had to be perfect, didn't You? To the disciples, on the mountain, when You gave that sermon. You said 'Be perfect, as your heavenly Father is perfect.'[122]'

Then I offloaded a million and one incoherent thoughts. About how I can't do it. I've trying to be perfect my whole life and all it did was make me sick.

'I know You wouldn't set a bar that we could never reach – that would be cruel, and I know You are not cruel. So, what the heck do You mean, by being 'perfect'?'

---

[122] Matthew 5:48.

He listens patiently as we walk. Then He tells me to read wide again. Go to the bit before He says the 'Be perfect' bit. I read it on my phone. While I'm walking.

'You have heard that it was said 'Love your neighbour and hate your enemy.' But I tell you, love your enemies and pray for those who persecute you, that you may be children of your Father in heaven. He causes His sun to rise on the evil and the good and sends rains on the righteous and the unrighteous. If you love those who love you, what reward will you get? Are not even the tax collectors doing that? And if you greet only your own people, what are you doing more than others? Do not even pagans do that? Be perfect therefore, as your heavenly Father is perfect.[123]'

I stop walking. I pause and take a breath. I think I see something.

Looks like being perfect is the summation of all that has gone before. It's the summation of the command to love, especially those who have hurt, offended or been 'against me' intentionally or otherwise.

He gets me to look up the same phrase in a different gospel, in Luke. So, I search, trying not to veer into a tree as I scroll and find it. He gives the same instruction as He does in the Matthew passage – about loving your enemies. But this time He finishes it off with a different phrase. '*Be merciful, just as your Father is merciful.*[124]'

Be perfect. Be merciful.

[123] Matthew 5:43-48.

[124] Luke 6:36.

'So...perfection is showing mercy. And mercy is... showing love to the undeserving. Is that it? Is that what You are saying?'

He is not finished.

He tells me to go to another story. The one about a 'sinful' woman who gatecrashes a dinner He has been invited to at a Pharisee's house[125].

I wonder what this woman has done. Slept with too many men? I guess I don't know, but I figure I can relate to her shame. Her sense of complete and public failure. That would be me all over.

She stands behind the Shepherd weeping, wetting His feet with her tears. Then she wipes them with her hair, kisses them and pours perfume on them.

Look how much I honour this woman's love.

I look and read on through the story – the bit where she has been laid into by the Pharisee who owns the place, and He defends her fiercely.

'Do you see this woman?' He says to the Pharisee. 'I came into your house. You did not give me any water for my feet, but she wet my feet with her tears and wiped them with her hair. You did not give me a kiss, but this woman, from the time I entered, has not stopped kissing my feet. You did not pour oil on my head, but she has poured perfume on my feet.[126]'

---

[125] Pharisee: a member of an ancient Jewish sect, distinguished by strict observance of the traditional and written law, and commonly held to have pretensions to superior sanctity. The story is found in Luke 7:36-50.

[126] Ibid.

What it must feel like to have Him honour you like that – honour your extravagant, over-the-top, breaking-all-social-etiquette, shameless kind of love. I would love that.

Now look for the reason why. Why I honour that woman's love.

I read the last bit, dodging the kerb and the postie's bike.

'Therefore, I tell you, her many sins have been forgiven – as her great love has shown. But whoever has been forgiven little, loves little.[127]'

Do you see it?

I do. It is brilliant.

The key to extravagant love, the kind of love that is 'perfect' is .... extravagant forgiveness. And for that – you actually *need* to be *imperfect.*

The 'perfect' is love - the kind of love that pours forth from forgiven mistakes. From hopeless imperfection. From this week's meltdowns and tears. And the hugs and apologies that came after.

But He still is not finished. It's my need to be perfect before I can come before Him thing. The thing I threw at Him in a feeble attempt to push Him away when we started walking.

Look at the woman again.

I do.

And now I see something else. Another layer to the story.

---

[127] Ibid, v 44-47.

I see that she is not perfect when she comes into that house. She is a sinner. She is steeped in sin. She invites eye rolls, scathing looks, tuts of disgust. Yet she throws herself into loving Him – in the most extravagant way. No holding back. No hesitation. She comes soiled, stained, shamed, into the throne room, and worships Him all the same.

I think He is done. I put my phone back in my pocket. My storm seems to have passed. I try resting in what He has said.

I do not have to be a perfect parent to come to Him, to talk to Him, to love Him. I don't have to have a perfect day or a perfect prayer time – whatever that is. I don't have to have perfect emotions and have perfectly repented of every sin. I don't have to have done my meal plan perfectly or, if the ED is having a field day, measured everything to perfection, eaten 'perfect' food (whatever that is), or arranged things perfectly on the plate.

I just need to see the instant grace, instant forgiveness, instant washing in His eyes. And throw myself at His feet in perfect, broken, imperfect love.

The bar is changing. Love is the new perfect.

Self-Hatred

'I'm such an idiot! I hate myself! Stupid piece of s***. Such a crap parent.'

I'm angrily thrusting breakfast dishes into the dishwasher. The words aren't pretty. They fall out of my mouth before I've even thought them, it seems.

The trigger? Sam had a difficult moment cleaning his teeth this morning. And I'm a slow learner at figuring out when a demand is one too many for him, and when it's good to push. Today I chose wrong. I pushed too hard. I provoked a tirade of swear words and anger from him that are still slashing at me inside, even though I know he doesn't really mean them. I can only imagine what it must be like – having to do something twice a day that is a sensory hell for your nervous system.

Somehow, we managed to miraculously salvage the situation by playing 'Mahna Mahna' from the Muppets on YouTube whilst he conceded to performing the dreaded task. So teeth are clean now. Sam is settled. I've apologised for pushing too hard. I've delivered all the emotion coaching and affirmations I can think of to help him heal up. We've hugged. Crisis over.

At least for now.

Enter my tirade of self-deprecating comments.

'It's all my fault.' Angry plate in. 'Such an idiot.' Angry cup in. 'So stupid.' Angry knife in. And on and on.

The logic behind them?

Self-hatred is my internal 'riot gear'. I erect it, often before I realise I'm doing it, when the chips are down. And even when they're not.

Why do I need riot gear? Because I get these pesky things called… emotions.

And for some reason, even in my forties, the ghosts in my head tell me that emotions are not okay. Often they hurt. And often they are judged. Sometimes by people on the outside. Always by the phantoms in my mind.

'You've got no reason to be angry with everything that we've done for you.'

'If you're going to ruin our Christmas by being sad then you can spend it somewhere else.'

'How can you be happy when I'm not?'

'The Bible tells us not to fear – so you shouldn't be anxious.'

There are quite a few. And all of them have made emotions for me, generally, unsafe. Hence the need for riot gear. Hence the need to armour up. If I can thrash myself for this emotion, nobody else can. And, bullseye, it means I can push away the emotion itself.

I'm not sure when I started putting on my riot gear. Maybe it was that evening washing dishes at the sink when I was thirteen when I found myself sobbing, 'I hate myself, I hate myself' and not knowing why. Maybe it was before then. I don't know.

All I know is that today, self-hatred is a drug I shoot up on without even choosing to. Like I have no control over it.

I break my clavicle and have to clean the house one-armed for 3 months. 'You're such a f****** idiot.'

I sit at my computer doing work for my boss. 'You can't honestly think that crap you're churning out is any good?'

I'm vacuuming the house picking up Mike and Sam's odd bits scattered everywhere. 'God you're so pathetic.' (Reference me, not them.)

I think people believe that anorexia is the ultimate expression of self-hatred. For me it wasn't. It was the only way I knew to medicate it.

What do you do with a ranting bully screaming at you in your head all day? Shrink. Hide.

What do you do with the plethora of emotions that seems to kick it into gear? Numb them. Starve them.

Works quite well.

I've finished attacking the dishwasher. I know I need some space. Mike is offering his usual kindness and love to support me and the only response I can give is what an idiot I am, how my hair looks stupid and I'm a s*** parent. My self-hatred isn't just harming me. It's pushing him away too. For both our sakes I need to go for a walk. I need to take the self-hatred to Him.

'I'm sorry. I know I shouldn't be like this. I'm not meant to hate myself. It's awful for Mike to have me throw back his love like that. And it's bad modelling for Sam. And I know You love me and all of that …I just… I just can't help it. I just freaking hate myself!'

We walk up George Street and turn the usual corner.

'And I can't handle nice words right now. I can't handle people reminding me that You love me, so I should love myself, or that I'm a great person, a great mum, doing the best I can bla bla bla. I can't handle affirmations. Any of that s***. *I just freaking hate myself.*'

It's taken me a while to realise I can be this honest with Him in these moments.

What's going on Al?

I stop for a moment with the ranting. I know the way He rolls with it. It's the only thing that has ever helped.

He invites me to take off the riot gear for one moment and see what lies beneath.

Five years ago, there was no way in high heaven I was going to do that for anyone. Today, I'm learning that it might be safe enough with Him.

'I just wish I could make life easier for Sam. I wish I could make school easier. Food easier. The sensory stuff easier. Everything easier.'

He listens.

'I hate that life is so hard for him. And I get tired of being a metaphorical… or literal … punch bag. Everyone says I am his safe place, that is why it happens. But I don't want to be the safe place all the time. I don't feel safe. I'm sorry. I shouldn't say that.'

It's okay.

'I feel sad. Tired. And worried.'

I know you are feeling this way. You're doing well to talk about it.

Pause.

That's a big load you're carrying, trying to make life easier for Sam. Do you think that's your job?

I realise how crazy that sounds. Like I can fix Sam's life – or anyone's for that matter.

'I guess not. I just feel like it is all my fault.'

He's autistic Al. I made him this way. And I love him this way. But it means life can be hard for him. That's not your fault.

'I know. I get it. I'm sorry. I shouldn't take it all so personally.'

You're sensitive. I like that. But it can be hard for you at times.

And so continues the conversation. New medicine for my self-hatred. I must take it often.

I discover something very precious about Him in these conversations. He reminds me that... no joke... He has emotions too. It says so, time and time again in His book.

And He doesn't hate Himself for it.

He weeps when His kids go through death. He rages when His love gets misrepresented as some kind of transactional deal that people can buy, or when vulnerable people get abused and injustice gets played out. He laughs with His friends at their parties and tells ridiculous stories to make a point. He glows with joy at the prospect of saving human beings. And He has a totally soft heart for cute kids (and lost sheep)[128].

He shows me that apparently, I was designed to be just like Him. I was made in His image. So those emotion things that I simultaneously defend and push away with self-hatred – they aren't a design fault. They're part of His plan.

Not only that. They can be, amazingly, a platform for intimacy with Him.

Each time I hurl the self-hatred at His feet, He unpeels it to reveal a feeling – a feeling that might invite a range of His wise and compassionate responses.

Perhaps a Truth of His that reframes everything. Like the idea that He's got Sam, so whilst my desire to be sensitive to his needs is good, it's not on me to make his life plain sailing and pain free.

Or the perspective that accidents like breaking your clavicle happen not because I'm evil, but because .... accidents happen. And I can be kind to myself about that.

Maybe it's the reminder that He is completely in control of everything right now, even if it doesn't feel that way, and if I just sit back, let go and trust in that, I might find the frequent panic attacks recede a little.

And sometimes His response is very simply.... just... Himself.

That silent, loving Presence that bathes every feeling I've just spewed out and little by little dissolves each of them in love – however many tears and self-hatred dumps that might take.

---

[128] John 11:35, Matthew 21:12-13, Matthew 11:19, Hebrews 12:2, Matthew 19:14, Matthew 18:10-14, Luke 15:1-7.

I turn the street corner after twenty minutes of this kind of talk. We walk up the drive. I breathe a bit easier.

As I step back into the house, I know the raging at myself has gone. I can go and embrace Mike and thank him for his kindness. Explain the emotions that were really going on for me beneath my self-destructive outburst. The grief for Sam when he struggles. The anxiety. The exhaustion.

I can apologise for hurting him as I hurt myself. And I can go and ruffle Sam's hair and tell him I love him. Not as the perfect-emotion-coach-trying-to-hold-it-altogether kind of mum. But as the human, wounded, rails-at-herself-under-stress-but-slowly-learning-to-change kind of mum.

It's taking a while, learning to treat my self-hatred with His kindness and wisdom. But as I do, I learn that when the riot gear goes up, it's not a sign I need to conjure up more self-love affirmations. Or angrily scrawl ten nice things I can('t) think about myself. Or get even more angry with myself because I'm angry with myself.

It's just a sign that I've got a feeling going on right now and He's okay with that. He can handle it, if I'll let Him.

A whole lot better than I ever could.

OCD, rules, rituals and rigidity[129]

I'm feeling frustrated.

My weight is slowly tracking to health again. It's a hard slog and we're getting there.

But I don't feel free.

I feel exhausted.

By a million and one rules I have no choice but to obey to get through my day.

It is 1030 am and I am breaking from work for a coffee. The rules are really bugging me today. So I pull out a writing pad and scrawl the title 'Weird shit I still do.' across the top of the page.

Then I start listing.

Have to eat stuff with the same spoon.

Have to use the same bowl and cup.

Have to put salt on everything, including cereal, yoghurt, biscuits…etc. (soooo embarrassing….)

Have to reheat my food 700 times before I can actually eat it.

Have to measure and remeasure everything – at least 3 times to be sure.

---

[129] Trigger alert: this chapter contains mention of some compulsive behaviours.

Have to wipe the kitchen surfaces myself even if Mike has already done it.

Have to clean bathrooms every day.

Have to touch the corners of places.

Have to check, recheck and recheck 5 times that I have taken my nausea medication.

Have to eat at the same time each day, or within a 15-minute window of that time max.

Have to walk the same route when I go for a walk.

Have to dust rooms in the house in same order.

Have to prepare my own food.

Have to get up at the same time come rain or shine.

On and on it goes.

I call it my Gulliver list. I feel like Gulliver pinned to the ground by a million compulsive ropes[130].

'This is ridiculous. I am ridiculous. Why do I still do all this stuff? Why can't I just chill out and go with the flow?!' I exclaim.

It's hard for you isn't it, Al? I know that.

---

130 From the novel, Gulliver's Travels by Jonathan Swift (1726), Chapter 1. After being shipwrecked, Lemuel Gulliver washes up on the shore of Lilliput, a land of tiny people (the Lilliputians), to find himself tied down with hundreds of miniscule ropes, unable to move.

'It's been hard for so long. I can't imagine surviving without doing all this shit. I'm exhausted. I can't keep going with it. But I'm terrified of change. I'm scared stiff to let them go. I'm so stupid.'

You're not stupid. There's a reason why you have these compulsions. It's not your fault.

'But I'm in recovery – I should be loosening up. Yet here I am drinking coffee out of the same cup, measured with the same measuring container, having a snack at the same time, in the same way, day in day out.'

Can you be kind to yourself for a moment in this? I am not judging you.

I think it over. OCD, ED rituals, rigid thinking patterns... whatever you want to call them – they paralyse me, still.

They seeped into every diagnosis I was given, and, in the case of self-harm, they were not just an inconvenience – they were lethal. It's a wonder I still have arms and legs.

But ERP – Exposure and Response Prevention – never fixed it for me.

ERP was the staple treatment for both my anorexia and OCD. It's a CBT intervention that is meant to help patients develop coping skills that prevent their compulsions from taking over.

You start with a particular ritual – a 'small' one that isn't too daunting. You identify the thing you fear – e.g. having full cream as opposed to skimmed milk, or eating a meal without getting up to reheat, or giving the cleaning a miss one morning. Then you go ahead and do the thing *without* compensating (e.g. via restriction, exercise, harming, excessive over-cleaning) in any shape or form. You're given suggestions like distraction and other distress tolerance activities to replace the compensatory behaviours. Once you have mastered flexibility with one compulsion or rigidity you graduate up the scale to the next one on the list.

The best example of ERP not really working for me would be the 'challenge days' we had to do on the ED day programs I attended. These were the days we all went out for a meal or a snack.

The event was perfect for disobeying a plethora of rules in the ED sphere. No opportunity to measure out or prepare your food. No guarantee what you ate would stick religiously to your meal plan. No familiar cutlery or plates. No promises you could avoid that 'fear' food.

It was the ideal environment for testing your capacity to let go of control.

And, I'm embarrassed to say, for me, it was a complete nightmare.

A bunch of us patients would rock up to some place most people go out to on a Friday night for a good time (before that became impossibly expensive) – let's call the restaurant 'Fried'. The people in the restaurant around us joke, laugh, enjoy themselves and their food. There's an air of conviviality, of joie de vivre.

But not amongst us. No.

We sit in silence around the table perusing the menu of torture we have to choose from. The slightly bemused waiter takes the orders. 15 minutes of awkwardness ensues while the staff try to engage us in 'distraction' from our anxiety. Conversation is often so sparse that they are forced to resort to the trivia card question box. Questions that most of us are too dissociated with anxiety to answer in any case.

The meals arrive and we all retreat into our own peculiar but distressing coping behaviours.

Some of us eat our meal one particle at a time. Others dismember it into coloured groups. Some wolf the stuff down to get it out of sight as quickly as possible. Others wait till it is stone cold before attempting the inevitable. Some stare at our plates with a glazed look of terror. Others disintegrate into uncontrollable tears and hyperventilation.

Eventually the ordeal is over, and we return to the program site. We evaluate how we all went, and what we will do tonight – or more specifically what we won't do (no compensating). Then home we go, usually dissociated from distress, to somehow pull off life as parents, daughters, sons, or whatever else we are. We get a pat on the back next day for increasing our flexibility.

But for me, I just vowed I'd never try go to 'Fried' again. (No offense, 'Fried'.)

One time we had completed a challenge meal and returned to the centre for our afternoon snack. More food. More exposure.

I broke down completely. I couldn't eat the snack. I was beyond dysregulated.

The nurse sat with me and said to me, passionately '*This* is where the recovery happens Alys. This is what you *must push through*. If you really want to get well, *this* is what it is going to take.'

I felt like I was in a gym with some boot camp trainer yelling at me, 'Try harder, try harder!' through the fear, the distress, the overwhelm. As if to say, 'if you're for real about this recovery thing you will push through this pain and break these rules and behave like a normal person.'

I still have flashbacks of my ERP treatment days.

There are admissions I can't bear to remember. Day programs I never want to talk about. I never found the promised land of freedom that all these exposure exercises were meant to give me. They simply elevated my fear of food, of going out to eat, of trying to cope without all my rigidities.

They confirmed what the ED and OCD had always told me – if you don't do this ritual, stick to this rule – ED or otherwise - you will fall apart, and it won't be pretty. ERP confirmed to me that if I wanted to get anywhere near being a half decent mum that didn't slide into disassociation or harming, I *had* to stick to my rituals and rules.

'How do I change all of these? Where do I begin? I get hives even thinking about it...'

I pause in another defeated slump on the kitchen chair.

'Not only that, but I'm constantly weighed down with guilt for having this problem in the first place. I know You say it's not my fault – but what about the books and pamphlets I've read in the Christian bookshop that talk about OCD and compulsions and EDs as sins? Not just sins, in fact, but idols! You can't get more cutting than that...'

I think of a tract on the topic I read that likened a compulsive behaviour to worshipping Baal[131] in the Old Testament. The only way through was to repent. And then not do it. Period.

Al, I am not judging you for your illness[132].

Really? I wonder how I can be sure I'm not just hearing my own voice.

I have indeed seen the misery of my people in Egypt. I have heard them crying out because of their slave drivers, and I am concerned about their suffering[133].

The words I hear Him say are from the Old Testament of His book. Even though they're spoken to a Middle Eastern group of people over 3000 years ago, they seem to speak directly to me.

I am concerned for what you go through each day with the rituals.

Concerned. Compassion. Care. That's different to what I thought…

Let Me help you see your compulsions in a different way to the way you are viewing them right now.

I shut my eyes.

He shows me a kid with high anxiety from the get-go, trying desperately to get a sense of control and safety in a world that so often felt out of control and unsafe. Like a toddler that clings to its threadbare, one-eyed teddy bear when its family has just escaped a house fire. The toddler will

---

131 Baal: A Canaanite and Phoenician deity referred to in the Old Testament, that the Israelites succumbed to worshipping at times, with dire consequences.

132 Romans 8:1.

133 Exodus 3:7.

not let go of that teddy bear, even though the teddy bear wasn't the thing that saved her and the housefire is now over. The fact that the toddler grows up still clinging to its teddy bear years later doesn't make it some sinful idol-worshipper. It just makes the kid scared – for understandable reasons.

To Me, when you feel the pull of your compulsions, you're no different in My eyes to that frightened toddler.

I think of the ramifications of His words.

That would make all my compulsive rules and rituals kind of like the one-eyed teddy bear (only perhaps a bit more noxious.)

Would I yell and scream at a toddler, now grown into a tween, to let go of their teddy bear? Would I tell them how stupid they were to still fear housefires? Would I demand they grow up and stop being such a sook?

I don't think I would. I think I would try my best to gently comfort them, soothe their fears, let them talk through the trauma of that fire however much they needed. I would hold them while they were still holding their teddy bear to such an extent that one day they would realise, the love they have in me is even better than the teddy bear.

And eventually one day they would let go of it.

If that is how much you would take care of your own child, think how much more I want to care like that for you[134].

I sit with what He is saying for a moment.

---

[134] Matthew 7:11.

'Okay… I guess the root of all my compulsions is fear. Paralysing, life-limiting fear.'

I know that there has only ever been one thing that has truly overcome my fears. And it wasn't the boot camp voice.

It was Love.

That's right. Perfect love casts out fear.

Here we are again on that one…

'So… You want to love me, rather than … I don't know… goad me?... into freedom?'

I sense His affirmative. And I reflect on some of the time-worn passages about love in His book.

Love does not drive. It does not threaten. It does not say, when you cower at a change, 'well are you for real or aren't you? Do you want to get well for your son or don't you?'

It doesn't boot you off the program if you fail. It is patient. It is kind. It does not envy or boast. It is not proud. It is not easily angered and keeps no record of wrongs. It does not hone in on the times you doubt, get confused, and succumb to a behaviour.

No, it rejoices in those moments we dare to believe and act upon the Truth. It always protects. Always trusts. Always hopes. Always perseveres. Even when we've tried and failed to put down a compulsion again and again.

Love never fails[135].

Do you remember Lazarus?

Lazarus… one of His dearest friends whom He raised from the dead after four days in a tomb. When Lazarus came out of that tomb, alive, he was still wearing grave clothes[136].

What did I say about the grave clothes?

'You told everyone to take the grave clothes off him and let him go.[137]'

Something clicks. I've always felt that, as long as I clung to ritualistic behaviours and compulsions, my healing and my recovery were not for real. I was a fake. No miracle had really happened. At least that was the taunt in my head – which loved to go wild each time I succumbed to one.

But this story suggests nothing could be further from the truth. The Shepherd had still given me new life – the moment I woke up to Him in the living room. Nothing could change that.

But, like Lazarus, I too had 'grave clothes' that needed to come off, one by one. My Gulliver's list was akin to those grave clothes. My rules and rituals couldn't take away the life and hope and strength He was giving me to move incrementally forward each day.

But nobody wants to walk around in grave clothes. So, it made sense to let Him slowly take them off.

---

135 1 Corinthians 13:4-8.

136 John 11:1-44.

137 Ibid. v. 44.

'Okay… well... I think I need You to change my 'want to' on this one. Because truly I don't feel like giving any of them up – it is all too scary.'

As I say those words, I'm immediately reminded how tiring these rules are. How complicated they make my life. How I'd love a break from them.

'Maybe You could show me just one item of grave clothing You might help me unpeel today. Like… maybe we could try not getting up and down when I eat so much.'

How about you consider that I give you permission to rest when you eat?

That feels different. I'm used to telling myself this is something I *should stop* doing. 'Should' feels hard – like I fail before I even try.

But He has replaced a language of 'shoulds' with…. the language of possibility. *I give you permission…*

I try it out and see how it feels.

I give you permission to take a break from cleaning today.

I give you permission to be flexible in the bowls and cutlery you use to eat – to not have to wash up the same one.

That would be nice.

I give you permission to let Mike cook for you.

Golly…

I give you permission to sleep in.

Imagine that…

The more I think about His reframe, the more it fits with other things I've heard Him say.

In his book of Psalms one of His beloved servants talks about being '*set free*' to run in the path of His commands.[138]

What if the path of His commands was simply a life free of all these onerous behaviours? And what if that was something He wants to *release* – not drive - me into, like letting a horse run loose in a wide expansive open pasture?

I'm setting you free to run in the path of My commands....

Coffee break is up. Time to get to work. My sense of frustration and defeat is giving way to hope.

*

Time passes, and peeling off the grave clothes, running in the path of His liberating commands, has become an ongoing work for me.

I still have little behaviours I cling to, or new ones that I pick up – particularly if Sam is doing it tough and my stress levels are high. But He never chides me when this happens. And when I'm tempted to beat myself up for vacuuming the house twice in one week, He gets me to take a rain check and have a look at what is going on in my life right now.

Usually something a bit stressful. When that's the case, His words are often to simply,

Ease up.

---

[138] Psalm 119:32, World English Bible (WEB).

Take a breather.

Give yourself a break.

Or,

You're doing behaviours – perhaps you're having a tough time right now. Let's go talk about it together.

We talk. He loves on me. I ask Him to change my 'want to' so that I can get a bit of freedom in that area of compulsion. And, one step at a time, He does.

Another grave cloth is peeled off.

There are behaviours I haven't done for years now that I never would have dreamed of being free of. And there are some in the pipeline to let go of this week.

For all of them, the nightmare of ERP – a treatment that maybe I was just not cut out for – has been replaced by a different, kinder path.

The path of Gentle.

Boundaries

'I feel completely out of control.' I blurt out in the bath. (Eyes open. Winning.)

Go on.

'Like I'm being pulled everywhere ...sucked dry... and I don't understand why I let life get this way.'

I submerge my head under and listen to the muffled silence in the water. Relief for a moment.

This week has been one of those 'going-under' kind of weeks. Lots of stupid little things, but still that kind of week.

A friend knocks on the door in the morning when I've just managed to get Sam to school and .... asks for a hug. Apparently, I am hugs-on-tap. I hate hugs. But I feel guilty, so I scrunch my eyes and give it all the same, cringing inside.

Sam falls apart when I try to go out for twenty minutes in the evening to make a phone call in private. The event is so apocalyptic I consider it not worth trying... ever... again. And cancel my once-a-year plan later in the week to try going to a writer's workshop. Maybe it's better I am just on tap in the evenings too.

I take a call from family on the pretext of catching up - and wind up after an hour completely wrung out by stresses and drama. I can't sleep that night.

Another friend casually reminds me what a miracle it is that I saw the light and came back to Mike. They throw in how grateful I must be that they kept praying for me all that time I was so lost and deluded. Innocent remark. True for sure. But can we not keep talking about it? It stings like crazy. The pain lingers on for days. I'm so goddamn sensitive.

There's more, but I halt the replay that has already done five reruns today.

'It's like I have no walls. Someone wants something and I can't say no. I get cut to the core by things people say that other people wouldn't care about. I seem to absorb stress around me like a Chux dish cloth, only I can't wring it out after…'

I try and let my shoulders relax.

'Mum!' I hear. Shucks. I thought he was settled on the computer.

'Mum! Mum! MUUUMMMMM!'

Nope, can't relax, get the towel on, downstairs I go.

'What is it love? I… I... I am trying to have a bath – I just need 10 minutes…' My tone of voice is slightly desperate. It's a tech issue, and ever since Covid I've acquired the nickname 'Technomumma' because, for the sake of all our lives, somebody had to work out how to fix the freaking computer if it went wrong.

I know I should draw a line. I should stay in the bath on a point of principle and get Sam to practice using his initiative with it. But I can't relax when he's calling out for me over and over. So, I figure it out quick (reboot… I'm a genius) and head back up to the bathroom, trying to reclaim my space with a feeble, 'I'm gonna be ten minutes and I can't come down before then now…'.

I get back in the bath, shoulders up again.

'I suck…' I say to Him

'...completely suck at boundaries. I just feel swamped – like I don't exist. And anyways that's okay because … like I don't *deserve* to exist so… that's it really.'

I throw the last comment out thoughtlessly.

'Sorry. I shouldn't say that.'

I start shaving my legs, carelessly. Blood in the bath. Darn it.

Tough day?

I sigh. 'Nothing on what some people deal with, I know. It's pathetic. But yeah… I guess it feels like a tough day…week... Sorry. I shouldn't complain.'

I feel selfish even talking about it. All this stuff is small fry compared to the news right now… seriously small fry.

Talk to me a bit about the boundaries thing.

So, I tell Him.

I've always struggled with boundaries. I still do as a parent. Saying no seems like the hardest thing in the world – actually, not so much saying no, but saying no in the right way, at the right time and dealing with the response from the other person when you do say no without retracting the no or apologising for it. Ug.

I never mastered the art of drawing boundaries skilfully, or at all, as a kid. And that was fertile soil for an eating disorder. Because if you can't say no, if you can't work out where you end and another person begins, it's not long before you feel pretty out of control in your life.

You're pulled in every direction, depending on what you perceive others want or need from you. That prompts a desperate need to control something – anything – to survive. Like food, weight and exercise.

'It's not just the external boundary though – like saying no to an external request or demand, saying what you can and can't do for someone. I feel like I don't have an internal boundary either. I'm like a pin cushion constantly asking to be skewered. Everything seems to affect me like …way too much…. I can't even watch kid movies for crying out loud without doubling up in stomach cramps because of some emotional response they elicit in me.'

You're sensitive. I love that.

'You're just being nice. It makes me hard work, being sensitive. I cry too much. Get sad too easily. Get scared too much. I hate it. It's exhausting. And embarrassing.'

I cried the other day watching the Smurf's movie. I mean, seriously.

I made you that way for a reason. Trust Me on that.

I try to hold His words. I get out the bath and start the tedious process of plastering all my shaving nicks. Sam – even though he's year's away from having a beard himself - thinks it's hilarious that girls get shaving cuts on a shape as straightforward as a leg when a man has clearly got his work cut out with the facial hair thing. Unco, I mutter to myself under my breath.

'But I feel like the only way to deal with not being able to draw a boundary around the outside or the inside of myself is to shrink away from both. Literally. That's why I've starved myself so often. I know You know that.'

Perhaps there is a better way – to draw the line. To protect yourself.

'But is that really in keeping with what You say in Your book? Like what about dying to self? Carrying each other's burdens? There was that girl I met at church when I was in my twenties who would say 'See a need – fill it.' I thought that was what You want us to do – to be 'yes' to everything and everyone.'

I have this intense fear that, if I say no to someone it'll come back to bite me at the pearly gates. I'll be one of those unfortunate goats that didn't recognise Him when He was in need, and I'll burn for it[139]. A bit extreme I know... but a genuine fear.

I'm all plastered up and ready to dress. Eyes still open.

Have you thought about Nehemiah?

'Nehemiah...What about him?'

I try to remember the details of his story – a prophet in the Old Testament who gets the go-ahead to return to Jerusalem - a city desecrated from Babylonian defeat - and repair its walls. It's a story of hope, healing and promise for a city ravaged by its own self-will coupled with the ruthless greed of neighbouring nations.

[139] A faulty interpretation of the parable of the goats and the sheep, found in Matthew 25:31-46.

Something in the story resonates with me. I come downstairs and boil the kettle for a snack. I have my virtual Bible open on my phone, and I pull it up.

'I guess… I guess it shows that You cared about rebuilding the walls of that city.'

Yes. Go on…

'Walls that determined what and who could come in, and what and who should stay out.'

What does that show you?

'I guess… those walls… they kind of helped re-establish the city's identity …

And what was that identity?

'…of being home to Your sanctuary ... the Temple.'

What does that tell you?

'That Jerusalem was no longer to be a free-for-all for neighbouring enemies. It was allowed to have a contained sense of …. self. You were allowing it to feel and be established and safe again.[140]'

If I would do that for Jerusalem, why would I not do it for you?

'So You're saying that, on one level we die to self – I guess our false, ego-constructed kind of self – but there's a deeper self, maybe our true self –

[140] The entire story is found in the book of… you guessed it… Nehemiah, in the Old Testament.

the one that is found *in* You - that You are keen to establish... to protect... to contain...?'

I'm worried I am theologising beyond the bounds of my limited understanding.

But… it kind of fits. He knows the numbers of hairs on our head. He knows when we rise and when we lie down. Our deepest desires and longings. Our tears and our joys[141]. And He cares about all of that – no, not just cares, He died for that[142]. To rescue us, awaken us.

So, there's a sense in which a true self, the self that, if we surrender, is found hidden within Him, really matters. Is worth protecting, worth defending and worth drawing a line around.

The boundary lines have fallen for me in pleasant places[143].

'Oh… that's one of the Psalms, isn't it? I love that line, but I never really understood it. Perhaps You could help me draw my boundary lines too…'

I would love to do that.

I finish my snack and our chat concludes, for now.

But in the sporadic moments I catch with Him over the coming weeks and months I start giving myself permission to try drawing the line – outside and in – with Him.

---

141 Psalm 139, Luke 12:7, Psalm 56:8, Psalm 37:4.

142 John 3:16.

143 Psalm 16:6.

The outside line is scary. Saying no to Sam when a no is what is needed, whatever the fallout might be. Declining a catchup with someone for whom I lack the emotional resource right now. Asking Mike to do something I need done to help in the house.

In all these instances I'm paranoid the line is wrong, unkind, unfair. I don't trust my wants and desires. I don't know if I've got it right.

So, the moment I start to get that panicky feeling – the overwhelm when there is an external need or demand that I can't meet – I have to talk with Him. Debrief the whole situation, completely uncensored, everything out, no matter which way it comes. Even if I'm doing the shopping at the same time.

'I can't deal with this friend and all the religious speak they throw at me! It drives me nuts! I know they've got a lot going on at the moment, but I literally feel like I don't want to hang out with them again after last time I saw them!'

'I'm so over getting Sam's food, drink, shoes, socks, everything, and getting it wrong when I do! I'm over it! I love him but I hate being a parent right now….'

'I love those family members, but I get triggered every time I speak with them on the phone - I feel like I can't make another phone call ever again.'

And so on.

The debrief is usually followed by a plethora of apologies. But I sense He's okay with my dump. I think He knows it's better out with Him than in with me and then out with anorexia or some other behaviour.

Talking through the situation uncensored is crucial. It's like identifying the breach in the wall.

After the dump, He helps me see a clearer perspective. Am I being reasonable or unreasonable? Is this my stuff or the other person's? Always with eyes of compassion.

Then – He never wastes a thing – we loot my common sense, DBT scripts, old therapy vaults, conflict resolution tips – whatever lies in the recess of my brain, to work out a reasonable boundary to draw and how to draw it.

Last, the check. He prompts me to run it past Mike, or someone I can trust - the boundary I was thinking of drawing. Which is good because it wounds my pride. And it's necessary. I'm like a bull in a china shop some days and, for everyone's sakes, I need all the stops and checks I can get.

What if, after all of that, I'm still cacking my pants about drawing the boundary?

He reminds me that when the dreaded moment comes, He'll be with me. He'll show me what to say, what to do, whispering guidance from behind[144]. I just need to stay tuned in. Dependent. Humble.

Learning to draw external boundaries in this way is a bit of a wobbly road. I'm a beginner with training wheels. But each time I try it, even if imperfectly, my need to control the way I eat, or to do some other compulsive behaviour, loosens.

I feel a little bit safer. A little less out of control.

And what about the internal boundary line? The pin-cushion defence? That's daunting too.

---

[144] Isaiah 30:21.

But His method here is surprisingly simple - which is good, because I need simple.

He reminds me of a passage in His book where He says I have a shield – a shield of faith[145]. And faith – in this context - is complete trust and confidence in Him.

So, when a painful arrow comes my way – an insensitive word, a forgetful remark, a judgement, or an out-and-out insult – I can raise that shield. I can make a conscious decision to put my complete trust and confidence, not in the arrow – however persuasive it might feel – but in Him and what He says about me.

Here's how it might look:

I say no to something Sam really wants in the moment that, I know deep down, would not be good for him. Sam says I'm the worst mum ever. Ouch. I raise the shield and ask Him what He thinks of me right now. He tells me He chose me to be Sam's Mum. He tells me I'm doing my best and He is proud of me. He tells me it's okay to make mistakes and sometimes drawing the right boundary with your child can result in some painful responses. But they're not the truth – He is.

Arrow deflected. Win.

My friend is disappointed I don't catch up because I want to write. I see the 'You are so selfish and self-indulgent!' arrow hurtling my way. I raise the shield and ask Him for His perspective. He tells me my friend will be okay, and it's okay for me to spend time on a project that He put on

145 Ephesians 6:16.

my heart to do right now. He tells me that saying no on this occasion doesn't make me a bad friend – it makes me focused and determined. I'm writing for Him and others. So, I can let go of 'you are so selfish'.

Boing.

A relative reminds me of the difficulties I have put Mike and Sam through. I see 'It's all your fault. You will never make up for the past' whistling through the air. I raise the shield, and He reminds me there is no condemnation for me – I belong to Him, He keeps no record of wrongs, so I have no need to either.

Away it flies. Phew.

It's amazing. I thought you could only armour up on the inside by numbing out, shrinking away, harming or taking benzos. I never imagined there was an alternative that might actually work.

Granted I'm a work in progress – I forget to ask His help to draw a line often. I cave to outside pressures. I still get shot by life's arrows. And I still cry watching Pixar movies.

But in time I think I will get the hang of this boundary thing. Hopefully by the time He comes to take me home.

Either way, they're making me feel secure – His 'boundary lines in pleasant places'. They're helping me feel precious – worth protecting. Like maybe I do…deserve to exist… after all.

And I would rather die learning to build His boundaries, the right kind of boundaries in my life, than lose myself to everything around me – and then anorexia - again.

Filling the Void

He's a tween ….and he still loves hide and seek.

It's a father-son thing (thankfully). The house goes eerily silent while Sam searches for his dad. Then an explosion of laughter as he finds Mike cowering in an old suitcase hidden in the spare room wardrobe. Turns are switched. The house shakes and quakes as Sam stampedes his way to the next location while the seeker counts to 10 (for the life of me I have no idea how a pint-sized kid makes so much noise).

Usually, I'm called on to assist in Sam's vanishing act. Our best effort was a few months ago, where, at his request, I tried to squeeze him into the cupboard under the kitchen sink. Didn't quite pull that one off, which is good because, to be honest, I didn't feel entirely comfortable attempting to compress my 12-year-old into the cubic volume of a waste-paper basket.

Fortunately, on this occasion, my recon scout skills are not required. I make a cuppa and sit down outside for a snack. A moment's quiet in the garden. No need to listen or talk or work or do anything. Something to be savoured.

So, what is my kneejerk instinct?

No surprises – it's to grab my phone. Which is dumb, because I know there's absolutely nothing I want to look at on it. Facebook and Insta bring out the worst in me. My YouTube account has been taken over by Sam's obsession with the Muppets and I can't be bothered to wade through his search history before I get to something that might interest me. My Google newsfeed is beyond depressing – it's disturbing. And I've read all the free book samples I downloaded on Kindle for now. So why the heck am I reaching for my phone?

I call it 'the Void'.

I'm not talking about the difficult emotions we run from with busyness or work or scrolling or whatever. We kind of touched on that with the exercise thing and I'm working on it. But the Void - it's a deeper thing. It's more than life's pain.

It's the existential question mark. Those moments when you suddenly find yourself asking, 'What's the point of everything?' or 'Why am I even here on this planet?'.

Anorexia, along with obsessive phone scrolling and a host of other mindless activities, was a gargantuan distraction from not only my feelings or my circumstances, but from the Void. And it worked pretty darn well. Because the unbelievable amount of willpower it takes to restrict your food against your body's inbuilt instinct to live is all consuming (pun not intended).

Starvation, fatigue, anxiety and obsessing about how to control the minimal food I could eat didn't only quell my intrusive voices and uncomfortable emotions. They papered over the Void. They took up my every waking moment. Yes, on the surface, I pulled off life – sometimes quite astoundingly well – attending to others needs, doing a great job as a youth worker, teacher, or whatever my occupation was.

But underneath, anorexia filled the gaps in my mind and soul that lay yearning for something more – something I feared didn't exist. And it distracted me from that yearning.

One of the hardest feelings to sit with during periods of treatment and weight restoration was that that distraction from the Void was taken away. I didn't feel hungry all the time. Pressure to be flexible around food types and meals meant I could no longer numb whatever I was feeling with the boring, predictable routine of what I ate. I didn't have the pain of muscle burn and exhaustion.

What faced me instead were a set of terrifying questions.

Who am I without this illness? How can you feel okay about life if you are not hungry? What do I fill my emotional and spiritual emptiness with if I'm not obsessing, planning and controlling my food, weight and body shape all along?

What is this life all about?

Without anorexia I faced a chasm that I couldn't bear to look at.

Treatment had a lot of methods to fill the Void. Work out what you value in life and then make a list of value-based activities you can fill your time with. Remind yourself of the people you love and how you want to contribute to their life. Do service. Make a vision board – have dreams and set goals to achieve them. Go to the list of 'pleasant' activities in the DBT manual and pick 1 or 2 or 25 to kill time.

And it should have been easy for me. I had a son I adored, a husband who loved me – though I lost sight of that treasure for a period of time. I had gifts and talents that I could use to do great things if I put my mind to it. But none of these methods or considerations were enough for me.

When I was practising Christianity during my 'survival' years, I tried repeating relentlessly 'who I am in Christ' affirmations from the Bible in the hope that that would fill the Void. I ran church projects to help other people (I cringe thinking of it given the state I was in...).

When those things failed to fill my hole, I jumped ship and tried filling it with other religious practices - chanting and mantras and pujas and offerings in the Buddhist sphere, or relentless visualisations in the hope of manifesting something that made me feel whole in other arenas of self-development.

I scrolled and scrolled social media, creating and recreating myself on a platform of emojis and likes in the hope that others approval and applause would work. I listened to podcast upon podcast of preachers, self-development speakers, and motivational personalities.

None of these filled it either.

I realise now you don't have to have anorexia to be in a state of constant distraction from the Void. I think we live in a world gone mad with distraction. I just found a particularly lethal method for the same.

I glance at the home screen of my phone, poised to punch in the pin access. I sigh and press the sleep button.

'I'm sorry... I don't know why I still do this - distract-distract-distract - thing. You give me a moment's peace, and I go straight to filling it with something pointless. When will I ever change? I mean can You imagine if I was a nun or something? I'd be climbing up the walls trying to feed my distraction vacuum.'

You're not a nun, Al.

I pause for a moment, acknowledging the obvious.

I'm just inviting you to spend a moment with Me[146].

I feel bad. Like a neglectful lover. He doesn't mean it that way, but it's what I feel.

In my early days of recovery, I would fill up on Him in planned ways. I worked hard at it. I would sing worship songs (badly) or write out His Truths and turn them over in my mind while Sam was playing Minecraft. I would list His attributes that I could thank Him for and then speak out those words of thanks.

On occasions these things felt like a time-filler, but the more I did them, the more they would stir within me a genuine love and desire for Him – a love and desire He would rush to meet, like two magnets flipped towards each other. The Void would disappear for a time.

But after my crash in recovery, and Sam's increased difficulties, I couldn't always put that kind of effort into filling the Void. As I climbed the weight-gain mountain all over again with constant nausea and cramps, emotionally wrecked as a parent, I wanted so desperately to distract and distract and distract from the pain around me and within.

I lacked any energy to pump out worship songs triumphantly to induce a sense of His presence. Or to pray bold declarations from His book. I lacked the time to write out anything amid Sam's distress. When I went for walks with the Shepherd it was all I could do to cry and swear. If I listened to my audio-Bible, its words ran off me – my brain cells couldn't absorb a thing.

---

[146] Mark 6:31.

Remember what I have taught you since then.

I stop reminiscing and come to.

He's right. He has shown me a different way to fill the 'anorexia-gap' since then. I think I like it better. It is a simpler way – one that involves less 'efforting', pushing and trying.

It's the way of His Presence.

Now's as good a time as any to try it.

I put the phone on silence and turn it over, face down.

'Okay... help me... help me see You right now.'

I start with the feel of my body where it is. I'm seated and I can feel the pressure on the bench that I'm sitting on. I feel it's warmth. Its solidity. I'm reminded of the energy that creates that warmth. Energy that permeates, enlivens the whole cosmos. I feel gratitude. I contemplate the molecules bound together that make that solidity. I'm not a scientist but I find myself imagining their microscopic structure. An intricate construct of quarks, leptons, electrons, photons and more. An invisible universe I cannot begin to fathom.

I find myself in awe of its Architect.

I scan my body from head to toe. I let myself feel the sensations of aliveness, rather than run from them as I always used to. I'm reminded of the Spirit that birthed them when I took my first breath. The One who enlivens them still, dwelling in me, through me.

More awe. More wonder.

I look around. Where is He? Where did He just go? Where can I spot His footprints?

There are the weeds in the garden bed in front of me. A thought interrupts me, telling me I'm a slacker because I haven't gardened for weeks. I roll it over to Him.

I go back to one weed. A tall, spindly piece of grass. Nothing exceptional in its appearance – and yet everything is exceptional. The green chlorophyll that turns sunlight into food. The network of cellulose and turgor pressure that enables it to stand. The aphids and thrips that find a home in its blades. One weed. A microcosm of wonder.

I hear Him whisper,

Do you see? Do you see that?

He is the child now. Eager to surprise me with His autograph in hidden places.

'Yes, I do, I do… it is wonderful... Show me something else...'

The sun goes in for a moment and I look up. Clouds are drifting. Carriers of water and life. I notice their patterns. Their ever-changing shape. We play cloud shapes together. Is that one an angel? No... a beetle! Look at her – she looks like a seahorse! That's just a blob… you can't make anything out of that one…

You think?

And we play on.

I hear a crash from inside the house. My body jars with the hypervigilance I've developed over the years with Sam. I hear His soothing whisper.

They're okay. They're playing.

And I'm overwhelmed with gratitude. For His comfort, ever present. And for the joy in our home in this moment. The playfulness.

I listen and I hear the breeze. Like His voice. Calling my name. It reminds me of how He is. Always there, but some days you don't know where He is coming from. Or where He is going[147].

I breathe and I'm reminded that He breathes me. We are intimately bound, He and I. The lungs that expand and the heart that pumps within me are entirely nurtured and held together by Him[148].

I notice the smell of a BBQ next door, and it reminds me of human community. Of relationship. He casts my mind back to the many times He hung out with His friends around meals, around conviviality. Perhaps the Jewish version of an Aussie barbeque – pork excluded - in the Gospel era. He was the life of the party so often. He must love it when His kids come together. When they share, they laugh, they tell stories, they love.

He is the author of that. Him – no-one else.

My monkey-mind tolerates this exercise of being, of awakening to Him all around me, for approximately five minutes. Then in it jumps with one-hundred-and-one things I should be doing. Concerns I should be worrying about. Words I could be writing.

---

147 John 3:8.

148 Colossians 1:17.

I notice the thoughts with Him. His gentle smile has a way of settling my leapfrog brain.

It's okay, you don't have to go yet Al. Stay a little while longer.

I return to the present via the taste in my mouth. The snack I have just eaten lingers. I marvel that I did just eat it, when years ago it would have been an impossibility. I marvel at the way, already, it is being assimilated by my body to sustain me, grow me, fuel me for whomever He would have me be today.

Gratitude, again.

'It's funny,' I say.

What's that?

'Well... Sam and Mike are playing hide and seek right now. But You and I – we kind of are as well.'

I sense Him chuckle. Who would have thought we have a playful God…

It is as if through my whole life, every present, breathing moment, He is beckoning me to come and look. Come and find Him.

Seek and you will find…[149]

Be still and know …[150]

The kingdom of God is in your midst…[151]

---

[149] Matthew 7:7.

[150] Psalm 46:10.

[151] Luke 17:21.

I halt the distraction drive for even one moment like this, and His presence fills the Void. Like water in a jar full of pebbles, He fills every gap, every space, every hole. The existential crisis that I've run from for so many years is arrested.

I find my purpose.... in knowing Him[152].

All the other purposes follow on from this. Because how can you not love when you have encountered Love? How can you not bring hope when you have just encountered Hope? How can you not speak truth - however imperfectly - when Truth has just spoken to you?

'Muuuuummm!'

Okay, time up.

'MUMMMMM!' Stomp, stomp, stomp. I get up from my seat of repose and go inside.

'Yes love?'

'Food.'

I haven't quite mastered the art of training Sam to say please, would you mind, thanks ever so much – yet. At least when it comes to food. Time to rustle up a crunchy smorgasbord of pretzels and popcorn for him.

But as I do so, He gently reminds me,

It doesn't have to stop there...

---

[152] Jeremiah 9:23-24.

I can practice His presence anytime, anywhere. While filling a container of pretzels. Pouring some lemonade. Sweeping the floor. Doing the dishes.

All are prisms of wonder. All is grist for the mill. The world is awash with Him.

I used to live to eat – that's what happens when you're starving. You are hanging on and on till the next tiny meal which isn't enough, and then the next, and then the next. That's your purpose. No rest. No lasting satisfaction. A Void that is never filled.

But now I eat to live – a life with simple, gentle purpose. A life with moments to pause. A life with gaps and holes and yearnings that I no longer fear and run from.

Because, if I'm up for a game of hide and seek, I'll find His Presence filling them, day in day out.

Befriending my anorexic self

I got the book because I thought I should. It's the staple for eating disorder recovery. They referenced it so often in treatment. Other patients recommended it. It has inspired hope and freedom for thousands where freedom felt impossible. I thought to myself, He has been helping me recover – so maybe I should read that book they were always banging on about, to see how far I've come. To see whether I am 'getting there'.

I start reading it one night in one of those ten minute slots Mike and I get once Sam has gone to bed. We try and kid ourselves we have a whole evening to relax, so we open a book on the couch to prove it.

But this one doesn't help me relax. I've read three paragraphs, and it has already pushed about thirty buttons.

It talks about seeing your eating disorder as an abusive partner. Male. Mean. Evil. One that you need to divorce, cast out, make a declaration of independence against.

I can already feel the panic rising. It throws me back to ward rounds and group intervention meetings. Always getting you to split your ED from yourself. Returning like a homing pigeon to the golden question, 'But is that *really* you talking, Alys, or your ED?'

Sometimes it wasn't a question, it was an assertion.

'I am terrified of this upcoming social eating challenge.'

- That is the ED talking.

'I can't eat ice-cream today. I just can't manage it.'

- ED – not you.

'I feel I like I won't cope if I don't exercise.'

- That's the ED lying to you.

'I want to go home. I miss my son, and he is not coping with me being in here.'

- Your ED is trying to sabotage your recovery.

I encountered a religious variant – casting out demons – that attempted the same. Repent of and rebuke the illness – and the plethora of its symptoms - and it, or they, will be gone.

But they stayed. I still struggled. Still do.

For sure, the author of the lies that underpin anorexia, self-harm, suicide and any other condition that leads to confusion, death and despair needs to be booted by Him with full force. I'm reminded of that every day I choose to surrender, lean on Him and put myself under His protection all over again[153].

But there is a difference between the Black, and the part of me that succumbed – and can still succumb - to the Black's lies. The eating disordered part of me. The suicidal part of me. The self-harming part of me.

---

[153] John 10:10

Neither of these conditions define who I am. But I am weak - the lies maimed me - and I still walk with a limp. And the part of me that limps longs for, and needs, to be heard, cared for, and validated. My anorexic self needs help, not exorcism. The campaign to 'divorce 'Ed'' felt, and still feels, like an attempt to silence that part of me and get rid of her.

And honestly, that's exactly why she started acting out in the first place.

I huff and puff as I read and Mike, in his gentle way, asks me what's going on.

'I just... this is *so not helpful*!' I explain what I am reading.

'I tried it – in therapy, in church – casting out the eating disorder. Walking away from it like some evil villain. But the break never lasted. The behaviour came back with a vengeance. I would always relapse, and relapse hard.'

I pause, remembering the frustration that brought both of us.

'When people say 'Oh... that's the ED talking,' it is like nothing you say is real. You don't exist. Everything is discounted. You can't be trusted. You don't have a voice – you are simply an eating disorder on legs.'

I feel sad and hopeless thinking about it.

'And the worst bit is, you only get your voice back once the eating disorder has gone. Once you're perfectly recovered and have written a book like this one that I'm reading. Then you have something to say, yes. But not before.'

I am such a hot head. Mike is tired. I bulldoze on.

'Like any other illness you can stand up, tell your story and express what you feel and think, whether you're sick or recovered. No one says 'Oh, that's the diabetes talking so we'll discount that' or 'Oh, you're having a bad episode of MS so no, we can't trust anything you say today..."

Mike patiently listens and validates, but I can tell he's fading fast.

'Sorry... you go to bed love. I'll be there in a minute.'

Mike dismissed; I continue the rant with the Shepherd.

'Like what about those of us who never get there – wherever there is? Can't we have a voice?'

He is silent. I know I don't need to say that kind of thing to Him. He always gives me a voice.

I shut the book down on my Kindle account and sigh, head in hands, trying not to revert to doom scrolling.

'It's the passengers-on-a-bus thing that works for me. But with Your twist on it. Not divorce proceedings or independence declarations.'

The metaphor comes from Acceptance and Commitment Therapy[154], another staple treatment for a host of mental health conditions. I found it had some helpful stuff, and the passengers-on-the-bus idea was one of them. But I had to tweak it a bit.

---

[154] Acceptance and Commitment Therapy (ACT) is a type of psychotherapy that combines mindfulness, acceptance, and behaviour change strategies to help individuals develop psychological flexibility. It was developed in the 1980s by Steven C. Hayes. Rus Harris further popularised this approach making it widely accessible to the public and therapists.

You think of your whole self like a bus driving from A to B. The bus has picked up a ragbag of passengers who have paid their ticket and will be staying for the ride. Passengers like anxiety, fear, self-doubt ...and anorexia (my addition).

Who's the bus driver? Well ideally the 'you' that is the wisest of the lot - your 'deeper' self. The you that tries to act according to your most deeply held values and beliefs. The aim of the game is for 'wise old you' to drive the bus to its destination – wherever that may be – without letting the passengers take over.

Good luck.

Let me introduce you to my bus.

It's batshit crazy. We have a hysterical three-year-old still convinced we need to hold the world together at all costs. There's a thirteen-year-old perfectionist that believes nothing is worth doing unless you do it for at least eight hours a day. An insecure eighteen-year-old that thinks you're not worth having unless you give a man everything, regardless of how you feel about it – and is quietly fuming about that. A thirty-four-year-old that insists we beat ourselves up FOREVER for being a mum with a mental health illness. And somewhere in the cacophony is a forty-year-old going on fourteen – let's call her 'Anna' – who thinks the only way to deal with life is by reducing her food or at least measuring it 45,000 times over to make sure it's not too much.

(And that's without mentioning the kamikaze dude that believes the apocalypse is coming so our best bet is driving off the next cliff. Or Edward Scissorhands, who is convinced this bus will drive a whole lot better if we just pause, slash the tyres completely, then keep going.)

The driver? Well, there's a problem, because the driver of this bus:

a. Has no clue whatsoever how to get the passengers under control,
b. Is tired of trying to do a. and
c. Lost the map as to where we are meant to be going some time back in the early 1990s.

That's why I have to tweak the metaphor. I need another driver.

You can imagine the relief when, one morning, the Shepherd gently suggested He take the wheel.

I was in a rush, Sam was stressed, and I found myself remeasuring my breakfast milk not once, not twice, but *seven* times for crying out loud before allowing myself to sit down and eat the darn thing. I mean seriously, who has time for this?

'Okay… but... what do You mean exactly? I thought You were in control anyway?'

You sure about that? How many times did you just measure your milk Al…?

'Oh... okay. Got it. But what do we do with her?' (I'm talking about Anna, the forty-year-old going on fourteen who thinks we need to remeasure the entire contents of the pantry....)

Well, why don't you tell Me what's happening?

'Okay… well… there's this stupid eating disorder part of me that is telling me if I don't remeasure this milk like fifty times, I'll end up puking and being nauseous all day.'

The first thing I notice is His quietness. I get the sense that the judgement is mine not His.

Do you want to know why she is doing that?

'...uh...okay... I guess. Is there something I need to know?'

As soon as I ask the question, I get a flash of insight.

Of course. Sam was super upset about school last night and saying he didn't want to go. He's looking tired and sad, with his head on the table, not wanting to eat any breakfast because that signals the next step towards going to school. I feel lost. I don't know how to solve it. I don't know what to advocate for anymore because I don't know what the solution is. I'm terrified we're going to have a repeat version of two years ago and it will be all my fault. I don't know if I'm a terrible mum for making him go, or a terrible mum for keeping him home.

'Ug. Well, what do I say to that? I mean no wonder she's remeasuring milk – but – like that's gonna help...'

How about something like...

And the words I would say to any stressed-out mother come to mind.

'Hey... you're stressed. It's okay. It's hard right now. I get that you're worried about him. I get what you're scared about. But we've got this. Sam is going to be okay – the Shepherd has Him in the palm of His hand, even if it doesn't feel like it. He'll be there when he gets to school, and He'll help you pick up the pieces when he gets back home. It's going to be okay.'

Good job. What's happening now?

My shoulders have gone down a little. Funny, Sam is suddenly laughing about something that happened yesterday at school – something good...

'The milk – it isn't morphing into different sizes anymore. It doesn't matter so much. I think we can just pour it and be done.'

'Anna' must have gone back to her passenger seat on the bus. He seemed to know what she needed, and He helped me work out how to give it to her.

And that's been how we roll these days on my nut-mobile of a bus. Lots of passengers muscling for the wheel, in lots of crazy ways, my anorexic self included.

But whenever they do, I don't have to fight them or get stressed or try to boot them off altogether. I just let Him know who is edging up. Ask Him if there is anything I need to know about them, or if there is anything I can do to help them. Then I follow His advice.

There's a verse in His book that a lot of folk talk about – says we are 'complete in Him'[155]. Sometimes I hear the word wholeness in its stead.

I could never grasp what that meant. Does it mean I was like a doughnut and now my hole is filled? Maybe.... but I found something else in the same letter, a few chapters later, that helped it make more sense. The writer speaks of all things 'holding together' in Him[156].

---

155 Colossians 2:10 (KJV).

156 Colossians 1:17.

Now that I've been a passenger in the bus with Him for a while, I think I'm starting to get it.

The wholeness in Him that I've yearned for all my life isn't simply the filling up of a hole in my heart – although that is part of it. It's the way He brings together all these disparate parts of myself. Stops them warring with each other. Calms them down. Meets their needs.

Which means I can become whole again. I can become at peace.

Oh – and the me not having a map thing? I never could come up with a set of values and long-term goals that didn't feel like they'd been pulled from a Pinterest crochet design. But we're good now – as long as I keep letting Him drive.

He knows where we're heading, even if I don't some days. He's given me enough clues to trust Him. It's somewhere where Love reigns. And the journey from A to B is simply about loving better – Him, others, and all these noisy parts of myself too.

Letting Him drive my bus seems to work a bit better for me than divorce litigation.

Thank goodness.

Leaning

I'm nearly a healthy weight now. And I'm okay with that. To be honest, the amount of effort it has taken to get this far - the amount of blood sweat and tears – I'm relieved.

But I feel like a duck paddling frantically underwater to pull off a seamless glide above surface.

People say 'How does it feel? You've come so far!' and I don't know how to answer. Maybe they're hoping for something like this:

'Yeah – I am doing *amazing*! I am a new person! I don't even think of acting out – Anorexia? It's in the past! I'm a born-again normal person! I laugh in the face of eating disorder thoughts - watch me eat cake now, just to prove it....'

But the truthful answer isn't that simple. Like the paddling duck, recovery can feel hard work.

And I have my days where I don't do it so well - where I know I'm keeping myself alive, fed and nourished, but I'm fighting against the current. I can't look in the mirror. I tune out of the sensation of my body to avoid it. The meals and snacks I need to continue to put into my body feel like chalk scraping down a blackboard.

I hate these days because I worry how this internal experience will affect the way I look and behave to others. It might make me oversensitive to Sam – and that will upset him because he hates to see me sad. No matter how hard I try to cover up, he has antennae that far surpass my ability to mask.

It might make me withdraw from Mike. I can't tolerate having his piercing gaze of love look into my eyes when my soul feels like shit.

It might make me careless at work or preoccupied when I try to listen to a friend.

These are the moments I think 'Why am I doing this?' or 'No way am I going to put up with feeling this way tomorrow. Let's restrict the remainder of today's meals.' Or even 'It would be better for everyone else if I just called it quits on recovery here. Then I wouldn't be so grumpy and irritable.'

Today is one of those days. I call it a struggle day. And He's the only place I can go to with it. It's too hard to explain to others – even Mike. Too hard to put your finger on it. All through the morning I spew out words of desperation to Him.

'I'm having that skin crawling feeling again.'

'I can't bear to look at myself in the mirror.'

'I can't eat these meals today – I just can't do it.'

'I feel completely useless to everyone today.'

Or simply,

'Please help me. I can't do this anymore.'

In the past I might have felt a failure to feel and say such things. But He has taught me to see it otherwise. He's not shocked or disappointed. He knows I'm having a struggle day even before I have twigged to it.

He's told me countless times that that my path of healing isn't the straight trajectory that others may have, and that is okay. It's a journey of fits and starts and falters and slips.

It is a journey of leaning.

And He loves that.

If I doubt it, He reminds me of words He has spoken in His book,

A broken and contrite heart, I will not reject[157].

I came for the weak ones. The broken ones. The ones who don't have it all together – not the 'sorted'[158].

Come to me, you who are weary...[159]

I have staggered through the morning chores and sat down at my desk, ready to start work. Before I do, I shut my eyes and imagine Him next to me.

He's holding out His arm as if for an elderly person. I grab hold and put my entire body weight on it.

I sigh. Breathe. Pause.

And I hand to Him a bundle of my thoughts, body sensations, together with my urges to restrict or harm or give up. Like a giant overladen backpack. I don't even try to converse with them, wield His word at them,

[157] Psalm 51:17.
[158] Luke 5:32.
[159] Matthew 11:28-30.

contradict them. I don't have the energy for that right now. I'm tired, we still need to keep going on this road and I need to conserve my energy.

So, I simply hand Him the backpack.

Then I lean.

All day long. When I work. When I eat. When I get Sam from school. When I make his lunch for tomorrow. When I ask Mike about his day. When I clear up dinner.

I lean, and lean, and lean.

I carry myself gently, because He carries me gently[160].

I discover that days like these make me more dependent on Him. I think that is why He allows them to happen. There's no muscling through, or 'you can do this if you're really committed to recovery…', and the rest.

No. He just lets me lean.

He whispers gentle encouragements as I attend to Sam or prepare a meal.

You've got this Al. You're doing great. I'm proud of you. I am here for you.

He provides simple suggestions when I freeze wondering what to focus on next with the fog in my head and the demands swirling around me.

How about you take a breath. Then do the dishes – just that for now. Then we can work out what next.

He reminds me of simple truths.

---

160 Isaiah 40:11.

These feelings will pass Al. Tomorrow will be a new day. And I love it when you depend on Me like this[161].

Or,

There is only one thing that matters right now – that is to trust in Me. That is all that counts[162].

At the end of the day, falling into bed, relieved the day is done, I reflect on what has gone before. The intimacy I've had with Him. Another layer of my pride and self-sufficiency peeled away. The tenderness of His comfort, support and encouragement.

A miraculous eradication of all ED thoughts and feelings would make a catchy recovery story. It might sell a whole lot better.

But it wouldn't be truthful. And if it were, I wouldn't get my leaning days. I'd go back to doing it all alone. I can't bear the idea of that.

Maybe I will always be that duck paddling like crazy to sail with grace. But if it keeps me grafted to Him, that's okay.

I think I was wired to lean on Him. It's my sweet spot. It is where I belong.

---

161 2 Corinthians 4:17-18.

162 John 6:29.

Suicidality

I see the poster in the doctor's waiting room. It is titled 'How to have a conversation'.

There are four steps, each accompanied by some happy looking stickmen. In the first two pictures they're talking whilst having a cuppa, little hearts throbbing as one listens to the other. In the next they're walking a dog, smiling, and in the third they're cooking a barbeque and still beaming.

Must be a nice conversation.

I guess we all could use a little help with talking to each other these days, given the way technology dominates our world. Real live talking, I mean.

So, I scan the poster for its rationale.

It's National Suicidal Awareness Day. Or maybe it was. That's why the poster is up.

The conversation? It's the one you might have with someone you think is doing it tough – someone who might be suicidal. I skim the recommended questions to ask:

1. How are you traveling?
2. Have you been feeling this way for a while?
3. Have you spoken to your doctor about this?
4. (Fast forward a few weeks) Have things improved since our last chat?

I imagine giving each question a whirl with my suicidal self, who can still show up on tough days.

'These questions... they're great… but... I don't know if I could get them to work for me. You know, when I'm really in the pit.'

We have a way to go before the doctor gets to us. Good time to talk.

Go on.

'You know what I mean… suicidality… it… it's complicated.'

I think about the timeline of my own suicidal thoughts and behaviours. They began at a young age – about the time I found myself looking wistfully out the window of a practice room each evening, wishing a bus would run me over. My brain formed a loop that became almost comforting, if sad. It was my go-to in thinking when everything became all too hard. If school is too hard, if Mum and Dad are arguing, if I can't get through this, if I fail this exam, if I can't go on anymore with this restriction, I will just take myself out. That'll do it. I'll just give up.

Anorexia fuelled that thinking, because the illness is so goddamn painful. But simultaneously, it was a slow-burn to the same end. Of course, I couldn't kill myself – I knew what that would do to my family. But maybe, just maybe, if I keep on starving, it'll happen anyway, and then the decision is out of my hands.

By early adulthood suicidal thoughts and urges became the repository of every feeling of dirt I carried from the multiple sexual traumas and relationship breakups I'd had. They short-fused the shame of having a visible and stigmatised illness. They absorbed a gnawing sense of failure and inadequacy that I had, despite pulling off a first-class university degree and a host of altruistic jobs.

After thirty years of struggling with the eating disorder, failing at treatment over and over again, and totally exhausted and depleted as a mum, suicidality seemed the only way out of a never-ending nightmare. I lived a life torn between fighting to stay alive for Sam and Mike and wishing for all of our sakes I was dead – despite the devastation that would cause.

But suicidal thoughts were a whole area of my illness that it seemed safest to hide in treatment.

Call triage and tell them you're suicidal, they call CATT, and you end up in a psych ward. Tell the psych ward team you're suicidal and not coping and they end up discharging you saying the treatment is not working for you.

So now you're back home feeling suicidal, still, and a failure, and your child is reeling from your unexpected absence.

And then there was the morphing of the suicidality with OCD. An urge to take my life was not one, but thousands of repeated thoughts, raining on me from thousands of vindictive directions. Each with their own cruel rationale.

'Sam really would be better off if you did this.'

'Just let Mike and Sam get on with their lives without you.'

'These thoughts won't leave you alone until you overdose. Overdosing is the only way to shut them up. Just do it – once you have done it, they will stop, and you will have peace.'

'You don't deserve to live anyway.'

Et cetera et cetera.

It might seem insane, but my not-quite-lethal suicidal actions – overdoses or harming to the extreme – were attempts to bypass the final act itself. They were my best effort at shutting up the cacophony in my mind and staying alive for Sam and Mike.

I come back to the poster tips.

'What kind of conversation can you have with someone with all of that going on in their mind? And what if their situation really is desperate, and can't be changed? Such as an eating disorder. The illness is hell. The treatment is hell. And there's no guarantee the treatment will work. If you relapse it'll simply be more, no, worse …hell. What's the follow up question to that?'

Now I'm irritated, eye-rolling at the poster despite its great intentions. I hate it when I do that.

You sound upset about it, Al.

He is right. I'm upset just thinking about all the times I've felt suicidal. About the shame and guilt I carry for those thoughts, and the fact that there is still a bug in my head that goes there when I'm under stress.

You know I don't judge you, or anyone, for having those thoughts. For feeling that way.

'But… on one level, maybe… and I wouldn't judge someone else, for sure. Yet... for me… I still have this sense that it's a *sin.* That if, God forbid, I ever caved to the urge, I wouldn't wind up in Your arms – I would burn in hell. That's the worst part of it.'

Al. You forget who I am sometimes.

I think about what I just said. The god that throws a human being into hell for giving up when there seemed no way out in their life is not the God that is sitting next to me.

'Sorry. I just still… default to fear of You sometimes. The wrong kind of fear.'

He places a hand on my shoulder as if to gesture understanding.

The waiting room clock makes a peculiar whirring sound. It has just passed the hour. We are twenty minutes late now, but I let it go. It's kind of peaceful, sitting here waiting. I like it.

Think of the way I was with anyone who came to Me sick or afflicted. In My book. Remember?

I do remember. I don't ever recall an occasion where He turned someone away whether they were tormented in their mind or in their body.

Think of how I responded to you yesterday, when you said you wished you were dead, in the kitchen.

I think back. Sam was having a tough time with his homework. He didn't have to do it – with his PDA[163] we know better than to put that demand on him. But he's a perfectionist, and he wanted to show he could do it and do it perfect.

---

[163] PDA: Pathological Demand Avoidance. A profile within the autism spectrum where the person experiences intense and crippling anxiety in response to demands placed upon them – perceived or real.

He got stuck. And unravelled into a ball of self-reprobation and anger. He punched the wall. He punched himself. He tore up his work and threw it on the floor. I offered comfort but he couldn't receive it and retaliated.

It was heart-breaking. There was nothing I could say or do to help. I felt like this situation, these situations, are never going to end. I can't bear it. I want it to be over. All over.

That's when the suicide bug kicked in.

I embraced you then. I didn't reprimand you. Do you remember My words?

I relax slightly as I bring them to mind. He told me that He knew how hard this was. How unbearable it felt. He told me that He was here for me. He was not going anywhere.

'Thanks … it really helped to hear that. The bug quietened down a bit then.'

I'm reminded how often He has told me that nothing I think or say will scare Him away from me. He knows my suicidal thoughts before I've even thought them. And He isn't freaked out, or offended, by them the way human beings can be: He doesn't go into all-alarms-ringing, emergency-safety-plan-activation mode.

And He definitely doesn't send me packing with them. He can handle it. He's got this.

You know, there are a lot of people in My book that felt suicidal.

I ask Him to remind me of who they were. Surprisingly, the ones that come to mind are the good guys. The exemplary ones. Job. Elijah. The psalmist - countless times. Even Jesus Himself expressed the kind of despair that can drive suicidal thoughts when He was on the cross[164].

So, it seems we're in reasonable company, those of us who are suicidal.

And you know, Al, that suicidal thoughts are not, and never were, who you are.

Yes. I remember. A moment a year or so back where I suddenly saw it clear as day…

I was standing at the kitchen table helping Sam sort papers for his delivery run. Back in the granny flat before we all moved in together. Sam was listing every Mega Man[165] boss and its attributes while we folded and piled and folded and piled. I had, I confess, zoned out from his tutorial and, for some reason my mind drifted to the suicidal thing. At just about the point that Sam was explaining Guts Man.

I suddenly realised that the thought 'I want to die' that my brain had defaulted to so often in my life was a lie. *Something* wanted me to die. But it was the Black. Not me. It had somehow lodged the thought 'I want to die' in my head – maybe when I was fourteen, or sixteen, I don't know – and convinced me that was *my thought.*

And I willingly took the bait. I thought it, and thought it, and thought it, thinking all along, 'This is me,' and then hating myself for it. What kind of a daughter, or friend, or partner, or mother am I – wanting to take

---

[164] See the entire book of Job. For Elijah, see 1 Kings 19:3-18. Matthew 27:46.

[165] Mega Man: A classic video game series from the 80s that has been remade for the Nintendo Switch.

my own life? Shame and guilt heaped on top of suicidal thought after suicidal thought, like an auto-destruct feeding frenzy.

But it wasn't me. It was never me. I had never wanted to die.

I just didn't know how to live. I didn't know how to keep going.

'Of course. I remember when You showed me that. Golly... what a difference that makes. When you realise how much the wool has been pulled over your eyes by him.'

I know. He sighs, sadly. I can see He is thinking of some of His other kids.

But think about when those thoughts show up.

'I guess it's when I am under duress.'

When I am pushed to the brink. When I can't see the way through. When something is hurting, and I don't know when it's going to stop. When I have lost hope.

Those thoughts need healing, not judgement.

It makes sense. Once I had taken the Black's bait, throughout the decades that followed, suicidal thoughts became my escape hatch from duress. They forged and reforged their pathways in my neural networks. A kind of brain damage, they were not something I could think or reason my way out of. They needed healing, not reprimand.

'What's the healing then? Because I know I get them less these days than five years ago, for sure. But I don't know how that has happened. And it hasn't been because I've been sticking my head in ice buckets and holding squeezy balls at the right time....[166]'

Well... what has suicidality really been about, Al, for you?

He gets me to dive deep. What has my heart been crying for in my darkest, most desperate moments?

'I think it is... needing hope and ...meaning... desperately. When you are in pain that you can't bear, you want to know when it will end. And if it doesn't look like it's going to end, you want to know there is some purpose in suffering it. If you don't have those – hope and purpose – despair takes over. Completely.'

So, the healing...?

'Would be hope... but... not any kind of hope.'

I'm not thinking of the hope of fully recovering from an eating disorder. Or being cured of cancer. Or getting your family back together. Or a child having an easier run at life.

Those things would be great, but you can't guarantee them. So it can't be that type of hope. It's got to be a different hope, much more powerful.

'It's the hope of... knowing You, I guess. A bit like when the children in Narnia meet Aslan[167] for the first time. They don't need Him to say anything or do anything. They just know that in meeting Him, everything

---

[166] Some of the methods suggested for extreme distress tolerance in DBT courses.

[167] C.S.Lewis, The Magician's Nephew, Chs. 8 & 9 (1955). Similar accounts are to be found in each of the Chronicles when the Lion is encountered by the children, or even His name mentioned.

has changed. Everything is different. And somehow, no matter what happens from hereon, everything is going to be okay.'

That's the hope that endures even if your worst nightmare happens.

It was with me even after the crash. I might not realise it at times, but it stays with me no matter how tricky a day Sam has had. It doesn't depend on things turning out okay right now. It knows there is better to come, and we can count on that. It's the hope that flows from Him and it is never ending.

Once you bring the darkness of your despair into that light, you just know, whatever is going on right now, we're going to be okay. We can keep going.

I pause and think some more.

'There's the other bit, though, the purpose… You give a purpose to the pain, no matter how bad it gets. No matter if it feels like it's never going to end.'

What do you mean?

'It's like, being yoked to You and Your cross - and everything that You did through it – turns all that pain and darkness into resurrection and life…'

I pause for a moment.

'I don't know how, but I just know that the pain I feel in any moment, even if it never goes away You… You can turn it to some good. It won't be wasted. Even the pain of eating on increase days, or the yuck feeling, or nausea… even the small fry like stubbed toes and headaches...[168]'

I can and do. Always.

'And I know... I know also... that You *promise* … one day... every tear, every pain, will be wiped away.[169] Pain might feel like it will never end. But it *will* end, won't it - when You come to take us home? I don't know how, but I believe that - I hold onto it so desperately some days...'

He squeezes me.

There is one more thing though, I think you have forgotten.

I'm curious.

Think about the ultimate end of suicide. And then think about who I am.

The ultimate end... then…who He is… my brain is whirring. I love His riddles.

'Oh… I think I got it. The end of suicide – it's death, obviously, tragically. But You, You are ... Life. You are the Way, the Truth and *the Life*[170]. You came that we should have *life* and *life* to the full[171]. So even if I can't manufacture my own desire to live – I can hook into Yours... however despairing the moment. I can hook into Your Life-drive. Because You are... Life.'

---

168 Romans 8:28, Matthew 16:24, Colossians 1:24. See also Catechism of the Catholic Church, 2nd Edition, Paragraphs 1505-1506, that speak of the opportunity given us in suffering to unite it with the Shepherd's redemptive Passion.

169 Revelation 21:4.

170 John 14:6.

171 John 10:10.

I remember. Over the past 18 months, every time I've had a moment of complete despair, when the suicidal bug is in full flow and I've become hypnotised into thinking I want to end it all, something in me – I guess His Spirit – has enabled me to weakly, pathetically call out His name.

And in that moment, I receive a flash of clarity. My thinking is instantaneously reconnected to His mind, His thinking – a mind that is wired for Life not death.

'So… really… it's You. You are the healing, aren't You? You are the Hope. You are the Purpose. You are the Life.'

I want to hug Him. Sometimes I wish He still had skin.

The doctor's door opens, and she calls my name. Big smiles. Hopeful. We're doing a weigh in today. Hopefully we hit the jackpot. I am not sure whether we will. But little by little we're getting there.

For all the suicidal bugs in my brain, the desire to live is winning.

Finding True Beauty

It's official. I have to go shopping. Ugh.

At the moment, I have three T-shirts I cycle through. I can't be bothered to choose anything different to wear, and they all have gaping holes in them. Mike is forever telling me I should go get myself some new clothes. Not just because, fast approaching a healthy weight, I've outgrown the ones I have been wearing for twenty years. But because (he is so polite in his wording) they're a bit 'tired looking' (half of them look like crochet blankets…).

Which means I have to go to the shops. And I can't stand clothes shopping. Never liked it. Never will.

My favourite solution to this unavoidable ordeal is to head for the charity shop, Second Chance. Because at least there,

1. You don't have the double sting of spending a fortune on top of putting yourself through clothes-shopping-torture.
2. There are minimal mirrors.
3. Fashion – however much they spin it – is *not* the name of the game. Which means you are spared from that super-awkward moment where an immaculately dressed, manicured shop assistant comes up to you and asks you 'Can I help you?' (Seriously, if we stand next to each other in front of a mirror – them in their Dion Lee outfit and me in my overworn tracky pants and hoodie – what help could they possibly give me?! I am a soul lost to the abyss of fashion doom, from which there is no return.)

Truth is, my hatred of clothes shopping – or any activity related to my appearance – is a symptom of a deeper issue. And I don't think I'm the only one who has it.

I never really felt beautiful. Ever.

Before I became sick, I saw myself as too chubby, too daggy, too geeky, too.... whatever other kids at school called me (which generally wasn't very complementary.)

When I was sick, I was too skinny, too gaunt, too emaciated. Boyfriends were happy to remind me of this. One said he had had to explain to his mates that the only reason he went out with me despite being so skinny was because I was such a nice, compliant girlfriend – not like other women (apparently... he wasn't a real big fan of women). But he reminded me all the same that more meat on me would mean better sex in bed, so that would be a win-win.

So no, with or without anorexia, I never felt beautiful.

Now I'm 46 and nearly physically recovered. The prospect of clothes shopping simply raises the same old question I admitted defeat over when I was fourteen. What's to find beautiful now?

Mike tells me there is much, but I'm sure he's just being nice. I mean, he's stuck with me, right? So I guess he has to think positive about the 'looks' situation. I'm past the age of bothering to aspire to be a supermodel (not that I ever considered that a realistic goal...). I'm sure I've got wrinkles coming, especially where I frown. My hair looks terrible whichever way I cut it. And my arms and legs are covered in scars.

At least that's what one voice in my head says.

Granted, there's a deeper part of me that knows well enough beauty is only skin deep. Some of the most stunning people I ever worked with had bodies and facial features that were shaped uniquely, differently, 'contorted' some might wrongly say, because of their cerebral palsy or other genetic conditions and disabilities. I never questioned their beauty.

But, for the part of myself that lapses too easily into self-hatred, the standards are different. My looks are ridiculous. No clothes can save me. And pity the person who would deign to be with me. This part of me would rather hug a porcupine than walk into a clothes shop.

I get in the car and head resignedly to Second Chance.

'It doesn't matter,' I say to the Shepherd as I drive, dreading what's to come. 'In, then out. We'll grab a couple of random T-shirts and be done in a flash.'

Silence. I know He's listening for the deeper stuff going on.

'Okay, seriously, the beautiful thing? I'll just not think about myself at all. I'm ugly and hey that's okay. I knew I never would be beautiful so - no surprises.'

I don't think He's going to let that one go.

It does matter.

It matters to Me.

'Why should it matter? What about dying to self and all that?' I throw back... callously.

It matters because I made you. You are precious – deeply precious to Me[172]*. And what you think about and say to yourself matters to Me. If you say you are ugly, no good, a waste of space, I hurt.*

As I know you do.

I pause. I know what He means. Sam lashed out at himself only yesterday, mortified after a mistake he had made. The torrent of insults he rained down on himself in his frustration cut me to the core just as they did him.

I guess it's not much different for my Maker.

'I'm sorry… but I don't know how to think differently! I know You help me with the self-hatred and all, letting me talk through the emotions underneath it. But when it comes to my looks, I can't think anything other than those kinds of thoughts.'

We turn onto the freeway at the top of our street.

'And I'm not going back to endlessly repeating Louise Hay[173] affirmations about myself day in day out. It never works and it just makes me self-preoccupied and embarrassed for devoting so much time to such a pointless exercise.'

I'm a bit cutting in my tone. I apologise.

---

[172] Genesis 1:27, Isaiah 43:4.

[173] Louise Hay (1926-2017), popular motivational self-help author and philanthropist. Founder of Hay House publishing and considered a significant contributor to the New Age movement. Publications include the immensely successful 'You Can Heal Your Life' Hay House Inc., 1984, which has sold more than 50 million copies around the world in 30 languages.

Did you hear Me suggest doing that?

Nope. But it's all I hear from the world some days. 'Love your body.' 'You're worth it.' 'You are beautiful inside and out.' Ugh. Hats off to those who can say that stuff. Me? Just makes me want to puke.

I'm slightly alarmed at my attitude on this one and apologise again. We swing into the Second Chance car park and ease into a spot. I turn the ignition off and sigh.

'So how do I change? How do I drop the self-hatred – when it comes to my looks? Mike wants me to get a dress today as well – that means trying the thing on in front of a mirror! Seriously, how am I ever going to do that at this rate?!'

Finally, I'm done with my monologue. We've got twenty minutes for this whole exercise. Enough time for me to listen for a moment.

He responds.

I don't think you realise how beautiful you are to Me when you love Me. When you worship.

You cannot imagine the beauty I see in you when you simply lift your eyes to Me and adore Me.

I try not to say it, but something in me mutters 'yeah…right.'

Do you remember Sam when he was a baby and a toddler – all those times that he would simply gaze into your eyes and smile? Just look up at you and beam?

'Why do You mention that? You know it makes me cry…'

A pang of grief stabs in my guts. I do remember. He would waddle over to me, drooling, covered in pen or play doh or whatever he was playing with, hands outstretched towards me, smiling.

Isn't it the most amazingly beautiful thing in the whole universe?

There's no doubt in my mind – the look of an adoring baby or toddler is more beautiful than the most glamorous supermodel.

That is how I see you every time you lift your eyes, in trust and love, to gaze at Me[174].

I know He's not saying this because He has some big ego that needs His kids looking up and adoring Him all the time to feel good. But because this is what I – or any person – am created to do. This relationship of completely dependent, gazing, adoring, heart-melting love is what I've been created for.

He has me in a corner. I can reject what He is saying and hold onto my current estimations of my own beauty. Or ease up a bit on them. Let Him prize them out of my hands.

He goes on.

He explains that this momentary act of adoration might only be uttering a few words – His name… I love You… I need You… Or it might be a full blown completely invested worship song. The point is, that as I assume a posture of loving Him, I'm fashioned more and more into His image, and I become more beautiful to Him than I could ever hope to be in the world's eyes.

---

[174] 2 Corinthians 3:18.

'So ...' I ask, hesitantly 'Does that mean I'm only beautiful to You when I'm consciously worshipping You? What about the rest of the time?'

I'm a bit concerned. I'm looking for the catch.

He is quick to respond. Not at all. He doesn't only see me as beautiful when I'm being a 'good girl' and worshipping. No - He always sees the beauty in me – even in my worst moments.

But when I love on Him, I take my eyes off the clothes, the mirror, the scales, the fake selfie or whatever form my warped self-image is feeding off that day, and I see my reflection in His eyes – His eyes of love.

And it is at that moment He sees beauty I could never conceive of on my own.

Something in me lifts – the heavy burden of trying to fix my own self-esteem.

And that is enough, He concludes.

You don't even need to dwell on it – just know that with your eyes off yourself, and onto Me you are liberated from self-hatred and filled with the Truth of My love for you.

'I'm sorry. I am such a slow learner. You have said this stuff to me about body image before. '

I'll say it as many times as you need to hear it.

'So... the solution to my feeling totally unbeautiful... is to ... is to love You?'

I feel His nod.

He whispers into my ear a verse from one of His Psalms as I get out the car and lock the door.

Listen daughter and pay careful attention: forget your people and your father's house. Let the king be enthralled by your beauty; honour him, for he is your lord[175].

A King gazing into a bride's eyes and being 'enthralled' by what He sees. The bride looking back and 'honouring' him. So much intimacy contained in these words.

'You know, it's scary – looking into Your eyes…'

And why is that?

'Because whenever anyone looks into my eyes it feels like they're looking right into my soul – they are seeing all of me... You know – I always shy away from Mike when he does it…'

But I ***am*** *the One who sees you*[176].

El Roi[177]. I remember it. In His book. With Hagar, in the desert.

All of you.

And I am enthralled by your beauty.

---

175 Psalm 45:10-11.

176 Genesis 16:13.

177 El Roi: one of the names of God in the Hebrew Bible meaning 'The God who sees me.'

For a moment I am amazed at what He is saying. Imagine that. The King, enthralled by my…beauty…

It feels a bit much to take in.

I take a breather from His heady words as we pass through the shop's sliding doors. The musty waft of second-hand clothes hits me. Not the greatest of smells. I make a beeline for the 'women's tops' rail. We've graduated to size M, which is kind of exciting. I find two, acceptable colours, acceptable cut and head straight to the till.

Al. The dress.

Darn it.

'Oh please - can't we just skip that one? It's not like I have a wedding to go to…'

He brings Mike's face to mind. The look of love in his eyes when he shared how much he would love to see me in one. I don't want to let him down.

'Okay... but You have to help me find something quick. I've got to get Sam in ten!'

I wince a bit. It's a trivial request. I'm sure He has more important things to be thinking about.

Over here.

He directs my gaze to a rail of dresses. Long, short. Ball gowns. Winter garments. Skimpy beach items. Things your granny would wear. Things your teenage daughter would go clubbing in.

I sigh. What a nightmare. Where do I begin...

One grabs my eye. Blue. Tye-died. Simple. I realise I could wear it over leggings. For some reason that kind of helps in the whole exercise.

Reluctantly I take it to the dressing rooms. I shut the door to be confronted by the usual, full body-length mirror.

'Oh God please help...'

I turn my back to it. Strip off the necessary layers. Throw the thing on. Turn around.

My first glance is with my eyes.

No surprises – it looks awful. But hey, it's a dress, it costs $8, I've done what Mike asked, so goal achieved.

Al. Wait.

'I just want to get out of here... I can't stand this!'

Why don't you ask me what I see?

I sigh impatiently. 'Okay... well... what *do* You see?'

I look again, but this time, with His eyes.

Something shifts. I am not any different. But the way I see me is.

The dress looks alright. But it is not so much the dress – it is the person wearing the dress. She is... okay. I almost like her. She has big blue eyes – I never knew they were so big. The frown crease is kind of cute. Shows she cares about stuff – perhaps a little too much sometimes, but still, it's a quality. Her hair is a bit wild. I kind of like that. It's fun. She has a few freckles. They're quirky. Unique. When she smiles, her teeth aren't perfectly straight – but that's okay. Her smile is warm. Compassionate. It's been through a lot. And there's health in her these days. She's got flesh on her arms – muscles even! And her cheeks have a bit of substance to them – they're nourished.

'Oh...'

I pause and take it in – this weird, looking-at-myself-without-hating-myself moment.

Then I remember the time.

'Shit, we're going to be late.' I strip off and reclothe frantically. We'll take the dress. We'll take the lot. We swipe through the till and head straight for the car.

Driving to school pickup, He has one last thing to say.

It's words from His book that His friend Peter said. I used to baulk at them big time. I thought the passage was basically a bloke bossing women around telling them what they should and shouldn't wear so the guys could walk all over them.

'Sorry about that.'

That's okay. You'd had a rough run with a few men back then. But remember what those words say.

I do. They read: 'Your beauty should not come from outward adornment, such as elaborate hairstyles and the wearing of gold jewellery or fine cloths. Rather it should be that of your inner self, the unfading beauty of a gentle and quiet spirit, which is of great worth in God's sight.[178]'

As I turn them over, I realise, He is not being chauvinistic or a prude telling me I should go out and wear tweed all day.

He is giving me freedom. It's as if He is saying:

You can let it all go – the world's standards of beauty. Because it is the inside, not the outside of you, that truly counts. That is where true beauty lies – the beauty that will remain beyond the grey hairs and wrinkled skin. The beauty of a spirit softened, quietened by My love. This kind of beauty will never fade. I see it in you. I am growing it in you. And I love it.

We turn left onto the road leading towards Sam's school gates.

I realise that, when I start getting the 'God, you're ugly' barrage, I don't have to buy it. Neither do I have to fight it with relentless, unnatural affirmations of the opposite.

All I need to do is rest in a posture of love, eyes up, mouth wide open like a toddler, uttering words like 'Dada' or 'Abba', even, if that's all I've got. And know that what He sees in that moment, He adores.

In this place - loving under His gaze, and seeing through His gaze - my beauty, on all levels, is totally taken care of.

---

[178] 1 Peter 3:3-4.

Is my recovery good enough

'Does that… does that mean that I am formally, officially, … in remission?'

The doctor's smile glows. She grabs my hand in excitement, which is sweet, but slightly uncomfortable. I try to focus on her words.

'It does, yes. You are in remission from anorexia. You have done it! All on your own – I could never have imagined, 6 months ago – but look at you! Well done!'

She is a petite doctor from Thailand. Incredibly kind, encouraging, dedicated, enthusiastic. Amazingly, she didn't freak out on me when I rocked up at her clinic earlier that year, back at an emaciated ground zero and desperate for nausea meds to help me weight restore. Most doctors would have sent me packing to ED. But Dr. Bui took a punt and let me give it a crack on my own again, with Him and the aid of domperidone.

Thank God for that drug. Literally.

I try and take in her words. 'Remission from anorexia.'

My weight has hit the official 'healthy BMI' number. The lower end, but still in the green band. I've got further than I ever did in hospital or day programs. I can't believe it. Is it for real? Did we really do this? I never thought we would. I don't know what to say to Him. I don't know whether to laugh or cry.

I leave the clinic in a daze. I'm still that way when I get home and throw my bag on the kitchen table. I pull my laptop out and attempt to snap back into reality before work.

I can't.

A sinking feeling is already setting in. Thoughts are starting to whisper.

'You're not really recovered.'

'You were dithering over breakfast again for goodness' sake – call that recovered?'

'You had a rough day three days ago – where's the consistency Alys?'

'You're still so rigid…'

'You haven't eaten out for ages…'

'You have different dinners some evenings to Mike…'

'You're a fake.'

'You're a fraud.'

Old voices. New situation. I should know better than to jump online to resolve them. But I'm grasping for tangibles, boxes I can tick to prove I am legit, good enough. I still feel like I will be sprung and sent back to a psych ward – even now.

I grab my phone and clumsily punch 'Definition for recovery from anorexia' into Google.

A plethora of results come up. It's evident no-one can agree.

Is it this BMI or that BMI? And how many years do you have to have maintained said BMI before you are considered, officially, normal (whatever that is)?

Some ED organisations talk about recovery being an 'individual journey', not easily defined and different for everyone. Yet a few pages down they insist on two years of that intangible if you want to volunteer for them.

I'm confused. I keep going, desperate for reassurance, and wind up with the inevitable.

Chat GPT.

Today's not-so-trustworthy AI assistant concedes that the DSM-5 does not explicitly define full recovery beyond remission. Nevertheless, 'here is a list of clinical considerations usually taken into account when determining whether or not a person is recovered.'

That'll do for my black-and-white brain. I read the list and commence a personal score-take.

A return to a healthy BMI.

- Golly. Did it. But I'm at the lower end – is that okay? Is it the 'set point' they used to talk about in treatment? How do I know?
  Score: Undecided.

Stabilization of vital signs.

- Yep. But then, my vital signs were weirdly stable even at my lowest weight...
  Score: Pass but consider it a cheat, because this was always the case.

Resolution of health complications caused by malnutrition.

- Score: Fail. Still have osteoporosis and neutropenia and neither seem to be going anywhere.

Improved body image.

- Depends… It's good when I look up at Him rather than down at me. But that could mean a fail because I don't tolerate a daily scrutiny in the mirror… but then who wants to spend each morning examining themselves in the mirror? Confused.
- Score: Undecided, likely fail.

Emotional stability.

- Um… well … my feelings have come back because I'm not starving them out. They're big, painful and ugly. Most days. And I have carer burnout. Which means I'm crying usually once, if not twice, per day. Sigh.
- Score: Fail.

Normalisation of eating behaviours.

- Okay…. Let's see… I eat regular meals, regular times, regular food. But I still have those Gulliver's list items in the pipeline… And spontaneity, flexibility…? I pull them off … on occasions… with extreme anxiety… when it's…planned… d'oh.
- Score: Fail. We're a work in progress.

Social and functional recovery.

- I'm not sure what the definition is of a functional human being… and I'm not sure I want to know. Let's go the social front. Right,

well... I'm a carer, and I don't have time to go to the toilet some days let alone become a born-again extrovert with the world of friends I don't have. Ouch. I guess that would be a ...
- Score: Fail.

Sustained change over time.

- Ah... the perennial piece of string... which change? And how long is 'sustained'? Are we just talking about weight, or is it the rest of the Gulliver's list too?
- Score: Undecided.

At this point, I stop the scorecard. I'm starting to get that panicky feeling I used to get every time we had a ward round in hospital. My mind jumps back to it.

The post-meal support room is silent as we all sit, each waiting our turn for this week's hearing. The clock ticks and whirs. Some of us scroll aimlessly on our phones. Others hide under a blanket trying to sleep off the jumble of panic, depression and self-loathing elicited by the 5:30 am weigh-in that morning. Every ten minutes or so, the duty nurse unlocks the door allowing a shaken, blotchy-faced patient to return to their seat before summoning the next on the list.

It's my turn. I'm swiped out of the ward's double doors, into a part of the building that is tantalisingly close to freedom – I can see the main entrance, the car park, people walking by with children they can see, making calls they can make and carrying bags they can carry unchecked.

I avert my eyes – it's masochistic to look. The nurse directs me left down the corridor and into an enormous conference room.

From the moment I step in, I feel like I'm on trial. The duty nurse directs me to a seat at the head of a conference table with 15 shiny suits complete with polished pointy shoes positioned in an arc around me. For a moment, I'm transported back to the weekly performance classes at music school where you'd get a grilling from teachers and peers after a mock recital. I'm not sure if it's better or worse.

I ground. My social anxiety is sky high, and all eyes are on me.

The purpose of the meeting? To discuss treatment progress. Let the questioning begin.

'We notice you've been sneaking warm water to have as a drink with your meals. Do you want to explain what is going on there?'

'Your weight has not tracked the target 1kg for this week, but we put you up a meal plan. Do you want to explain why?'

'We noticed you were scratching your arms during mealtimes. Do you know the policy of no tolerance we have here when it comes to self-harm?'

'We see you've been asking for smaller cutlery for your yoghurt. Do you understand that this is an eating disorder behaviour and contrary to your treatment goals for recovery?'

'The nurses have noticed you've been doing yoga some mornings in your room. We've decided therefore that you will be asked to get up at 630am and sit in the main ward area until the purple room is opened at 8am, so you can be monitored and protected from yourself. Is there anything you would like to say about this?'

The sense of shame and failure is excruciating. The standards are so high. Will I ever be good enough to get out of this place? Will I ever hit the bar to go home?

On one occasion I crumple. Completely. I say I can't do this. I want to go home. I want to be with my son.

'Are you really serious about recovery? Do you want your son to be without his mum – do you want to stay alive or don't you? Do you realise that is just your eating disorder speaking?'

It feels impossible. To prove you are recovered enough to get out.

Gain the weight. Keep your hands on the table. Participate in mealtime conversation. Stay seated, always, everywhere. Be emotionally regulated. Talk positive recovery talk. Ask for help if you want to harm. Don't have harming urges. Look yourself in the mirror. Don't body check. Do this right thing or that right thing – more and more, better and better.

Always the bar is that little bit higher than what you've achieved. And when you finally do get out, the understanding is that you're by no means fully recovered. You still can't be trusted. You still can't trust yourself. You leave haunted by the question that never goes away - is that you or is that your eating disorder speaking right now?

So I don't – trust myself. Ever. I just ricochet from one person's opinion of what I should be doing to be recovered to another's. And I never hit the bar. I never hit recovery. I never have a story that's worth telling because I can't tick all the boxes.

These are the thoughts and feelings that come up for me as I do my self-inflicted scorecard.

I return to the present.

Is this helping you, Al?

Of course it isn't. What am I thinking of, even doing this stupid exercise of self-appraisal.

'I'm sorry. I know I shouldn't have scrolled. I shouldn't be searching for answers, seeking reassurance, trying to get human approval. I'm sorry.'

Why don't you ask Me how I see it?

Always the best question. Too often the one I leave till last.

'Okay... well … what about You then? What *do* You think? What *is* good enough recovery? I had a flop day yesterday. The nausea was so bad when I woke up, I couldn't do it – I couldn't do my full meal plan. Or Monday when I exercised on a rest day – I failed again. Does that mean I've failed You? Don't I have to be perfectly recovered to be of any worth to You, to have a story that is worth telling? A story that shows people how amazing You are, that gives other people hope and inspiration? Because if I can't even do that, what is the point of all of this, all this fighting against the grain with this illness … what's the point?'

My exasperation is not pretty. He waits as I take a breath. Then lets me go on.

'I have friends who have a strong faith in You. They have that kind of 'breakthrough' faith – they are always praying for a breakthrough – mine, theirs, the dog's, everyone's… But I'm too tired to talk to those friends these days. If breakthrough is to hit all these medical bars of recovery, no symptoms, no hard thoughts, no behaviours, then I feel like I've failed before I even get out of bed each day. And… and… to be honest I feel scared, defeated by that kind of faith. It makes me scared of You – because I feel I let You down each day being a struggler, a leaner. A broken vessel that has to ask for help to eat two biscuits. Still.'

I stop. I'm crying. Again.

'I just want to do You proud.' I snivel. 'I just want to be *good enough* – to have a healing that is good enough. I'm nothing if I'm not good enough for You. Some days I'm scared You're going to interrogate me like they do in ward round - about my thoughts and behaviours. I'm frightened to talk to You, because I'm worried You will question me and question me so that I have to admit that yes, I'm still a walking pathology. An ED on two legs, even if I look good on the surface. I'm scared You're just waiting for me to stop and listen so You can point out the gaps, the failures, the slip-ups.'

I let it all out, all these questions and insecurities about my failed, 'not-good-enough' recovery. The veiled anger I feel with all those unattainable treatment goals and regimes. My resentment towards kind prayer warriors that have encouraged me to muscle on through to the triumphant victory and healing that is my due to claim.

Finally, I'm done. I breathe. I exhale the last of my emotion into Him.

Why in the world would I do that, Al?

He is not arguing – He is pointing out the blindingly obvious.

He is Love. Love is not standing in the wings ready to pick holes in its children. It keeps no record of wrongs – if struggling with an illness were to be a wrong.

I slowly start to melt into that ever-present 'hold' He encases me in so often.

And as I do, I sense that He knows the feeling of failure and discouragement that I'm speaking of. He brings to my mind a moment when He was on the cross, bleeding and dying. Surrounded by people shouting and yelling at Him to work a miracle for Himself, come down from the cross if He really was who He said He was[179].

This image of Him is a far cry from me in my human weakness. But it gives me a sense that He knows what it is to feel this way – to feel powerless to do any better than you're doing right now. To feel 'not good enough' in the eyes of the world.

I love you.

Right where I am, in my imperfect recovery.

It feels like several minutes that we stay in this listening stillness, with the hold and the Love.

Then come the words.

I am always with you. Every step of the way along this journey. I have all the time in the world. I am the Alpha and the Omega. ***I am*** *what this is all about. Not perfect recovery. Not the DSM-5 criteria fulfilled or no longer fulfilled. Not the perfect testimony. Just knowing Me, trusting in Me, loving Me, more and more each day*[180].

---

179 Matthew 27:40.

180 Matthew 28:20, Revelation 22:13, Exodus 3:14, Matthew 22:36-40.

'But...' I exclaim, '...aren't I a failure, an embarrassment to You if I'm not fully recovered? How can I be useful to You if I've not 'made it'?'

He tells me no. His strength is made perfect in my weaknesses – not my successes. That a broken vessel is good enough for Him because His light can shine through the cracks, the vulnerability. That He's not so much interested in how perfectly I can recover as in how much I can love. And weakness and imperfection seem to be fertile ground for love, compassion, gentleness and empathy[181].

'What about good enough, though? That beast haunts me even now on this journey, where I have sought to give up on satisfying the world's standards, demands. Aren't Yours infinitely more important and far-reaching? How can I know that my recovery – not just that, but *I myself* – am ever good enough for You? *How can I be good enough*?'

After all those conversations about perfectionism, here I am again on the same old topic.

His answer is firm. It is directly from His book.

The work of God is this: to believe in the One He sent[182].

I keep pushing.

'So what do You mean by 'believing in You'? Is it to hold to the correct principles of faith? To pray 'the sinners' prayer'? Once? Twice? Daily? To show real change, or change in this or that aspect of my life? To manifest

---

181 2 Corinthians 12:8-10.
182 John 6:29.

the gifts of the Spirit? To help a hundred people come to know You? To be super helpful at church? To be a better person because I know You?'

I reel off a hundred possible 'bars' that my human brain can come up with to fabricate a standard I can hold onto again.

To believe in the One He sent...

I turn the phrase over in my mind. My human eyes don't get it.

I'm like the blind man at Bethsaida. It's a story in one of His gospels. The Shepherd put His own spit on the guy's eyes so he could see again. Only, the first-time round, it didn't quite work. So, He asks the guy, 'Can you see anything?' and the response He gets is crushingly honest: 'Um...I can see the people, but they look like trees on legs...'

Doesn't stop the Shepherd. He spits again. Rubs it on. And then the guy can see clearly[183].

I'm like that blind man with this verse. I see trees not people. I need more of His spittle.

So, I ask. I wait.

Then I see.

This is the work that I require. This is what 'good enough' is.

To believe in Me. That I loved you that much that I died for you, and that I have risen, am risen, to bring you a hope that can never be robbed from you whether you get through this illness or not.

---

183 Mark 8:22-25.

To believe in My words – every single one of them.

To believe in My love for you, day in day out, no matter what kind of day you have had.

To believe that I am for you, not against you, no matter how many times you relapse.

To believe that I am the love that never fails, always hopes, always trusts, always perseveres. The love that never gives up on you – even when you give up.

To believe that I will always welcome you into My arms no matter what state you are in.

To believe that I forgive you again and again and again, whether others do or don't.

To believe that I am rooting for you every day of your life – whether you are fully recovered or not.

This is the work I require. To believe in me[184].

I let it sink in.

Whether I'm in a hospital bed on an NG tube. Whether I'm confined, again, to a gruelling psych ward regime. Whether I'm heroically attempting my fifth - or fifteenth - day program.

---

[184] John 3:16, John 5:24-27, Ephesians 3:17-20, Romans 8:31-33, 1 Corinthians 4-8, Psalm 103:11-14, Hebrews 4:15-16.

Or if I'm just struggling along as I am now, a messy mum trying to figure out recovery on their own with Him at home. With good days and not so good days.

I boot up the laptop.

To believe in Him. Period. That is a good enough recovery. A good enough life. A good enough anything.

That is good enough.

Letting Him rewrite my story

It's a monster form. They always are - but this one tops the lot.

It's the enrolment form for Sam's secondary school and I've been working on it for days. We're going alternative – I just can't bear to wait for him to fall apart all over again before the supports he needs, which may still fall short, are put in place.

It's good they ask the questions they do. They haven't missed a beat. Family background history. Attachment issues. Early exposure to trauma. And more. Lots more.

I slip into a persona whenever I fill out forms like these – I call it the Fall Guy.

I fear people will blame me for Sam's challenges. So, I beat them to it. I fill in the entire form as a litany of my errors.

Don't get me wrong – I make sure they know absolutely everything they need to know about Sam, his needs, his strengths, his qualities, his sensory profile, his learning trajectory, his triggers – everything they ask. I'm thorough like you can't imagine. The form is 10 pages long by the time I'm done.

But if Sam's struggles point to any harm done in his life, that harm is on me. My eating disorder. My borderline. My OCD. My hospitalisations. My self-harm. My separation. My identity confusion.

It makes for brutal reading. But I'm too scared to do otherwise. I've been shot down enough times as a mum with a mental health illness to know it's not worth waiting for. Best to do it yourself.

It's not just Sam-forms that the Fall Guy steps in for. These days, I switch him on the moment I connect with anyone I haven't seen for a while.

Here's his core message, as per a recent rerun:

'What an idiot I was - trying treatment after treatment, forcing Sam through agonizing separation anxiety, with nothing to show for it. Everything he suffers now – autism and complex needs aside – is entirely my fault. If Sam were ever to take his own life, the blame would be mine. Completely.

And Mike – how could I have put him through such hell? After all the support he gave me, I decided I was gay?! Without ever having had a same-sex relationship? What kind of half-brained idiot does that? I never deserved him, and I never will. The damage is done and I will never be able to make it right. Not only that, my enslavement to rigidity, introversion, and anxiety have pushed him away time and time again. I'll forever be indebted to his goodness. And I'll never be good enough. I can never make it up.

What a totally dumb idea it was of me as a teenager to choose to stop eating. I'd heard of anorexia and knew how debilitating it would be as an illness. But there I went, voluntarily walking down that path and hurting everyone that loved me in the process. I had it all – talent, brains, a good education – and I threw it away. If I'd been anything like person X I would have handled life so much better. I would have made my parents proud. You would be able to find me on LinkedIn and Wikipedia like my other accomplished relatives, with trophies to share and achievements to glow in. What a waste. All those gifts God gave me, and I threw them all away. '

I don't think I would ever put this narrative on someone else.

But The Fall Guy version of events has felt like the safest way to give an account. It's my armour against others' judgements.

And the narrative hasn't come from nowhere. For all the compassionate perspectives suggested to me by therapists, it's the throw away comments from innocent passersby that have stuck:

'You're not like the other patients here. You've got no reason to have this illness – you have a wonderful husband.'

'How could you do this to your mum?'

'This is the one sickness you can get yourself well from – so just pull yourself together and start eating.'

'Never underestimate the impact having a psych admission has on your family, particularly your children.'

'You've publicly shamed your husband. If I were him, I would never forgive you.'

'Mike might have you back but I wouldn't.'

'It's not surprising Sam has all the issues he has, given your history.'

They were just trying to help. But the words cut me to the core. They're lodged in my heart. Still.

And the story I spin works well – it does beat people to it. They don't get a chance to judge me this time, because I already have. Phew.

Problem is that the story I weave for myself is not a life-giving story. It's a life-sucking one.

It is hard to be a solid, compassionate, gracious mum or wife when this is how you think of yourself. It's hard to do what it takes to stay well with an eating disorder if you've never forgiven yourself for having it in the first place.

I realised my story was crippling me one day when I was riding my bike down the creek after Sam had had a particularly painful meltdown. Tears streaming, I blurted out to the Shepherd everything you just read. Again. Heaven knows what other people on the path seeing me hurtle by would have thought.

I could hear His gentle invitation to forgive myself. But I couldn't do it, and I told Him so.

'How the heck do I forgive myself for that? Nothing can change the past, what I've done, how I've been! Nothing can bring those years back for Sam or Mike. How can I just 'let it go'?'

I knew I should just be able to look at the cross and have all my shame and berating self-narrative washed away. But I felt like they were completely stuck on me. I couldn't shake them, for all the theology in the world.

After exhausting my self-directed expletives I collapsed in a mental heap, still pedalling, asking Him what to do. It wouldn't do Sam any good, or Mike, me returning home in this state.

That's when I heard Him say,

Why don't you ask Me how I see your story?

I tensed. I did not want another therapeutic trick played on me to try and make me feel better about so many messes. I was past trusting in cognitive reframes or other tools of the trade.

But then it occurred to me that seeing things through His eyes might carry a bit more weight than all the conversations I've had with psychiatrists. Theirs was a well-meaning but fundamentally human perspective. And human perspectives, like 'positive thoughts' to challenge the ED, were not powerful and weighty enough to overshadow the immense shame and regret I carried.

But He – He was in a different class. He made me. He made this whole world.

It occurred to me that His perspective might actually be more valid than other people's, including my own. I reflected that He *is* Truth – so it would be impossible for Him to present a perspective of my story that was false, a feel-good spin or something similar. That would go against His intrinsic nature.

I took a deep breath, pedalled on, and asked Him to show me.

And this is what He said.

Where you see a precocious teenage girl at a privileged school obstinately refusing to eat and throwing away her gifts and potential in the process, I see....

A child desperately trying to survive. A child with no clear way out, no safe place to turn, under incredible pressure with no tools to cope. A child whose gifts and talents – and her veiled autism – may have looked enviable to others but were, for her, a tremendous burden. They were used, with the best of intentions, by adults, schools and TV companies in ways that could only have induced an unbearable sense of pressure and exhaustion. A child who resisted growing up not out of immaturity, but because she didn't have the chance to be at home the way other kids did – and when she was there, home was far from easy. I see a child who fought with every inch of her being to keep going in the only way she knew how, and who continued to fight even when the illness she had ripped everything from her.

Where you see a mum indulgently trying hospitalisation after hospitalisation to fix herself and maiming her son in the process, I see ....

A mum fighting for her child. Doing everything she possibly could to survive because, for all the pain of the treatment she went through, she knew it would at least keep her alive, and that her death would be an irreparable wound to her son. A mum that never asked to be sick. Who only wanted to be the best she could for her boy. A mum with the sensitivity to recognise his special needs and push through professionals who were so eager to pin his autism on her own mental health challenges, for the sake of getting him the help he needed.

Where you see a wife shamelessly and publicly rejecting her husband for the sake of a new-fangled identity that might help her feel good, I see...

A woman who was deeply torn not only about who she was, but about how to help her family come to some semblance of calm amid Covid lockdowns and autistic meltdowns. A mum who endured her son begging for separation on account of his own insecurity and attachment issues, night in and night out. A woman who was trying desperately to find some way to diffuse the tension that existed in their home - tension that was resulting in explosions, holes in the wall and heartache for all her family – not just her alone. A woman who would rather wear the blame for that decision by calling herself gay than have either her son or husband feel responsible.

I paused trying not to rebut everything He was saying to me. I wanted to push this compassionate story away because it felt too risky.

'Someone surely would hear that story and knock it to pieces. Isn't it nonsense? I can't just give myself a break like that. It's self-pity, of the worst kind!'

He simply said,

That is the way I see it.

He was not judging anyone in those narratives. His gaze of compassion extended not only to me, but Sam, Mike, my parents, the music teachers – everyone in my life. But it was a much wider, grace-filled perspective than the one I was clinging to. And from that perspective I heard Him speak further:

Where you see an idiot, I see a fighter who will keep going at all costs.

Where you see a selfish mum, I see a fierce protector for her child.

Where you see a stupid wife, I see a woman chosen and precious.

Brave. Strong. Chosen. Precious.

I did everything I could to let those words sit in my soul.

'Help me – I can't hold this.' I exclaimed to Him. The temptation to chastise myself was so alluring.

But He whispered that He knew. That it would take a lifetime to learn a new story about myself. His story. A story that gave me my dignity back and the ability to hold my head high – not in egotistical, self-righteous pride, but in the mercy and love of His grace.

I'm still learning to sit with this story.

But doing so has shown me how He is - way beyond any earthly psychotherapist, author or social media influencer - the Master Storyteller.

He rewrites the stories we tell ourselves and beat ourselves down with. He does the same for those who have hurt us. The same for our children. For those in the corridors of power. For the stranger we pass on the street who we may never see again.

For each of us, He is willing to draw a new story of grace, hope and life out of the old tale of shame, regret and defeat.

What gives Him the license to do this?

Because He is the one who wrote our stories in the first place. He created us within full knowledge of everything that would happen to us and through us. And He was confident He could make something beautiful out of that however messy it might be[185].

Not by simply wiping the slate clean and washing away the bad stuff – though His forgiveness is lavish. He is more creative than that - He wastes nothing.

---

[185] Psalm 139:16, Romans 8:28-30.

When we hand our past to Him, He takes our every thought, our every move, our every decision – no matter how disastrous – and weaves them like an artist into a vast cosmic tapestry of love. A story whose ending – though we may not know it now – will be good.

So very good.

I think it may take a little while before I have the courage to let His version of events show up in the forms I fill out for Sam. I'm still too scared of what others will say. It's weak, I know, but I sense His gentleness and patience with me on that. He knows I'm feeling my way – in this new mind, this new body, this new life.

But every time I do step into His Truth about me – just for one moment, even – He quietly cheers me on. I hold my head a little higher. I can look my fellow man in the eye a little longer. Shame retreats for a while.

And slowly, slowly, my heart begins to heal.

Eucharist

I pull into a space in front of the golf shop that neighbours the church.

'We love the game as much as you do.' reads the sign. Makes me smile – last time we played mini-golf as a family we had to evacuate the entire course as Sam, in frustration, started catapulting his club into the decorative bush arrangement, narrowly missing other players.

I check the time. 4:57pm. Hopefully they haven't started. Maybe it's my OCD but, all the same, I hate getting there after they've started. I feel like every word counts.

I semi-walk/run and swing through the doors. Thankfully people are still seated. Some on their knees praying. Others quietly talking. There is a hushed babble from a group gathered around the priest as they talk and laugh about the week, the weather, their lives.

I amble over to an empty end of a pew, bow at the cross, and kneel.

'I always feel so rushed when I get here… so not ready for this. So distracted. I'm sorry.'

It's okay. You're here. You would not believe how much joy that brings Me.

'There must be a million things I need to apologise about – to get my heart ready for You.'

I ferret around in my memory. The countless judgemental thoughts I've had. Loud opinionated statements I've made about others. Moments of losing my patience with Sam. Controlling manoeuvres with Mike. And then just the forgetting – the plain forgetting Him for hours or days on end some weeks. After all He has done …. why am I like that? I hate it in myself.

Gentle Al. I am here to heal not chide.

'Okay... But I'm sorry – for all of it. All my flops and failures to love and weaknesses. Please, clean me up, make me ready to receive You now…'

The bell rings. The entrance song starts. The procession of the gifts – His book, a cross – followed by the priest himself, moves slowly, solemnly, but joyfully towards the altar.

It is awash with light flooding in through the stained glass – glass that depicts an ocean with a sun rising on its horizon. My eyes track from this horizon up to the crucifix that is suspended above, forward to a golden cupboard containing last week's bread. Then back to the cross again.

Father Dispin bows. He turns towards us. He smiles. And so, the Mass begins.

Throughout the entire service, my mind is its usual leapfrog self. It jumps from one thing I have to do to another. Then one memory of something done to another. Gently, time and time again He brings it back to the words that are being spoken, the ceremony that is underway.

I used to stress about being so distracted. These days He's reassured me enough to no longer beat myself up about it. I'm learning to recognise that in this space I'm held, not only by Him, but by the web of human beings standing alongside me. When I drift, I know someone in that web is gazing upward, and their gaze is the tug I need to refocus on Him. Hopefully I do the same for them.

Prayers are spoken. Scriptures read. A homily given. Then Father Dispin commences the final liturgical steps that will culminate in the climax of this gathering.

'Blessed are You, Lord God of all creation… the bread we offer You…it will become for us the bread of life….' Then the wine. '…it will become our spiritual drink...'

Humbly, we're invited to pray that this sacrifice – the priest's and ours - 'may be acceptable to God, the almighty Father[186].'

My mind jumps back to a conversation I had with the Shepherd only a few days ago. It was about worship – the act of loving Him.

I was troubled.

How could I possibly offer the love, the worship, that was due His name? That was worthy in the light of the wonder that He is and the love that He has given me and every human being? What could possibly be adequate for this, the King of Love?

Songs come and they go, and so often they worship Him for something He has done for us. Something He has given. Or something we want Him to do. And those songs that do worship Him for Him alone – how often have I sung them distracted, thinking of the washing, or an email I need to send Sam's teacher, or what I should get for dinner tonight?

'How can I possibly honour You the way You deserve? What act of worship could be good enough? What sacrifice – if sacrifice is required – could come anywhere near what You have given?'

[186] Words taken from the Order of Mass, St Pauls Sunday Missal (2012).

He spoke words to me that He had spoken three millennia ago. They were uttered through a man called Abraham, in a slightly desperate situation.

God had asked him to sacrifice his son, Isaac, as a burnt offering. Scary stuff.

Carrying a bundle of wood on their way up the mountain, Isaac asks his dad (nervously?) 'Dad, the fire and wood are here, but where is the lamb for the burnt offering?' To which Abraham responds,

God himself will provide the lamb for the burnt offering[187].

Heaven knows what Abraham felt as he sheepishly spoke those words. At that point, things weren't looking hopeful.

(Spoiler alert for today. An angel averts the crisis. Abraham, knife raised over his son, is prevented from filicide just in time. It's a wonder Isaac didn't have to do therapy for the rest of his life ...)

But God does provide. At just the right moment, a ram pops out of the bushes to take Isaac's place.

So, Abraham names the place 'The Lord will Provide.'

As I reflected on this story, those were the words that echoed in my mind.

God Himself will provide the lamb.

What is the perfect sacrifice to offer Him? What can I give as the most perfect gesture of worship?

---

[187] Genesis 22:8. The entire story can be found in Genesis 22: 1-19.

I myself will provide. I am the lamb. I am the offering. Bring Me to the altar.

The sacrifice, the offering, the act of love that is most fitting for the One who loved each one of us into being, is the very One He provides. Himself. On a cross. His body. His blood.

And here I am, kneeling in this church, looking at it before my very eyes.

Perhaps that is why I seem to tear up every time the Priest raises the round circular host[188] that we will all consume, and states the words:

'Behold, the Lamb of God, behold Him who takes away the sins of the world. Blessed are those called to the supper of the Lamb.'

The peace is given. We say the Lord's prayer. The procession to the altar to receive the host begins. As I shuffle along with the rest of my brothers and sisters, I reflect on what this moment means to me.

In this bread, He is made real – so real I can touch Him, eat Him.

I am so fickle. No matter the enormity of all He has done for me, the richness of the conversations I've had with Him, the power of the words He has spoken to me. The idea that He is with me seems true one moment and a fairy tale the next.

But here, I have something tangible. Here He is, in that bread. And when, in the days that follow, I'm tempted to doubt His presence with me and in me, I will tell myself, 'No, Al. Remember Sunday. You ate Him. He is in your blood, your cells, your very being – closer to you than your own skin.'

---

[188] Host: The name given to the wafer, or bread, used at every Mass.

Some may baulk at such a notion. I don't mind. For me it is Life.

In this bread, too, I am cleansed.

I have thrust shame deep down inside me all my life. I cannot bear to think, still, of the things that have happened in my past, particularly in the area of intimacy. By myself, I've never been able to rid myself of the feeling of being forever a soiled woman. A woman who could never wash away, starve away, harm away, the things she had done and that had been done to her.

But when I take that bread, I seem to be able to trust more deeply the cleansing of His body and blood, shed for me[189]. I hold onto the memory of receiving it and swallowing it like a medicine that obliterates every spot of dirt from the past. Nothing else gives me that reassurance. Nothing else makes me clean.

And in this bread, I find all over again, a Love beyond imagining.

For many years, one of the beliefs that pushed me away from the Christian faith was the idea of a wrathful God. One that took out His fury towards a sinful mankind on His own perfect Son in order to somehow 'get it out of His system'. And that by this act, I was now saved and owed Him my love and trust.

I found it close to impossible to trust such a god whose character appeared positively sadist, worse than any child abuser I had ever heard of.

This little wafer, and all that has been spoken of it in the priest's Eucharistic prayer, frees me once and for all of that appalling image of

[189] Hebrews 9:14, 1 John 1:7-9.

God. Both transport us back to the last supper the Shepherd shared with His friends before His death.

Knowing all that He was about to endure, He took bread, broke it, and gave it to those with Him, saying,

This is My body ***given*** *for you...*

Given.

Not forced out of His hand – however much the human beings culpable for His death might imagine that to be the case. Not self-inflicted as an act of divine infanticide to placate a monstrous god.

But *given*[190].

Willingly. In an act of complete selfless, and total love.

For you.

If He had not given it, His love would never have been known. The darkness and hopelessness we see in this world would have had the last word. The Black would have won. We would never be able to wake up. We would never be able to return home.

But He was not pleased to let that happen. He wants His kids home – every one of us.

And for that, He gave everything.

---

190 Luke 22:18-20.

It is my turn. I bow before receiving. I take the host in my hand. I make the sign of the cross. All small, weak, broken acts of solemnity, the best I can do to honour the One I am about to take in.

Then I consume.

I return to my seat, still chewing on Him, speechless. I fall on my knees. Gratitude feels a pathetically small response. But it's all I have got.

Who would imagine that this is the worship He desires – the offering He Himself provides. My broken and contrite heart will do. Because His body and blood are enough.

Every time I can make it here to do this thing, I am reminded that it is a King of Love that carries me.

It is a King of Love that gives me strength to do today, to eat breakfast, to keep going, to keep loving as best I can.

It is a King of Love whom I choose to trust not just with my recovery, but with my whole life.

It is Love, and Love alone, that bids me eat.

SIXTH INTERLUDE – HOW DO WE TELL THEM?

'I think we're nearly done... I mean, in so far as anyone's story is nearly done...'

I'm laminating cards for a game Sam has designed. He is the mastermind. I am the back office. But it's okay because I have a fetish for laminating.

'But there's one thing...'

What's that?

'How do we tell them... how can we show them that You are not just mine; You are theirs too? And that we – they and I – together belong to You? What if they are reading this whole thing and thinking I'm just one of the lucky ones who get to go to Never Never land each day, seeing You, hearing You, chatting with You and all, but that would never happen for them?'

I remove sheet number 1 of four freshly sealed pages and insert the next. I am a whizz at preventing overlap - the cardinal sin of laminating.

'What can I say... to help... to help them see You? To help them know You are with them right now as they thumb these pages, and think about the shopping they have to get done, or a meeting they have tomorrow or the ward round that is coming or...whatever is going on in their lives?'

Well, what have I put on your heart? Why not try that?

I start cutting the cards in sheet number 1 while sheet number 2 creaks to its sealed destination.

I imagine writing a letter. It goes something like this.

*

Dear Reader,

This entire story may have made you cringe. All those sentimental, cheesy descriptions of Him, our chats, my rants, His embraces. I'm sorry if that's so. I'm not good at faking stuff. I prefer to be real.

All the same, you've made it this far so I guess you're not completely triggered, grossed out or fed up. Winning.

But maybe the reason you've reached this point is because something is tugging on your heart for more than what you have right now. More than this illness perhaps, or this life of doing it alone, or this daily grind.

Something yearning to let go, to quit the fight – whatever that is for you today. Something tired of coping and fixing and surviving and controlling and figuring it all out every day on your own.

And maybe that part of you – that yearning part – looks at this story and thinks it's too good to be true. A Shepherd showing up in your living room. Scooping you up. Taking the load. Showing you the way. Loving you back to life.

But really, it's not. I'm not special. He doesn't have favourites. He said that in His book[191].

---

[191] Romans 2:11.

He's been with me all along – I just didn't see Him.

And so it is with anyone else. Perhaps, like me, you just never knew it or believed it.

He's an absolute master at opening people's eyes when they can't quite see Him. All it took for me was a few fumbling words. To some, they probably were the wrong ones, but He didn't seem to be bothered.

There are a lot of prayers out there for how to invite Him in, how to own the stuff-ups, the messes, let Him rescue, take over, lead. I get dizzy and confused looking at them all...

But you know what, maybe just start by calling out His name[192].

And let Him take it from there.

You might be surprised how He shows up. Don't be afraid to let Him work with your imagination – He gave it to you, after all.

The Name? Ah.... you've known it all along, haven't you...?

His name is Jesus.

---

[192] Romans 10:13-15.

Encore

I press the buzzer and wait. There's a crackle and a voice with an Indian lilt responds.

'Hello, who is it?'

'Hi, it's Alys, I'm here for the music.'

'Sorry?'

'I'm the volunteer – for the memory support unit. Bev knows.'

'Ah, yes, come on in.'

I'm nervous. The keyboard is pulling on my shoulder, and it's bucketing with rain.

'Seriously, I can't believe I'm doing this. I am going to sound terrible.'

It's not a performance Al.

'I know, I know… I just... I'm really not sure this is a good idea...'

Trust Me.

I pivot through the double doors, careful not to knock over a tall, decorative pot plant at the entrance and sign in. I can feel the thing slipping – I swear it is going to break the carrier handles one of these days. I have to get a trolley or something.

I make my way down the corridor and hit the code for Kookaburra. Each area is named after an Australian bird species. The door swings open.

I see them. My fear evaporates. I feel like I'm seeing a bunch of long-lost friends, even though I'm only just getting to know them. I can't remember everyone's names, but I barrel over and greet them anyway.

'Hi, how are you going?' 'You're looking great Greg – nice hair cut!' 'Dorothy how have you been? Hey Terry - good to see you! Daphne – I've a few specials for you today, but you gotta sing with me, because my voice sucks.'

For some reason, when I get there, the intrusive voices that have harassed me about touching the piano again recede.

I put the Yamaha on a wheelie table and plug it in. Pedal connected. Seat loaded up with pillows, so I am at the right height. Phone tabs up. I'm as good to go as I ever will be.

'Okay, what do we start with today?'

I'm talking to Him right now. I have that shaky feeling I used to get before a concert where you don't know if your hands are going to do what you want them to do.

Somewhere over a rainbow – it's Dorothy's favourite.

Dorothy is crying and trying to get out of her recliner. She's convinced she needs to go to the toilet, even though I think the nurses are all over it and she has only just been.

I take a deep breath.

Just play it for me, Al.

I start. Dorothy pauses. She looks directly at me. She raises her right hand and starts conducting. We get to the chorus. Dorothy sings, in and out of the lines. '…over the rainbow……up high…. that I've heard of…. Lulla-by…'

I tell her she sounds beautiful, and we go again. This time Greg joins in. He's been talking to me while I am playing. I'm not so good at playing and talking at the same time and I can't quite understand what Greg is saying. But it's okay now, because he is singing too.

I tell him his voice is beautiful as well, keep going Greg.

He claps himself and nods intently at me.

There's a disturbance in the corner of the room – Dulce, who has just come on the ward, is upset about something involving Bruce, who is both bemused and offended by her words. The nurses are trying to separate both by distracting Dulce.

I've no idea whether I will make things worse or not, but I throw caution to the wind and call out 'Dulce, I've got the song – the one you asked for!' She looks at me and can't remember. 'That's okay Dulce, it's a long way to Tipperary – the one you love - I learnt it this week!' She walks away from Bruce and towards me.

'It goes like this,' she says, helping me out. She says different numbers as her fingers play the keys. They aren't the right keys, and I am not sure what the numbers are referring to, but I can see she knows – she knows what she is trying to play.

'Okay, let's do this… do you know the verse?'

‘Oh no, no..’ she shakes her head.

‘Brilliant, because I’m not good at the verse, so we just sing it once to get in the zone, and then we go the chorus, right?’

She smiles and nods. A nurse is standing next to her, and they start swaying as I start singing the verse. Badly. I slow it as we get to the cadence leading to the chorus. Then I draw her in. She sings. It is beautiful. Her words are jumbled, not the ones on the page, but it doesn’t matter. She is singing – that’s all that matters.

‘You sound great Dulce!’ I say, trying to hold the tune as I encourage her. We come round to the second chorus, and we go again. This time she gets quite a few of the correct words. I try not to be over-enthusiastic, but she is doing great, and she is smiling, which is a change from two minutes ago.

Tipperary finishes and we get a clap from around the room. Dulce blushes, and modestly says she can’t sing very well. ‘Oh, don’t be silly,’ I exclaim. ‘You’re better than me! Next time I will bring big, giant words, so you can see.’

‘That would be great,’ she says. I notice she and the nurse have started lifting their feet, left, right, left, right, in between their sways. The mood is kind of upbeat, so I figure I better seize the day.

We go with ‘Stand by me’.

I start with the opening riff, and they start clapping, which is great, but also a problem, because they are not in time, and this song – it all hangs on the beat. Got it and you jive, lose it you dive.

'You gotta help me…' I say to Him. He knows how much I was practising this week, trying to sing it with the syncopated rhythm whilst holding the riff in my left hand. I mean, man, I'm classically trained, not soul-trained.

Tap your foot.

'Okay, got it.' I tap and use the pedalling to keep the beat. Now it's not just Dulce dancing, Dorothy has started swaying side to side in her recliner, and Rodney, a beautiful man from Bangladesh, is conducting from his walker. We're becoming quite a groovy little group.

The afternoon rolls on – we do rainbow songs galore – the Rainbow Connection, Somewhere over the rainbow again, and again, and again... Hallelujah. Something inside so strong (I try not to cry). Oh Danny Boy. Moon River. You were always on my mind. Amazing Grace. And on and on.

Karl, a German ex-footballer who has been a ward of state here for the past two decades, rocks back and forth smiling with each song. Bruce looks like he is relaxing and joins in 'What a Wonderful World' from the kitchen corner, waving discretely every time I catch his eye and nod him on in encouragement. Poor Amir, from Iran, tolerates the cacophony by covering his head with a tea-towel throughout. 'You have to help me find some Middle Eastern stuff for him next time,' I whisper to the Shepherd.

We are 40 minutes in and my voice is starting to croak. This could turn ugly.

At that moment, I see Neville shuffle his way to a seat helped by a nurse. He is short, hunched over, with tired, blood-shot eyes. He looks agitated. I think the current repertoire may not have been his preferred style.

The nurse looks at me with beseeching eyes and says 'He loves classical.'

Classical?!.

'Oh... okay...' I smile politely.

'I said I'd do this if we don't do classical – remember?' I whisper to the Shepherd. 'That was the deal with playing again, right? Yes, if we *never* do classical again – and I thought You were cool with that!'

He is silent. Clearly, they were my terms not His.

My brain races. 'Well what do I do? There is only one piece I can remember.... And ... You know which one that is...'

It is the 'do it again' song.

Miss Stanford's repeated demands may have frozen my ten-year-old hands all those years ago. But they sure etched that Chopin Nocturne in my brain.

'I should have practiced more than I have, to play that stuff – I haven't done the hours... I'll have a memory lapse, stuff it up, just like I used to...'

Al.

Look at him.

I glance at Neville. He's blind. Blind with advanced dementia. He's so troubled that he can't stay seated, but he's unstable on his feet, so the nurse is repeatedly having to get him to sit back down again. I can see his distress, frustration and confusion elevate. I can't imagine what it must be like, being him right now.

Let Me play it, through you.

'Seriously?'

Don't think it. Feel it. We've got this.

'Okay.' I take a deep breath. 'Neville, this one is for you.' I say, cheerily.

Feel it, don't think it. Feel it, don't think it.

I start with the C# minor chord, right hand, left hand C# bass. The intro. The first phrase is repeated twice. I watch Neville like a hawk to see if we have him.

We do.

He stops getting up and down with the first, slow, deliberate chord. With the second, his eyes track upward, like he is seeing something no-one else can see. We move into the main melody of the nocturne and the entire room quietens. All eyes on me. My skin pricks with self-consciousness.

Keep going Al. Don't worry about everyone else. Just play it for Neville.

I follow His lead, and I lose myself. I think only of Neville, and I reach for his soul with the notes. This nocturne rips my heart out each time I play it. Maybe that was why, in the end, it won me so many competitions. It sings sadness, grief, pain, and beauty all wrapped into one. It speaks words without using words. Words I have always had but can never find.

I drop the worry, the 'self' that holds me down and I find myself free of the childhood glitch I always feared.

I feel my hands move and I feel through them. We climb, we soar, we caress, we soften. Hills and valleys of notes and music, touch and emotion. I see the faster scales approaching – the flurries and ornaments that make this nocturne so beautiful.

Self encroaches again. I hesitate, fearful I might miss them.

He whispers,

We can do it, Al. We've got this.

I let go and I release the notes.

We hit all of them. Every single one. The way I want them to sound. The way I want Neville to hear them.

We have lift.

We are flying again.

*

Bibliography

Holy Bible: New International Version (2011 text). (2025). Biblica. Digital edition via YouVersion app.

Holy Bible: English Standard Version. (2016). Crossway. Digital edition via YouVersion app.

Holy Bible: King James Version (n.d.). Public Domain. Digital edition via YouVersion app.

Holy Bible: World English Bible (n.d.). Public Domain. Digital edition via YouVersion app.

Catholic Church. (2000). *Catechism of the Catholic Church: Second edition.* United States Conference of Catholic Bishops. ISBN 9781574551105

Lewis, C. S. (2001). *The chronicles of Narnia.* New York: HarperCollins. ISBN 9780066238500

St Pauls Publications. (2012). *St Pauls Sunday Missal.* Strathfield, NSW: St Pauls Publications. ISBN 9781921946007

van der Kolk, B. (2015). *The body keeps the score: Brain, mind, and body in the healing of trauma.* New York, NY: Viking. ISBN 9780143127741

www.ingramcontent.com/pod-product-compliance
Lightning Source LLC
LaVergne TN
LVHW041101080826
845145LV00007B/1646